# Getting The Most Out of Life

# Getting the Most Out of Life

## An Exegetical Commentary on First Corinthians Three

By

Spiros Zodhiates, Th.D.

AMG
PUBLISHERS
Chattanooga, TN 37422

Getting the Most Out of Life
An Exegetical Commentary on
First Corinthians Three



*ISBN 0-89957-515-3*

*Printed in the United States of America*
03 02 01 00 99 98 –R– 6 5 4 3 2 1

*To my beloved friends*
*George and Anna Kafalas:*
*George was led to the Lord by his wife*
*Anna who grew up and came to know*
*the Lord in our orphanage in Greece.*

# Contents

# Preface

In this life you have the freedom to choose, not the freedom to choose the consequences of your choice. You may rebel against the laws of nature, but if you fail to cooperate with the most elementary of them, such as the need for food and drink, you will die. Such laws are fixed, not by some inscrutable life force but by God Himself.

Similarly, Scripture teaches that what you sow you reap. Or to change the metaphor, the house you build now is the one you will live in the future. That is what is known as the doctrine of works and rewards. Do not misunderstand me. Christ died for you, and you do not have to do anything except believe and appropriate His work on the cross for your salvation. That is the foundation of the Christian life. You did not lay it; He did.

But the apostle Paul challenged the Corinthian Christians, and challenges us all, to build a worthy house on that foundation. You are building it with what you say and do. How well you have built will show up in the future. But Paul gives you certain guidelines to help you determine what kind of superstructure you are now building. He does not want you to wait until it is too late, and you cannot do it over.

It is wise to find out the guidelines Scripture sets forth for self-examination here and now, while there is still time to make needed changes. Since the works of Christians must undergo the test of fire at the judgment for that purpose (although this will not affect your salvation), it is a good idea to use "fire-proof" materials. What these are Paul tells you in 1 Corinthians 3.

In writing this book, I have tried to examine every significant word of this life-changing chapter as Paul wrote it in the Greek. The English translation you are using may not have caught the full implication of every Greek word or phrase. It will pay to find out whether what you thought these verses said is really so.

SPIROS ZODHIATES

# An Overview of First Corinthians

**Author:** Paul the apostle, author of thirteen other epistles to various individuals and congregations.

**Date:** About A.D. 55.

**Recipients:** The congregation Paul had established in Corinth.

**Place:** From Ephesus

**Theme:** Paul had received news about the Corinthian brethren from several sources (1 Cor. 1:11; 7:1; 16:17). The church was afflicted with many of the problems that face young churches and new converts. The apostle, under the inspiration of the Holy Spirit, decided to write this urgent letter to admonish and instruct the church. Among other topics he discussed: the necessity of church discipline (5:1–13); divisions and disputes among Christians (1:10–16; 6:1–11); matters of conscience (8:1–13; 10:19–33); the support of preachers (9:1–27); abuses of the Lord's Supper (10:16–17, 21; 11:17–34); the misuse of spiritual gifts (12:1—14:40); and the importance of the resurrection of Jesus Christ (15:1–58).

# An Outline of First Corinthians

In the days of the apostle Paul, Corinth was the capital city of the Roman province of Achaia and the glory of Greece. Though its great ancient splendor had been destroyed by the Romans in 120 B.C., the city was rebuilt under Julius Caesar and restored to wealth and luxury under Augustus. Among all the cities of the world, however, it was most well known for its lewdness. The apostle Paul lived in Corinth for eighteen months (Acts 18:11). After his departure, Paul went to Ephesus. During his three-year stay there, he heard reports of wickedness and division within the Corinthian church. In an effort to correct these evils, Paul wrote several letters to them, including the epistle of First Corinthians.

| | |
|---|---|
| 1:1–9 | The introductory remarks of Paul. |
| 1:10–16 | Paul condemns the divisions in the church and exhorts its members to unity. |
| 1:17—2:16 | Paul defends his ministry. He has preached the wisdom of Christ crucified. This wisdom is foolishness to the world, but is the glory of all those to whom the Spirit of God has revealed the truthfulness of it. |
| 3:1–5 | Paul declares that the simplicity of his teaching was due to the carnal state of the Corinthians, which state is clearly evidenced by their divisions. |
| 3:6–23 | Jesus Christ is the only foundation. Ministers are mere servants; the work is God's. |
| 4:1–6 | The duty of ministers is faithfulness. |
| 4:6–21 | Paul contrasts the arrogance and conceit of the false teachers to the humility and sacrifice of the apostles. Using his unique position as their spiritual father, Paul calls on the Corinthian believers to be discerning. |
| 5:1–13 | Flagrant, sexual immorality was being practiced by one of the members of the congregation. Paul reproves |

| | |
|---|---|
| | their lack of discipline and calls for expulsion of the guilty party. |
| 6:1–11 | Christians should not bring their legal disputes before heathen judges. |
| 6:12–20 | Paul reprimands the perversion of the principle of Christian liberty to excuse fornication. Our bodies belong to the Lord and should be devoted to His glory. |
| 7:1–17 | Paul answers questions about marriage. |
| 7:18–24 | Paul advises that, provided they are not immoral or unlawful, our social positions should remain intact after coming to Christ. |
| 7:25–40 | Paul answers questions about virgins and widows. |
| 8:1–13 | Christian liberty and conscience: was it lawful to eat meat that had been sacrificed to false gods? |
| 9:1–23 | Paul declares the right of ministers to be faithfully supported by their congregation. |
| 9:24—10:13 | Exhortations to self-denial. |
| 10:14—11:1 | While the purchase of meat offered to idols is a matter of conscience, attendance at the heathen feasts of sacrifice is idolatry, even if such was not their intention. |
| 11:2–16 | Men and women should take care to conform to the customs of dress in their community that assure modesty and properly reflect the man to be "the glory of God" and the woman to be "the glory of the man." |
| 11:17–34 | Paul exhorts the Corinthians to properly partake of the Lord's Supper. |
| 12:1–31 | Paul answers their questions about spiritual gifts. He reminds them that they are all members of one body. God has distributed these gifts so that each member may perform the function it is designed for. |

| | |
|---|---|
| 13:1–13 | Love [*agápe* {26}] is superior to all other gifts. |
| 14:1–25 | The gift of prophecy is more valuable than the gift of tongues. |
| 14:26–40 | Principles for orderly public worship. |
| 15:1–34 | Paul proves the resurrection of Christ is fact. It is the foundation of our faith and the surety of our resurrection. |
| 15:35–58 | Paul explains the nature of our resurrection. |
| 16:1–9 | Paul's specific instructions for the collection of monies from several Greek congregations for the poverty-stricken saints in Palestine. |
| 16:10–12 | Recommendations for Timothy and Apollos to be accepted by the Corinthians. |
| 16:13–24 | Paul's final admonition to them to stand firm in the faith. Salutation. |

# 1 Cor. 3:1 | *Your Food Must Fit Your Nature*

*And I, brethren, could not speak unto you as unto spiritual but as unto carnal, even as unto babes in Christ.*

How often we hear church members blame their preacher for their own lack of spiritual growth—their lukewarmness, their attachment to others, or their carnal natures. "We just don't get fed," is their complaint. Yet oftentimes what they really want is to have their ears tickled. The apostle Paul sensed this same tendency in the members of the church at Corinth. In the second chapter of his first epistle to them, he had told them that when he came to them it was not in the power of natural wisdom, in spite of the fact that their present situation was affected by their placing too great importance on natural wisdom. He wanted to make it clear that he was in no way responsible for their present condition as far as spiritual things were concerned.

Now, in the third chapter, he wants to absolve himself of all responsibility for their present infantile state, which he proceeds to describe and which he tries to correct. It is as if he were saying, "I realize that there is a very personal relationship between you, the believers in Corinth, and me who brought the gospel to you in the first place. However, I cannot be held responsible for your present condition. There are other factors that you have allowed to come into your life which have hindered your spiritual growth. The responsibility is clearly yours." Paul's responsibility on the other hand was to tell them of their spiritual need, and how it could be met in Christ.

How much better Paul would have felt if he could have said to these Corinthians what he told the Philippians: "Therefore, my brethren dearly beloved and longed for, my joy and crown, so stand fast in the Lord, my dearly beloved" (Phil. 4:1). Nothing breaks a pastor's heart more than to minister the word of truth to his congregation and see that it makes absolutely no change in their lives.

The Corinthian church numbered many proud individuals in its membership. Their pride, however, was not centered upon Christ but upon their own superiority of intellect, of knowledge, and the abundance of their material possessions. They prided themselves on their wisdom. Paul was determined to take them down a peg. Read 2 Corinthians 8:1–5 carefully to note how the Corinthians prided themselves on the large gifts they were making to God's work—though these were far less than they were capable of giving. Paul reserved his commendation for the Macedonians, people of Northern Greece, including the Philippians, who, although they gave substantially less than the Corinthians, were willing to give more than they were able to (see 2 Cor. 8:3).

The trouble with the Corinthians was that they thought too highly of themselves, and Paul is about to tell them what he thinks of them and to disclaim any responsibility for their condition. A growing Christian should be like a church steeple: the closer he gets to heaven the smaller he should look in his own estimation.

Observe, however, how the apostle Paul addresses these Christians whom he is about to chide and to some degree humiliate. "And I, brethren," is what he says in both 1 Corinthians 2:1 and 3:1. He is about to call them carnal Christians and babes in Christ; nevertheless he calls them brethren, which indicates that they were born-again believers. Paul presents himself to the Corinthians as a spiritual brother. He evaluates their spiritual condition and says it is carnal. Nevertheless he does not reject them or exclude them from the kingdom of God. A weak brother does not cease to be a brother. As Paul says in Galatians 6:1, "Brethren, if a man be overtaken in a fault, ye which are spiritual, restore such a one in the spirit of meekness; considering thyself, lest thou also be tempted." There is a fellow-feeling for the erring one that is the true mark of Christian love.

A man was passing a group of half a dozen children who were all crying noisily. He stopped one lad and asked, "What's the trouble? Why are you all crying?" Between sobs the boy answered, "We all have a pain in Billy's stomach." That is real sympathy for the one who is suffering. Paul was possessed of such sympathy for the Christian brethren who should have been spiritual but were actually carnal. He still calls them brethren. His desire is not to condemn but to lift them up. This is the spirit of his third chapter of 1 Corinthians.

Paul then goes on to tell these Corinthians that he was unable to teach them all that he wanted to. He says, "I . . . could not speak unto you as unto spiritual, but as unto carnal." The Greek verb translated "could not" is *ēdunḗthēn*, which is in the second aorist tense, taking Paul back to the time when he was among them ministering the Word of God. It does not mean that Paul was incapable of preaching spiritual realities to them, but that they were unable to receive them, nor did they desire to receive them. He could have been far more blunt by chiding them, but in Christian love he rather chose the road of soft rebuke instead of the knockout blow.

This statement should be read with 1 Corinthians 2:6, 7, which says, "Howbeit we speak the wisdom of God in a mystery, even the hidden wisdom, which God ordained before the world unto our glory." Yes, Paul was perfectly capable of revealing the mysteries, the deep things of God, but only to those who were "perfect"—in other words to those who were spiritually mature enough to receive them. As he said in 1 Corinthians 2:14, spiritual things are spiritually discerned; and since the Corinthians were not spiritual, they could not discern the depths of God's revelation that Paul wanted to bring to them; they were simply incapable of understanding them.

Spurgeon says, "We have the likenesses of our boys taken on every birthday . . . so that we see them at a glance from their babyhood to their youth. Suppose such photographic memorials of our own spiritual life had been taken and preserved, would there be a regular advance, as in these boys, or would we still have been exhibited in the perambulator? Have not some grown awhile, and then suddenly dwarfed? Have not others gone back to babyhood? Here is a wide field for reflection."

And Andrew Murray comments on believers who evidence little growth in spirituality: "You come into contact with them, and you feel at once there is something wanting; there is none of the beauty of holiness or of the power of God's Spirit in them. Is it not sad to see a believer who has been converted five, ten, twenty years, and who has yet no growth and no strength and no joy of holiness!"

## Are You Still in the First Grade, Spiritually Speaking?

When the apostle Paul told the Corinthians he could not speak to them as mature Christians but as babes, he was stating a basic principle of the ministry. Just as a parent cannot give steak to a baby because he cannot assimilate that kind of food, so a spiritual leader cannot impart spiritual teaching in depth to Christians who have no spiritual depth.

Paul recognized two basic principles in his ministry: 1) A preacher must analyze the condition of his people, not for the purpose of criticizing them, but for the purpose of giving them food that they can assimilate. This is not compromise but realistic behavior. He must give each one only what will permit him to grow, even if this is "baby food" rather than "strong meat" that might cause him to get sick. And 2) a preacher finds it a painful experience to give baby food to an adult. But if an adult is sickly and weak, then he must be given food that his constitution can take. This was the condition of the Corinthians; and since Paul had to give them some form of spiritual nourishment, it had to be baby food.

We must realize that the Christian is composed of two natures that strive against one another. This is made clear in Galatians 5:17, 24, 25: "For the flesh lusteth against the Spirit, and the Spirit against the flesh: and these are contrary the one to the other: so that ye cannot do the things that ye would. . . . And they that are Christ's have crucified the flesh with the affections and lusts. If we live in the Spirit, let us also walk in the Spirit" (see also Gal. 6:8; Eph. 4:22, 24; Col. 3:9, 10; 1 Pet. 4:2).

The New Testament clearly teaches that every Christian has the Spirit and lives by the Spirit, but not every Christian walks by the Spirit. Paul understood that, in dealing with such persons, a wise teacher does not give his pupils more than they can assimilate, anymore than a farmer would scatter his seed indiscriminately on just any ground, instead of suiting the seed to the soil.

The teacher of spiritual truth must be governed by the same principle. It was the Lord Himself who said, "Give not that which is holy unto the dogs, neither cast ye your pearls before swine, lest they trample them under their feet, and turn again and rend you" (Matt. 7:6). So Paul in 1 Corinthians 3:1 says, "And I, brethren, could not speak unto you as unto spiritual, but as unto carnal, even as unto babes in Christ." He recognized that there were some in Corinth who, in spite of the time they had spent in Christ's school, were still first graders. Somehow they could not move to a higher grade in that school, so Paul was obliged to continue teaching them first grade lessons.

This does not mean, of course, that there were not more advanced and mature Christians in Corinth, who could receive higher teaching. You will recollect that in 1 Corinthians 1:5 Paul spoke of those who were enriched by Christ in all utterance and in all knowledge. But he was saddened by those who had the Spirit of God but did not walk in the Spirit, and therefore had to be kept on a diet of milk, so to speak. Of necessity he told them, "I am unable to teach you what I would like to, and which would greatly benefit you because you are unable to take it in because of your spiritual immaturity."

To a degree all of us who have the Spirit of God, but are still in the flesh, are first graders when it comes to God's revelation to us. Paul did not reveal to the Corinthians all he knew because of their carnal state. Similarly, the Lord Jesus Himself told the disciples at one time that He could not reveal to them all that was revealable. Why? Because they were still in the flesh, and in their carnal environment they were incapable of coming to a full comprehension of all the truth that is in God and that will one day be ours to know.

When our Lord was revealing to His disciples the fact of His coming departure from this earth and the continuing work He would be doing in heaven, He said, "I have yet many things to say unto you, but ye cannot bear them now" (John 16:12). They wanted to know more, and the Lord could have told them what they wanted to know, but He did not consider it wise to do so because such revelations would have been a burden rather than a help to them. This is just how Paul felt when he wrote to the Corinthians, "And I, brethren, could not speak unto you as unto spiritual, but as unto carnal, even as unto babes in Christ."

The Lord was acting out of sympathy for His disciples in their continued ignorance, and so was Paul in his attitude toward the carnal Corinthians. This was the sympathy of a father who knows what is wrong with his child but is reluctant to tell him because the child would neither understand nor heed his instructions or the information he wanted to impart.

The disciples were to a large extent earthly-minded in their conception of Jesus and His mission, even to the very end. It took those awful heart-deepening hours of His passion, the splendid mystery of the first Easter morning, the Ascension, and the great day of the coming of the Holy Spirit at Pentecost to prepare them for the advanced doctrine reflected in these events.

All knowledge of Christian truth has a relation to experience and most of all to the experience of love. To understand God better you must come to love Him more, even as in your human relations. To those closest to Him the Lord Jesus revealed the most. Pray for more love to Christ, and you will be taken more deeply into His knowledge. You cannot separate the two.

Instead of rebelling against God because you think He is arbitrarily withholding truth from you, you must fall down and worship Him. Men are so apt to ask, "Why in our perplexity and distress are we left in darkness?" But they forget that the darkness is not above them but within them. When God looks at hearts still not surrendered to His Spirit's control, He is reticent about revealing that which could make life so much more blessed to them. The silence of the Lord Jesus and of the apostle Paul regarding the deeper truths of God was not due to their limited knowledge but to the limited power of reception and response in those whom they sought to teach. As F. B. Meyer said, "God can do no more for you than He has done. All that God has is within your reach, but you must learn to take it."

## Indwelt by the Holy Spirit, yet Not Spiritual

One of the most cutting things that can be said to a born-again believer is, "You call yourself a Christian, and yet you act like that!" And the speaker goes on to say that no one calling himself a Christian should ever lose his temper, or act selfishly, or be vengeful, or break any of the Ten Commandments—and so on. In fact, the world often has a higher standard for the Christian than he himself has. They clearly expect perfection.

Be that as it may, the apostle Paul in 1 Corinthians 3:1 recognized that there are two stages of the Christian life, two types of Christians. "I could not speak unto you as unto spiritual," he tells the Corinthians, "but as unto carnal, even as unto babes in Christ." It is obvious that he considers both of these classes, the spiritual and the carnal, to be born-again believers. They were both "in Christ," as he repeatedly states in 1 Corinthians 1:1–9.

## The Natural or Soulish Man

There is yet a third classification of people to whom Paul refers, in chapter 2, and that is the natural man. In Greek, as we saw in previous studies, the word translated "natural" is *psuchikós*, which literally means "psychic." The *psuchḗ* or soul is held in common by man and animal. The spirit is the exclusive possession of man; it is the element by which he knows God, and that distinguishes him from the animal. A psychic or natural person is one who is governed by his natural instincts, by his soul, by his immaterial animal nature, so to speak—that is, his Adamic nature. He is the man in whom the Spirit of God has not come to dwell. In him the spirit is dead. It is to this state that Paul refers when he says that we are dead in our sins (Col. 2:13). Death is separation. Our spirit is separated from the Spirit of God and is therefore dormant, ineffective upon the personality.

The natural man does not receive the things of the Spirit of God nor can he know them. He is not in Christ—not a Christian.

### The Spiritual and the Carnal Man

The other two types of persons that Paul describes in 1 Corinthians 3:1 as "spiritual" and "carnal" are both Christians, however. The Spirit of God dwells in them, and both can discern the things of the Spirit. But the spiritual Christian can discern far more than the carnal Christian. The spiritual Christian is overwhelmingly led by the Spirit of God while the carnal Christian is directed and influenced by his Adamic nature. This in turn acts upon his material being, his flesh. Both spiritual and carnal Christians are in the body and are affected to a certain degree by their body and the desires of the flesh. However, in the spiritual man the Spirit has the supremacy, whereas in the carnal Christian his fallen nature, his *psuchḗ* or animal nature, has supremacy.

### Who is a Carnal Christian?

This is not necessarily the newly born-again believer who has had no chance to mature in the Christian life. Babes in Christ are not necessarily carnal Christians. That term was applied to the Corinthians not because they were new believers but because they had been Christians long enough to have evidenced spiritual maturity, and yet had failed to grow.

What is translated as the "carnal man" is *sarkikós* or *sárkinos* in Greek. This is the adjectival form of the noun *sarx*, which means "flesh." Of course, in this context the word does not refer just to the material element of man, his body, but also to his fallen nature. The body of itself cannot think or sin. The body simply externalizes the command of the sinful nonmaterial part of man, his soul. The flesh, therefore, is his inclination to do evil, which, when he becomes a child of God through the Holy Spirit's entering his heart, is not completely eradicated. The inclination toward evil is inherent in man's material self, the flesh. As long as we are in the body we are liable to temptation and transgression. As Christians we do not become exempt from the possibility of sin. We can, however, be exempt from the mastery of sin, and thus be counted as spiritual people.

As long as we are in the body, our redemption is only partial. It is a redemption from the power and supremacy of evil but not from the existence of evil. The Christian has a real struggle with evil in this life. If Satan did not hesitate to approach the Lord Jesus for the purpose of tempting Him, how shall we who seek to be His disciples expect to be spared by Satan?

Certainly there was a time in the life of Paul when he felt the power of the flesh, the propensity to do evil, so strongly that he confessed, "But I am carnal, sold under sin" (Rom. 7:14). That did not mean that Paul was not a born-again believer. We all have our struggles with the flesh and the tendency to satisfy it.

As Andrew Murray says:

> The young Christian is still carnal. Regeneration is a birth: the center and root of the personality, the spirit, has been renewed and taken possession of by the Spirit of God. But time is needed for its power from that center to extend through all the circumference of our being. The kingdom of God is like unto a seed; the life in Christ is a growth; and it would be against the laws of nature and grace alike if we expected from the babe in Christ the strength that can only be found in the young men, or the rich experience of the fathers.
>
> Even where in the young convert there is great singleness of heart and faith, with true love and devotion to the Savior, time is needed for a deeper knowledge of self and sin, for a spiritual insight into what God's will and grace are. With the young believer it is not unnatural that the emotions are deeply stirred, and that the mind delights in the contemplation of divine truth; with the growth in grace, the will becomes the more important thing, and the waiting for the Spirit's power in the life and character more than the delight in those thoughts and images of the life which alone the mind could give. We need not wonder if the babe in Christ is still carnal [Murray 1888, 225, 226].

So do not be discouraged, young Christian, if someone throws up your immaturity to you as grounds for disbelief in your being a Christian. You have to allow yourself time to grow and develop in the Christian life; and you are a Christian at every stage of your development. But if you are content to remain a spiritual baby, not striving for growth in grace and Christian virtues, you need not wonder when people doubt your Christianity. You may even come to doubt it yourself, for as James says, "Faith, if it hath not works, is dead" (James 2:17).

## Do Not Blame Your Environment for Your Failures

When two children in the same family turn out differently—one good and one bad, though both received the same parental care or lack of it—what makes the difference? When some individuals given the same spiritual training in a church turn out to be spiritual and some carnal, what makes the difference?

It is apparent from what the apostle Paul says in his letters to the Corinthians that many Christians remained carnal even though some time had elapsed since they were born-again. The fact, however, that there were spiritual Christians in Corinth shows that it is not the environment, or the body, or the flesh, or the sinful nature within a man that is to be blamed, but the will of man himself.

God has not only called us to grow, but He has also provided all the conditions and powers needed for growth. The environment, of course, plays a great part. That is why the born-again Christian must seek a church where he is more likely to grow spiritually than one where the worldly atmosphere tends to draw him toward a carnal life.

An elderly woman was being conducted through a great cathedral in Europe. The guide spoke of its beauty of design, calling attention to the statues and paintings. The woman was unimpressed. At the conclusion of the tour she asked the guide,

"How many souls have been saved here this year? How many people have drawn near to God here?" "My dear lady," said the embarrassed guide, "this is a cathedral, not a chapel." That is the trouble. Unfortunately we have too many cathedrals and too few chapels where the warmth of the Spirit of God is felt, conducive to a spiritual life that enhances our knowledge of God.

### Lack of Christian Fellowship May Contribute to Carnality

It is quite possible that your carnality can be blamed on your aloofness from other Christians, or your attendance at a church where the Spirit of God is not at work.

A Christian once said to his minister, "I can worship God and enter into the Holy of Holies just as easily in my garden as I can in a church pew." Later on the two men were sitting before a fireplace in which the embers glowed cheerily. Silently the minister went to the fireplace, took the tongs, and lifted a single glowing coal from the fire and placed it alone on the hearth. Soon it became black ash. The church-neglecting Christian said, "Ah, you need not say a word. I understand what you mean. I cannot worship alone anymore than I can live alone. I'll be in my place at the church next Sunday." The environment of the church is basic to Christian growth, providing it is the right kind of church. Ask yourself two questions before joining: Is Christ preeminent there? Is the Holy Spirit at work?

### The Church Contains Both Spiritual and Carnal Christians

When the apostle Paul diagnosed the condition of the Christians at Corinth, he found some of them to be spiritual and some to be carnal. He did not hesitate to call this to their attention so that they would examine themselves and find out for themselves what they really were. To think yourself spiritual when you are really carnal is a self-deception that can deprive you of great blessing. There is a feast of spiritual food and revelation from

God that you are missing. Examine yourself to find out whether you are spiritual or carnal. The fact that you are "in Christ" does not necessarily mean that you are spiritual. The fact that the Spirit of God is within you does not necessarily mean that you are walking in the Spirit. To the Galatians Paul said, "Walk in the Spirit, and ye shall not fulfill the lust of the flesh. For the flesh lusteth against the Spirit, and the Spirit against the flesh: and these are contrary the one to the other: so that ye cannot do the things that ye would" (Gal. 5:16, 17).

### The Characteristics of the Carnal Christian

To give us a concrete idea of what the carnal Christian is like, Paul tells us that the carnal Christian is a babe in Christ. He is a born-again person who is still a child in his spiritual development; he has not grown. This is a condition of protracted infancy. We do not become alarmed at the childish behavior of a youngster of five or six. But if we observe a teenager still acting like a baby, we become concerned. If a child does not grow, there is something wrong, and we must find out what it is. It is appropriate to give baby food to a baby but not to an adult. This is what Paul is concerned about—adults who have been Christians for a number of years and are still acting like spiritual babies.

This is the condition of the carnal Christians referred to in Hebrews 5:10–14:

> For when for the time ye ought to be teachers, ye have need that one teach you again which be the first principles of the oracles of God; and are become such as have need of milk, and not of strong meat. . . . But strong meat belongeth to them that are of full age.

### Marks of Infantile Behavior

Now what are the marks of a baby? He cannot help himself, but is always keeping others occupied to serve him. If he stays in the house, nobody can get any rest. If you find yourself demanding that everybody serve you, then know that you are a carnal Christian.

The second characteristic of a baby is that he can do nothing to help his fellow-man. A selfish Christian is a carnal Christian. He is unwilling to deny himself and in practice crucify the flesh. Heed the call of the Lord, who says, "If any man will come after me, let him deny himself" (Matt. 16:24). That is basic to service which pleases God. When you quit wanting others to cater to your needs and desires all the time and instead find yourself eager to serve others, then know that you are a full-grown man, a spiritual Christian.

A young man left the church of his parents for another church. Someone asked, "What was the matter with the church you left?" "Nothing," he answered, "except they do a lot more for a fellow over there where I go now. They give you a splendid present at Christmas, and a social with refreshments once a month, and a chance to get in with folk who can help you socially." That was his idea of the mission of the church. It was not long, however, before he changed churches again. The same man asked him why. "Oh, they didn't re-elect me president of the social league of the church, and I won't stand for being slighted." That is the kind of Christian that Paul would call a carnal Christian.

LESSONS:

1. Like other ministers, the apostle Paul's heart was heavy when he ministered the word of truth to the church in Corinth and saw no change in the lives of its members. He sensed that the Corinthians thought too highly of themselves.
2. The Corinthians were not able to discern the things of the Spirit (see 1 Cor. 2:14) and therefore were unable to discern the depths of God's revelation that Paul wanted to bring them.
3. The New Testament teaches that every Christian has and lives by the Spirit but not every Christian walks by the Spirit. The disciples had

trouble walking by the Spirit since their conception of Jesus and His mission was still to a large extent earthly-minded. Thus, the Lord Jesus could not reveal to them all that He might have revealed.

4. Knowledge of the truth is related to the experience of love. To know God better, we must love Him more. He reveals deep truths to those hearts that are surrendered to His Spirit.
5. Although the Spirit of God dwells in both the "spiritual" and "carnal' Christian, the spiritual Christian is led by the Spirit of God within him while the carnal Christian is predominantly led by his Adamic nature.
6. Carnal Christians are born-again people who need spiritual development. Such development, or growth, is found in the environment of the church, in Christian fellowship.

# 1 Cor. 3:2 — *Carnality, the Reason For Spiritual Ignorance*

*I have fed you with milk, and not with meat: for hitherto ye were not able to bear it, neither yet now are ye able.*

A baby requires a lot of attention. He wants recognition for every new achievement. Being praised is part of childhood. But a truly mature person is not always looking for praise, but can work toward a goal for the sake of a job well done.

An Egyptian architect was commissioned by one of the Pharaohs to build a lighthouse at the mouth of the Nile. On a piece of rock, duly selected, Cnidus, the architect, erected a fine edifice. Engraved upon the cement that was covering the outside of the lighthouse was the name Pharaoh. In a few years the effect of wind and rain had worn the cement away and Pharaoh's name had vanished. Then it was discovered that the wily Cnidus had engraved his own name in the masonry beneath.

Even Christian work may be done outwardly for the glory of God, but, when the underlying motive is laid bare, our own glory often turns out to be the real aim. This is sadly evident in the Christian church when a worker quits because things do not go his way, or he does not get the appreciation he feels he deserves. If that is the case with you, then you are, in that respect at least, a carnal Christian. A carnal Christian may be a very gifted Christian. He may possess any number of gifts of the Spirit. In fact, the very possession of such gifts may cause pride, which in turn engenders jealousy, causes dissensions, and brings about divisions in the body of Christ.

Andrew Murray makes an interesting distinction between grace and gift (*cháris* and *chárisma*). "This carnal state may be found in existence in connection with great spiritual gifts and graces. The graces of the Spirit are humility and love, like the humility and love of Christ. The graces of the Spirit are to make a man free from self; the gifts of the Spirit are to fit a man for work. We see this illustrated among the Corinthians. In the first chapter Paul says, 'I thank God that you are enriched unto all utterance, and all wisdom.' In the 12th and 14th chapters we see that the gifts of prophecy and of working miracles were in great power among them, but the graces of the Spirit were noticeably absent.

> And this may be in our days as well as in the time of the Corinthians. I may be a minister of the gospel; I may teach God's Word beautifully; I may have influence, and gather a large congregation, and yet, alas! I may be a carnal man; a man who may be used by God, and may be a blessing to others, and yet the carnal life may still mark me. You all know the law that a thing is named according to what is its most prominent characteristic. Now, in these carnal Corinthians there was a little of God's Spirit, but the flesh predominated; the Spirit had not the rule of their whole life. And the spiritual men are not called so because there is no flesh in them, but because the Spirit in them has obtained dominance, and when you meet them and have fellowship with them, you feel that the Spirit of God has sanctified them. Ah, let us beware lest the blessing God gives us in our work deceive us and lead us to think that because He has blessed us, we must be spiritual men. God may give us gifts that we use, and yet our lives may not be wholly in the power of the Holy Ghost [Murray 1896, 12, 13].

Since the apostle Paul recognized the spiritual immaturity of some of the Christians in Corinth, he fed them accordingly. "I fed you with milk, and not with meat," he tells them in

1 Corinthians 3:2. Milk here undoubtedly refers to the simpler, more elementary doctrines of Christianity, such as the new birth, repentance, faith, and the like, which Paul had taught these Corinthians when he first ministered among them. Actually the Greek text says, "I gave you to drink milk." Milk is liquid food, especially suited for the early stages of one's life. Solid food in Greek is *brṓma,* and of course there is a great difference between solid food and liquid. As one grows, he certainly needs more than milk. Paul knew that the Corinthians needed solid food, but he could not give it to them because they were not ready to assimilate it. He goes on to tell them why he could not give them solid food: "For hitherto ye were not able to bear it." In fact, the Greek simply states, "You were not able" (*ouk ēdúnasthe*); using exactly the same verb as we find in the first verse of chapter 3, "I was not able (*ouk ēdunḗthēn*) to speak to you as spiritual ones." The inability, Paul declares, lay with them and not with him. He could give them plenty of solid food if they could assimilate it.

The problem that the prophets and apostles faced, and which the preacher today faces, is not that of the brilliant natural mind but of the unprepared heart of the people. Willingness to listen is not always equivalent to ability to understand. Have you ever tried to explain something that in your own mind is most important for the conduct of life to a person who is willing to listen, yet who in the end cannot comprehend your viewpoint? Especially if you are talking of spiritual matters, it is as though you were speaking a different language. You do not keep on speaking in a language people do not understand; if you did you would merely indicate how foolish you were.

If we with our limited knowledge feel like sealing our lips in the presence of those who cannot understand us, how much more must the omniscient, eternal God see the futility of breaking His silence in the presence of those who have no ability to comprehend spiritual truths? His silence is conditioned by the darkness of men's minds and the hardness of their hearts.

The general Christian public knows little of intimate fellowship with God because they are carnal, even as many of the Corinthian Christians were. So it was with the majority of believers in Christ's day. But the Lord selected a few to whom He revealed a great deal. So did Paul in Corinth. But with the majority he could not share the spiritual wealth he longed to impart. We today would not have the wealth of spiritual knowledge available to us in God's Word if Christ had not chosen out of the many just a few souls who, by their attachment to Him, were comparatively teachable. And even these He could not teach as much as He wanted to. That which seemed complete to them was fragmentary to Him. They counted Him to have said all when there was much more to say. He was always sounding out their thoughts and hopes and sympathies. And, alas, many a thought of His He dared not launch because it would straightway have gone aground and have been stranded and useless in the shallows of their lives.

### Are You a Tree or a Post?

Life is a never-ending process of learning. In fact, one of the great ends of life is to make us able to know. And the highest truth man can come to know is who God is, and what His purposes and will are in regard to us human beings. We learn by precept, by example, and by experience. But experience does not make us wise simply by the measure of the experience itself. It is meant to affect our character in such a way that we will be put in touch with a better understanding of that divine truth ever waiting at the door of our hearts. Experience by itself cannot make us wise, but it can make us teachable.

As we study our Lord's teaching methods, we find that His revelation was not mechanical and ours should not be either. It is not just a set truth that must be taught. It is a seed that must be implanted in proper ground. As Christ told His disciples, "I have yet many things to say unto you, but ye cannot bear them now" (John 16:12). He realized that the day would come when they could comprehend spiritual truths they were unable to take in at that particular time. Observe the word "now" in John 16:12 and in 1 Corinthians 3:2, "I have fed you with milk, and not with meat: for hitherto ye were not able to bear it, neither yet now are ye able." But the fact that Paul is writing to them indicates that he is not giving up hope of their being able to assimilate the spiritual truths he desired to impart at some time in the future. He hopes, but it would depend on their relationship with the Lord Jesus Christ.

The lesson for preachers, teachers, and Christians in all walks of life is that we must never give up, either on ourselves or on others. We must always be inspired by hope. As the disciples were enabled by the coming of the Holy Spirit to know more than they did before His coming, so the believer can know more and more as he walks with the Spirit (see Ainsworth 1912, 45–52).

Although Paul disclaims any responsibility for being unable to feed the Corinthians meat instead of milk, there are preachers today who cannot give solid food to their congregations because they themselves are not spiritual but carnal. How can a preacher provide his congregation with solid food if he has no appetite for it himself? In a Florentine art gallery a student sat before one of Raphael's masterpieces trying to copy it. When his work was nearly done he stood back to compare the two. Then with his brush he daubed over the face of his picture and exclaimed tragically, "How can I do what Raphael has done, without the mind of Raphael!"

Of course, a preacher must always preach better than he lives, for none of us have attained perfection. The aim is what counts—as Paul said, "not as though I had already attained, either were already perfect . . . but . . . I press toward the mark" (Phil. 3:12–14). No preacher can give out the solid food about Christ unless he himself is pressing on to attain all the fullness of Christ. You cannot picture the spiritual life convincingly unless you are seeking to live it.

How patiently Paul must have waited for the day when he could give the Corinthians solid spiritual food, but how regretfully he concludes that he could not do it yet. That is why the greater part of his epistles to the Corinthians were concerned with their internal strifes and with the correction of their carnal attitudes. Just compare Paul's letter to the spiritually minded Philippians with his letter to the Corinthians and you will see the difference.

He goes on in the third verse to say, "For ye are yet carnal." This verse begins with the Greek word *éti*, meaning "yet, still." Paul refers to the present as a time when they should have grown up spiritually, so that they would no longer be governed by their natural desires but rather by the Spirit of God. By his use of the word "yet," it is as though Paul were telling them that the state of carnality is understandable and somewhat to be expected when one is just born-again. An infant needs time to grow. But though it is cute to see a baby sucking on a bottle of milk, the same action in a grownup is disgusting.

That is how it was with the Corinthians. They were no longer babies; they had been Christians long enough to have grown up; and yet they were still acting like spiritual infants. Many of them must have been like that person who, when offended by a rebuke, said, "I want you to know that I have been standing at my post in this church for forty years." The friend who thought enough of this dear brother to correct him, though he had been in the church and in Christ so long, yet without growing in the things of the Spirit, said, "It's time you unhitched yourself and got going."

In every congregation there are saved and unsaved people. (Of course, as we have noted previously, the unsaved people are to be distinguished from the carnal Christians.) Someone has aptly likened them to trees and posts. When you plant a tree, it begins to grow. When you stick a post in the ground, it begins to rot. A Christian is a tree that must grow; otherwise it does not fulfill its reason for being.

As J. C. Ryle says:

> There is a generation of Christians in this age who grieve me to the heart. They make my blood run cold. I cannot understand them. For anything that man's eye can see, they make no progress. They never seem to get on. Years roll on, and they are just the same—the same besetting sins, the same infirmities of disposition, the same weakness in trial, the same chilliness of heart, the same apathy, the same faint resemblance to Christ—but no new knowledge, no increased interest in the kingdom, no freshness, no new strength, no new fruits. Are they not forgetting that growth is a proof of life? . . . Are they not forgetting how awfully far man may go, and yet not be a true Christian? He may be like a waxwork figure, the very image of a believer, and yet not have within him the breath of God: he may have a name to live, and be dead after all. We ought to have looked on this world as an inn, and we have settled down in it as if it were our home: it ought to have been counted our school of training for eternity, and we have been at ease in it as if it were our continuing city, or trifled away time in it, as if we were meant to play and not to learn. . . . We have been careful and troubled about many things—we have allowed the affairs of this life to eat out the heart of our spirituality.

Wordsworth put his finger on it when he said, "The world is too much with us: late and soon, getting and spending, we lay waste our powers."

**LESSONS:**

1. A carnal Christian may be a gifted Christian and possess gifts of the Spirit. In fact, the very possession of such gifts may cause pride, which in turn engenders jealousy, causes dissensions, and brings about divisions in the body of Christ.
2. Spiritually immature Christians need to be taught the elementary doctrines of Christianity. As the Christian grows, he needs to assimilate more spiritual food.
3. Life is a process of learning. The experience of life itself cannot make us wise, but can make us teachable, and it is meant to affect our character in such a way that we better understand the divine truth that is waiting at our heart's door.
4. Preachers, teachers and Christians of all walks of life must always be inspired by hope. As the disciples were enabled by the Holy Spirit to know more than they did before His coming, so can the believer know more as he walks with the Spirit.

# 1 Cor. 3:3 | *How to Overcome Defeat in the Christian Life*

*For ye are yet carnal: for whereas there is among you envying, and strife, and divisions, are ye not carnal, and walk as men?*

When Paul was writing his letters to the Corinthians, the one purpose that stands out is his desire for them to cease being carnal and to become spiritual. Only then could they receive spiritual truth. "You are still carnal," he says in effect, "but after this admonition, I hope things will be different."

How can one make the transition from being a carnal Christian to a spiritual one? If you read the 6th chapter of Paul's letter to the Galatians, you will find that, like the Corinthian church, that church too was full of strife and division. Look at the first verse: "Brethren, if a man be overtaken in a fault, ye which are spiritual, restore such a one in the spirit of meekness; considering thyself, lest thou also be tempted." Meekness should be characteristic of the spiritual man, who is in duty bound to help his carnal brother.

## The Spiritual Life Possible for All Christians

Andrew Murray gives four answers to the question of how a carnal Christian can become a spiritual one: First, we must know that there is such a spiritual life to be lived by men on earth. This is primarily the result of the indwelling of the Holy Spirit and His having the supremacy. "Be filled with the Spirit" Paul says in Ephesians 5:18. But the English translation is inadequate to convey the full meaning. The Greek text says *plēroústhe*, "be continuously filled." It is not a once-and-for-all experience. The Holy Spirit enters the believer when he first believes. In fact, he could not believe at all without the energizing power of the Holy Spirit. But then, as the Spirit manifests Himself externally through the believer, there is need of constant replenishing. The believer who is content to receive the Holy Spirit just for his salvation and not for holy living is a carnal Christian. To become a spiritual Christian he needs a continuous filling of the Spirit.

As Andrew Murray points out:

> We do not want the Holy Spirit only when we go to preach, or when we have some special temptation of the devil to meet or some great burden to bear; God says: "My child cannot live a right life unless he is guided by my Spirit every minute." That is the mark of the child of God: "As many as are led by the Spirit of God, they are the sons of God" (Rom. 8:14). In Romans 5:5 we read "The love of God is shed abroad in our hearts by the Holy Spirit given unto us." That is to be the common, everyday experience of the believer, not his life at set times only. Did ever a father or mother think, "For today I want my child to love me"? No, they expect the love every day. And so God wants His child every moment to have a heart filled with love of the Spirit. In the eyes of God, it is most unnatural to expect a man to love as he should if he is not filled with the Spirit.
>
> Oh, let us believe a man can be a spiritual man. Thank God, there is now the blessing waiting us. 'Be filled with the Spirit' (Eph. 5:18). Be "led by the Spirit" (Gal. 5:18). There is the blessing. If you have to say, "Oh, God, I have not this blessing," say it, but also say, "Lord, I know it is my duty, my solemn obligation, to have it, for without it I can not live in perfect peace with Thee all the day; without it I can not glorify Thee, and do the work Thou wouldst have me do." This is our first step from carnal to spiritual—to recognize a spiritual life, a walk in the Spirit, is within our reach. How can we ask God to guide us into spir-

itual life, a walk in the Spirit, if we have not a clear, confident conviction that there is such a life to be had?

Observe that the word "filling" implies the occupation of every nook and cranny of the heart and life. It is predominant. For Paul to say, "Be ye constantly filled with the Spirit," there must have been Christians—and there still are—who were only partially indwelt by the Spirit and were therefore confused. Such Christians have two masters within them, a situation that causes them to be divided in their loyalties.

## A Second Conviction Needed

"Then comes the second step; a man must see the shame and guilt of his having lived such a life." He sees spiritual life in others and recognizes that he lacks it. He is sorry for this lack. As in order to be converted one needs conviction of sin, so to be converted from carnality to spirituality one needs a second conviction of the sin of carnality.

The sins of an unconverted man are different from the sins of a believer. An unconverted man, for instance, is not ordinarily convicted of the corruption of his nature; he thinks principally about external sins: "I have sworn, been a liar, and I am on the way to hell." He is then convicted for conversion. But the believer is in quite a different condition. His sins are far more blamable, for he has had the light and the love of the Spirit of God given to him. His sins are far deeper. Until this conviction of the wrongness of our carnal state as believers comes to each one of us; until we are willing to get this conviction from God, to take time before God to be humbled and convicted, we never can become spiritual men and women.

## One Step

Third, the transition out of the carnal state into the spiritual is only one step. Was not conversion only one step? So it is when a man passes from carnal to spiritual. Do not confuse two states: that of the spiritual man and that of the spiritually mature man. To become spiritually mature takes a long time, but not to move from the circle of carnality to the circle of spirituality. Growth is one thing and spiritual life is another. You have to possess spiritual life in order to grow. There has to be that initial step of becoming spiritual from being carnal.

As Andrew Murray describes it:

> It is when a man utterly breaks with the flesh; when he gives up the flesh into the crucifixion death of Christ; when he sees that everything about it is accursed and that he cannot deliver himself from it; and then claims the slaying power of Christ's cross within him—it is when a man does this and says: "This spiritual life prepared for me is the free gift of my God in Christ Jesus," that he understands how one step can bring him out of the carnal into the spiritual state.

### One Step That Can Change Your Life

Ever get discouraged when you look at eminently spiritual men and women of God, and then at your own anemic spiritual life? You hear a missionary or a great evangelist speak, and you wish you could have their spirit of consecration and self-giving to the Lord.

So far we have been considering three of the four steps necessary to the changeover from a carnal Christian, possessing the Holy Spirit only to the degree that ensures our salvation, to becoming filled to overflowing with God's Spirit. We have seen first of all that it takes a conviction on our part that such a life is possible. Second, it takes the conviction of being a Christian and at the same time carnal. And third, it takes a recognition of the fact that to leave this sinful carnal state and become a truly spiritual Christian takes just one step.

Let us pursue this last step a little further, as we continue listening to that eminently spiritual man of God, Andrew Murray. He says that when we enter upon the spiritual life,

> there will be much still to be learned. There will still be imperfections. Spiritual life is not perfect, but the predominant characteristic will be spiritual. When a man has given himself up to the real, living, acting, ruling power of God's Spirit, he has got into the right position in which he can grow. You never think of growing out of sickness into health; you may grow out of feebleness into strength, as the little babe can grow to be a strong man, but where there is disease, there must healing come if there is to be a cure effected. There are Christians who think that they must grow out of the carnal state into the spiritual state. You never can. What could help those carnal Corinthians? To give them milk could not help them, for milk was a proof they were in the wrong state. To give them meat would not help them, for they were unfit to eat it. What they needed was the knife of the surgeon. Paul says that the carnal life must be cut out. "They that are Christ's have crucified the flesh" (Gal. 5:24). When a man understands what that means, and accepts it in the faith of what Christ can do, then one step can bring him from carnal to spiritual. One simple act of faith in the power of Christ's death, one act of surrender to the fellowship of Christ's death as the Holy Spirit can make it ours, will bring deliverance from the power of your efforts.
>
> What brought deliverance to that poor condemned sinner who was most dark and wretched in his unconverted state? He felt he could do nothing good of himself. What did he do? He saw set before him the almighty Savior and he cast himself into His arms; he trusted himself to that omnipotent love and cried, "Lord have mercy upon me." That was salvation. It was not for what he did that Christ accepted him. Oh, believers, if any of us who are conscious that the carnal state predominates have to say: "It marks me; I am a religious man, an earnest man, a friend of missions; I work for Christ in my church, but, alas! temper and sin and worldliness have still the mastery over my soul," hear the word of God. If any will come and say: "I have struggled, I have prayed, I have wept, and it has not helped me," then you must do one other thing. You must see that the living Christ is God's provision for your holy, spiritual life. You must believe that Christ who accepted you once, at conversion, in His wonderful love is now waiting to say to you that you may become a spiritual man, entirely given up to God. If you will believe that, your

> fear will vanish and you will say: "It can be done; if Christ will accept and take charge, it shall be done."

The final point Andrew Murray brings out is that a man must take that step of becoming spiritual. We cannot expect the Lord to take away the ugly fruits of carnality while the poisonous root stays in us. We must ask Him to nail our flesh to His cross and must give up self entirely to the power of the Holy Spirit.

> There is deliverance, but not in the way we seek it. Suppose a painter had a piece of canvas, on which he desired to work out some beautiful picture. Suppose that piece of canvas does not belong to him and anyone has a right to take it and to use it for any other purpose; do you think the painter would bestow much work on that? No. Yet people want Jesus Christ to bestow His trouble upon them in taking away this temper, or that other sin, though in their hearts they have not yielded themselves utterly to His command and His keeping. It can not be. But if you will come and give your whole life into His charge, Christ Jesus waits to be gracious; Christ Jesus waits to fill you with His Spirit. . . . It is the Holy Spirit alone who by His indwelling can make a spiritual man [see Murray 1896, 16–24].

In the horse and buggy days, a man was driving with his wife along a dangerous road. At a very narrow place the wife became frightened and seized the rein nearest to her. Her husband quietly passed her the other rein and let go. Then she was more frightened than ever, and said, "Oh, don't you let go!" He answered, "Two people cannot drive one and the same horse; either I must drive or you must." Then she gave him the reins and he drove safely past the danger.

If we wish God to rule over us, we must give everything into His hands and let Him manage for us. Either God must be our King or self will rule our lives.

The spirit to obey is a ready solution of most of the practical problems of knowing and doing God's will. Once you have come to regard yourself purely in the light of a servant of Christ, with absolutely no desire but to know His will and do it, you may be sure that He will not leave you in the dark, but will lead you "in the paths of righteousness for his name's sake" (Ps. 23:3).

Make this beautiful hymn your prayer:

> My Jesus, as Thou wilt!
> Oh, may Thy will be mine!
> Into Thy hand of love
> I now my all resign.
> Through sorrow, or through joy,
> Conduct me as Thine own,
> And help me still to say,
> My Lord, Thy will be done!

## Growth, the Mark of a Spiritual Christian

What is the first thought that comes into your mind when you hear the word "carnal"? It is probably the dictionary definition of "relating to or given to crude bodily pleasures." But let us examine how the apostle Paul applied the word in chapter 3 of his first letter to the Corinthians.

There are two similar Greek words translated in this chapter as "carnal." The first is *sarkínois*, in verse 1: "And I, brethren, could not speak unto you as unto spiritual, but as unto carnal." This is the dative plural of *sárkinos*. It comes from the substantive *sarx*, which means, "flesh," and the suffix *-inos*, which designates the stuff of which anything is made. For instance, if something is made of skin, it is called *dermátinos*, *dérma* being "skin" and *-inos* the stuff of which something is made. *Sárkinos*, therefore, means "that which is made of flesh." It denounces its constitution, not necessarily its ethical propensity. It simply means something that has flesh for its material. If we wanted to translate *sárkinos* correctly we should say "fleshy, made of flesh." We are all carnal, all *sarkínoi* (pl.) in this sense, for we are all made of flesh. This is unavoidable. It is part of our make-up. And because we are made of flesh we are indeed affected by our body. We all recognize this when we quote Christ's words, "The spirit indeed is willing, but the flesh is weak" (Matt. 26:41).

But to be *sarkikoí* (pl.), "carnal or fleshly," is something entirely different. (Notice the change from *n* to *k* in the spelling.) This is the word used in verse 3 in all the texts, including the Textus Receptus. The latter, however, used *sarkikoís* in the first verse, though the latest Greek text of the United Bible Society has *sarkinoís. Sarkikoí* pertains to our sinful desires that move and stir in the ethical domain of the flesh. When Peter, in 1 Peter 2:11, speaks of "fleshly lusts" (*sarkikṓn epithumiṓn*), he is referring to lusts that begin with our animal soul and express themselves through our body. The body itself does not have to act in an evil way. The fact that we are *sarkínoi* made of flesh, does not mean that we must act as *sarkikoí*, fleshly, doing those sinful things through our body that are prompted by our fallen nature.

Thus, when the apostle Paul speaks of the Corinthians as being *sarkínoi* "fleshy," instead of *pneumatikoî*, "spiritual," in 1 Corinthians 3:1, he finds serious fault indeed with them, but the accusation is far less grave than if he had called them *sarkikoí*, "carnal or fleshly." (Again note the difference of one letter here in the words "fleshy" and "fleshly.")

As R. C. H. Lenski says, "At one time, in their early days, they were *sarkínoi* (fleshy), still largely made up of flesh because their spiritual part was still in the infant stage. They could then not help it." And Trench says:

> He does not hereby charge them with positive active opposition to the Spirit of God—this is evident from the *hṓs nḗpioi*, as unto babes, with which he proceeds to explain it—but only that they were intellectually as well as spiritually tarrying at the threshold of the faith (Heb. 5:11, 12). A baby has no malice. He acts like a baby because he is one, and he cannot help being one. There is no moral responsibility to being a baby. Every newly born-again Christian is a baby and acts as *sarkinós* ac-

> cording to his body nature. This is constitutional immaturity because of lack of time in order to grow. But *sarkikós* indicates moral responsibility. You are a baby spiritually because you wanted to be such, not because you had to.
>
> He [Paul] charges them as making no progress, that they were content to remain where they were, when they might have been carried far onward by the mighty transforming powers of that Spirit freely given to them of God. He does not charge them in this word [*sarkínoi* in v. 1] with being anti-spiritual but only with being unspiritual, with being flesh and little more, when they might have been much more. He goes on indeed, at verses 3 and 4, to charge them with the graver guilt of allowing the *sarx* (flesh) to work actively as a ruling principle in them; and he consequently changes his word to *sarkikoí*, carnal. They were not simply sarkínoi, fleshy only as all of us are when we are born into the kingdom of God, for no man and no church can long tarry at this point, but *sarkikoí* (carnal) as well, and as such, full of envying and strife and divisions. These are active sinful propensities, not mere passive characteristics of one's nature. You never accuse a baby of being evil simply because he or she acts like a baby.

As Lenski says:

> The difference between the two terms is: "fleshy" (*sarkinós*), and you cannot help it; "fleshly" (*sarkikós*), and you can but do not help it. "Fleshy" (*sarkinós*), you carry a bad load but will soon be rid of most of it; "fleshly" (*sarkikós*), you follow a bad norm and refuse to get rid of it. Paul approves of neither condition but cannot especially blame them for the former whereas he must decidedly blame them for the latter. Our versions erase the difference by using the one word, "carnal," as a translation of both Greek terms (*sarkinós, sarkikós*) [Lenski 1961, 123, 124].

A friend asked Longfellow the secret of his continued interest in life. Pointing to a nearby apple tree he said, "The purpose of that apple tree is to grow a little new wood each year. That is what I plan to do." Longfellow also expressed the thought poetically:

> Not enjoyment and not sorrow
> Is our destined end alway;

But to live that each tomorrow
Finds us further than today.

The Christian life, Paul asserts to the Corinthians, must be a continuous progress toward perfection. "Let us cleanse ourselves from all filthiness of the flesh and spirit, perfecting holiness in the fear of God" (2 Cor. 7:1; see Trench 1953, 272–74).

### Encouraging Spiritual Growth

Non-Christians are often puzzled, as Nicodemus was, by the meaning of the term "born-again." Very simply, to be born-again means that God's life enters our life, somewhat like a spiritual seed—and like a seed it must grow. The gods of the ancients were born full-grown. That is how we know they were fictitious. But the Spirit-indwelt Christian does not suddenly become full-grown. Christians begin as babes in Christ (*sarkínoi*) and advance through certain stages of normal growth to "the measure of the stature of the fulness of Christ" (Eph. 4:13).

There are many parallels between the physical and the spiritual. Just as there is natural growth in the physical seed so there must be in the spiritual. It is not growth by accumulation but development from within. An example of development by accumulation is what happens to a snowball that boys roll downhill in the wintertime. "See how big it grows!" they exclaim. That is not really growing. That is enlargement by accretion from without.

That is not the development Paul wanted to see in the Corinthians. The seed of the Holy Spirit planted in them had given them new life. But it remained undeveloped from within. It did not spring up into the works and fruits of the Spirit. Even as the ground baked hard by a drought covers a seed and does not allow it to spring up into the vision of the outside world, so the flesh often dominates in a Christian's life and acts in much the same manner to prevent the shooting forth of the Spirit in power.

Paul insists that the Christian life must be characterized by growth because the life of the Spirit indwells the believer. Such growth is not expected of the natural man, the unbeliever because God's life is not in him. How futile it would be for you to look for plants to spring up in ground where you had not placed any seed. Paul had planted the seed in Corinth (1 Cor. 3:7) and like a good farmer he expected to see something come of it. Even as he wrote this epistle, it was in the hope that the seed of the Spirit would begin to grow.

Neither the Spirit nor Paul could be blamed for the spiritual infantilism of the Corinthians; it was their own fault. True growth is spontaneous. The soul or spirit grows as the lily grows, without trying, without fretting, without ever thinking. No child grows by effort. No man "by taking thought can add one cubit unto his stature" (Matt. 6:27). And yet growth is commanded. Peter writes. "But grow in grace, and in the knowledge of our Lord and Savior Jesus Christ" (2 Pet. 3:18).

Growth is dependent upon health, and health is conditioned to a great extent by what we do for ourselves: the air we breathe, the food we eat, the cleanliness we maintain, the exercise we take. You never think of commanding a plant to grow; you water it and expose it to sunlight in order to encourage its growth. So when Paul is distressed about the stunted growth of the Corinthians, and Peter commands the Christians to grow, they indicate that they are not like plants with no say in the matter, but they are men with wills that can resist or encourage growth, who can either further or hinder their progress. The state of being *sarkínoi,* "fleshly," is a condition of inaction, of passivity; the state of being *sarkikoí* is one of resistance to the elements that cause growth.

Two children resolved to share the night between them watching over their mother who was sick. The order given to each child was important: whatever else they did, they were not to let the fire go out or to let the room become too heated. Life depended on their watchful obedience. Ample fuel was close by for each to use. The first child, who had a thoughtful, loving nature, watched and fed the fire with unsleeping vigilance. The second made the fire up once, and toward morning slept, neglected it, and let it go out. This is an apt illustration of the *sárkinos* (fleshy) Christian in contrast to the *pneumatikṓs* (spiritual) one.

Your heart is the hearth prepared to receive the holy fire; the fuel is abundant; the command is imperative that you feed life's spiritual flame and force. Neglect, want of interest, or unsuitable fuel explain the *sárkinos*, "fleshy," Christian who remains an undeveloped baby, cold and impoverished within.

As we explained in previous studies, the apostle Paul was complaining that the Corinthians, in spite of the fact that they were not new Christians, were carnal, *sarkikoí*. And we saw that the word "carnal" in 1 Corinthians 3:3 was to be differentiated from the word *sarkínoi* in the first verse, which means "fleshy, or made of flesh."

Paul realized that every person who is indwelt by the Spirit of God, while not "in the flesh" (Rom. 8:9) is still impacted by the flesh and must cope with its weaknesses. He does not have to give ascendancy to his fallen nature over his spiritual nature. When he does this he is *sarkikós,* "carnal." Of course, it is difficult to know the quality of a person's soul. We must not be too quick to judge others in this respect, but should first pass judgment on ourselves. *Sarkikós,* "carnal," actually describes the one who suffers defeat in his Christian life. Is that your state?

## External Characteristics of a Carnal Christian

Paul enumerates three of them here in 1 Corinthians 3:3. It is apparent that the Corinthian Christians were trying to deny Paul's accusation that they were carnal. They considered themselves spiritual and actually far superior to Christians elsewhere. It is so easy for us to be self-deceived in these matters and to think more highly of ourselves than we ought.

A humble layman, talking to a young minister, asked, "What do you consider the greatest hindrance to spiritual growth?" The minister replied, "A failure to renounce our sinful self." "No, no," quickly replied the layman. "The greatest hindrance to spiritual growth is our failure to renounce our righteous self and acknowledge that all our righteousnesses, apart from Christ, are as filthy rags in His sight." The carnal Corinthians could not see this. They prided themselves on their supposed spirituality and the "gifts" they possessed, which they considered heaven-sent, but which they used in a carnal manner. Paul comes right out and says, "Ye are yet carnal." And how do I know it? Here is the reason: "For whereas there is among you envying, and strife, and divisions, are ye not carnal, and walk as men?"

## Noble and Ignoble Zeal

The first reason Paul gives for calling the Corinthian Christians carnal is that there was envying among them. The Greek word translated "envying" in 1 Corinthians 3:3 is *zḗlos*. It is one of two Greek words commonly translated "envy." The other is *phthónos*, found in Matthew 27:18; Mark 15:10; Romans 1:29; Galatians 5:21; Philippians 1:15; 1 Timothy 6:4; Titus 3:3; James 4:5; and 1 Peter 2:1. *Phthónos* always has a bad connotation. It refers to the desire to deprive another person of what he has. But this is not the word used in 1 Corinthians 3:3, *zḗlos*, which can have either a bad or a good meaning. It is the word from which we derive the English "zeal" in its good connotation, and "jealousy" in its bad connotation. This word is also found in Acts 13:45; Romans 13:13; 2 Corinthians 12:20; and James 3:14, 16, where it denotes a sinful attitude.

Aristotle used the word exclusively in the noble sense, as that active emulation or ambition which grieves, not that another has that which is good, but that you do not have it. You see something that you admire in another person. You regret that you do not have it, but you do not envy the person who has it. You become ambitious to acquire a similar virtue or possession, without wishing to deprive the other of that which you do not possess. *Zḗlos* (zeal) according to Aristotle is that wonderful ambition that causes people to climb upward. Thus, Paul spoke of a "godly jealousy" (2 Cor. 11:2).

Paul uses it in this sense, in its noun form, in Titus 2:14 when he says that we, as a peculiar people of God, must be "zealous of good works" (*zēlōtḗn*). We know of the good works God requires of us, and we see good works in others. We are to desire these ourselves without in any way being jealous of those who excel us in this matter. How tragic if we lack this zeal for growth in our Christian experience! Over the life of each Christian should be written the words inscribed on a monument erected to an Alpine guide who perished while attempting to ascend a peak: "He died climbing."

It is evident, however, that Paul does not use the word here in a good but in a bad sense. Zeal is an emotion that you can channel either for good or for evil. It can harm others or it can benefit yourself. But it should never benefit you at the expense of harm to another person. As a Christian you can never elevate yourself by stepping on someone you have knocked down. It is so easy for good zeal and honorable rivalry to degenerate into a mean passion. Zeal becomes jealousy when you desire to have the same thing someone else has simply because you want to be equal to or superior to him. It does not spring from a sense of humility but from pride.

This word *zẽlos* is enumerated as one of the works of the flesh in Galatians 5:20, but is translated "emulations," though the word is singular and should be translated "jealousy." There are few sins that create a greater torture of unhappiness than jealousy. To have a jealous nature is to be exposed to an incessant gnawing of the heart. It accompanies many through life and exerts a most baneful influence on Christians.

Cain's rash act was triggered by jealousy. It angered him that Abel's worship was more acceptable to God than his own. And down through the ages we see jealousy cropping out in the relations of God's children. It was especially prevalent among the Corinthian Christians. They were characterized by a zeal that, when it came to the boiling point, became jealousy, a carnal distortion of Christian zeal.

How can you tell whether or not you have a jealous nature? When you are sorry over the promotion or progress of another person, then you are jealous. If you rejoice when someone gets ahead, then you are not jealous.

In a home where there were canary cages, one on either side of a window, a visitor made some comment about the birds. Whereupon the hostess remarked that one of the canaries was exceedingly jealous. She then proved her statement. Going to the cage of the bird that was not jealous, she began petting it, calling it pretty names and chatting with it. The reaction of the other canary was remarkable. Its feathers ruffled up, it fluttered all about the cage, and made angry squawks of protest. There was no question about its jealous nature.

Maybe you do not squawk angrily when a brother of yours is well-spoken-of, but are you ever tempted to make some belittling remark to lower him in the other person's esteem? That is jealousy, whether you recognize it or not. Dr. F. B. Meyer told the following experience to a few personal friends:

> It was easy, to pray for the success of Campbell Morgan when he was in America, but when he came back to England and took a church near to mine it was somewhat different. The old Adam in me was inclined to jealousy, but I got my heel upon his head, and, whether I felt right toward my friend or not, I determined to act right.
>
> My church gave a reception for him, and I acknowledged that if it was not necessary for me to preach Sunday evenings, I would dearly love to go and hear him myself. Well, that made me feel right toward him. But just see how the dear Lord helped me out of my difficulty. There was Thomas Spurgeon preaching wonderfully on the other side of me. He and Mr. Morgan were so popular and drew such crowds that our church caught the overflow, and we had all we could accommodate.

It really does not seem from the human standpoint that any logical man can rejoice when another is more successful than he. But this is what a Christian should do, and the overflow of the blessing that comes upon others will often come upon yourself. Jealousy always injures you more than the one of whom you are jealous.

Dwight. L. Moody told of two merchants between whom there was great rivalry and bitter feeling. One of them was converted. He went to his minister and said, "I'm still jealous of that man, and I don't know how to overcome it." "Well," said the minister, "if a man comes into your store to buy goods, and you cannot supply him, just send him over to your neighbor." He said he would not like to do that. "Well," said the minister, "you do it, and you will kill jealousy." Sure enough, when he began sending customers over to his rival for goods he himself could not supply, the other man began to send his customers over to this man's store, and the breach was healed. Why not try that philosophy to find that it will kill the spirit of jealousy in you?

## Fighting among Christians

When the Holy Spirit enters your heart and life, He produces a basic change in you to conform you to the image of Christ. Nevertheless, your own spirit, soul, and body do not change their particular and personal characteristics. When you become a Christian, Christ may put a smile on your face and add sweetness to your voice, but your physical characteristics and personal idiosyncrasies remain the same to a great extent. You become attached to the Lord Jesus Christ, but you do not become identical with every other believer. There is no uniform or stereotyped mold into which the Christian is compressed. Of course, in a certain way we are all like Christ because He indwells us.

Take a look at the disciples of Christ. Each one was a different personality when the Lord called him. They remained basically the same personalities, though sanctified by the Spirit of God. In their walk with Christ we find them exhibiting vastly different behavioral traits. Simon Peter was headstrong, impulsive, opinionated. Andrew was quiet, unassuming, willing to work behind the scenes. James was enthusiastic, ardent, vehement. John was loving and sympathetic. Matthew, a man with a "past," did all in his power to live it down and succeeded admirably. James the son of Alphaeus seemed to prefer to be in the background. Thaddaeus exhibited a spirit of bigotry. Philip was a realist, slow, calculating, and somewhat lacking in faith. Bartholomew was quick-witted. Thomas will be remembered as a doubter. Simon the Canaanite, or Zealot, was somewhat of a politician and nationalist. Judas Iscariot was selfish, greedy, and a traitor. Is it not true that all of us can find our counterpart to some degree in this group of disciples?

## Strife between Christians

Our individuality, however, should not lead us into conflict with one another. If it does, the apostle Paul tells us, we are carnal. In 1 Corinthians 3:3 he says to the Corinthians, "Ye are yet carnal: for whereas there is among you envying, and strife, and divisions, are ye not carnal, and walk as men?" We have seen that the word "envying" is the word *zē̃los* in Greek, which would better be translated "jealousy." It is misguided enthusiasm in the life of the Christian.

But what is "strife"? The Greek word is *éris*, which means "contention" and is an expression of enmity. Observe that this follows the word *zē̃los*, "zeal or jealousy," which is actually a state of emotional excitement. *Éris*, "strife," is what follows this emotional excitement. A carnal Christian can become so excited about how different he is from others that he begins to quarrel with them in his endeavor to make them like himself. Naturally, he encounters resistance because it is only human nature to resent being told what we should or should not do or be. In such a situation, you have two Christians, one saying that he is better than the other, and the other disputing this fact and insisting that he is going to remain what he is. This comparison of one's self with others—the attitude that says, "I am better than you are, and you ought to become like me"—is a frequent cause of trouble among Christians and in the church.

Paul brings up a third external characteristic of Corinthian Christian carnality, in addition to jealousy and fighting, and that is "divisions." It is interesting to note that the words "jealousy" (*zē̃los*) and "fighting or strife" (*éris*) are in the singular, whereas "divisions" (*dichostasíai*) is plural. There is a progressiveness to these evils. The first, "jealousy," is a disposition of the soul. You may feel jealous of someone and wish he were not so elevated and you so low, but you may not actually get into a fight about it. But "jealousy" leads to "strife," which is more overt. A jealous person is the most likely to fight. And when fighting erupts, the observers are likely to take sides. They begin to stand together in support of or opposition to the various elements of strife. One person may start one fight, but this can ramify into many divisions.

The word in Greek is *dichostasíai,* which is made up of *dichḗ*, meaning "in two ways," implying "asunder, apart," and *stásis*, "standing." Actually, the root *di* in *dichḗ* is used in English and other languages to indicate division, as in the word "division" itself. It means to stand separate from others. This is the same word Paul uses in Romans 16:17 when he says, "Now I beseech you, brethren, mark them which cause divisions [*dichostasías*, in the acc.] and offenses contrary to the doctrine which ye have learned; and avoid them." These are those who deny apostolic teaching and form their own apostate groups or denominations. They are not even Christian believers, and they are to be avoided by believers. Romans 16:20 equates them with Satan.

When such people separate themselves, denying the truth of the apostles and of Christ, we are not to approach them with a view to fellowship. Avoid them, Paul says. Are you avoiding apostates or do you fraternize with them? It is as much a sign of carnality to have fellowship with those who deny Christ as it is to cause unwarranted divisions. This does not mean that we can have nothing at all to do with them in the course of our daily lives, but that we are not to be on such friendly terms with them as to indicate that we condone or overlook their apostate condition.

As the *Berean Expositor* says:

> While we must ever watch our hearts and words lest Faction should be encouraged, we must equally weigh over the teaching of the Word as to Fellowship. Many who have sought to avoid the evil of a party spirit

> have, however, overstepped the scriptural bounds of Fellowship. We are urged to "put up no bar," and not to sit in judgment upon fellow believers. . . . But we must not allow ourselves to become entangled in a fellowship that is contrary to the Word, merely for sentimental or other feelings. While we are enjoined to "receive him that is weak in the faith," and not to despise the one whose weakness caused him to act very differently to ourselves, there are occasions when continued fellowship becomes a betrayal of our trust. John in his second epistle 9–11 says: "Whoso leadeth forward [*proágōn*—lit. translation] and abideth not in the doctrine of Christ hath not God. . . . If there come any unto you and bring not this doctrine, receive him not into your house, and greet him not; for he who greets him has fellowship [*koinōneí*] with his evil deeds" [*The Berean Expositor* 1918, 92].

## Divisions in the Church

Have you ever heard anyone say, "One religion is as good as another; after all, we all worship the same God, don't we?" What always amazes me when people make a statement like that is that they never seem to think God has anything to say about it. "We'll worship God in our own way, and He'll surely accept us," is their implicit assumption. Yet as far back as the book of Genesis that attitude led to tragic consequences. You remember that Cain killed Abel out of jealousy because Abel's worship was acceptable to God and Cain's was not. This should surely give pause to those who claim that all modes of worship are acceptable to God.

In writing to Timothy, the apostle Paul gave him sound advice that would preserve him from this very mistake. "If any man teach otherwise, and consent not to wholesome words, even the words of our Lord Jesus Christ, and to the doctrine which is according to godliness . . . from such withdraw thyself" (1 Tim. 6:3–6; see also 2 Tim. 4:3; Titus 1:11; 2 Pet. 2:1).

Clearly we see that Christians are to stand distinctively apart from those who teach or embrace false doctrine, who reject the basic teaching of the Word of God concerning the Lord Jesus Christ and His atonement for sinful man. Refusal to be aligned with those who disregard or pervert God's Word is not a sign of carnality but is the outcome of spirituality. A spiritual person must be able to discern who has and who does not have the Spirit of God. Paul spoke of this spirit of sound judgment and spiritual discernment in 1 Corinthians 2:15, "But the spiritual [person] discerns all"—including discernment of the natural man who considers the fundamental doctrines of the Word of God foolishness.

We have scriptural ground for such division. For instance, read 1 Corinthians 11:18, 19. "For first of all, when ye come together in the church, I hear that there be divisions [*schísmata*] among you; and I partly believe it." Paul is not happy about these schisms or divisions. He wishes they did not exist. But he goes on to tell the Corinthians of the inevitability of divisions, since they are based on matters of important doctrines. In the 19th verse he says, "For there must be also heresies among you, that they which are approved may be made manifest among you." That expression, "there must be," is *deí* in Greek, indicating the necessary consequence of an evil course after it has been chosen. Some people have decided to renounce fundamental Christian doctrines. That is an evil. The Christian believers in a church are not responsible for it. But they must do something about it. They must separate themselves from the unbelievers who are promoting heresies in the church. "For there must be heresies among you, that they which are approved may be made manifest among you." The Greek word for "heresies" here comes from the verb *hairéō*, which means "to choose or select." When unbelief comes into the local church it is an evil. The Christian in the Spirit discerns it. He is not supposed to tolerate it but to expose it, even as Paul is doing. The result is a schism, a rending or splitting of the church. There are those who choose (*hairoúsin*) to leave. These may be the believing or the unbelieving ones.

It is bad, of course, for any split to occur in a local congregation, but it is a must when unbelief is disrupting the unity of the Spirit, without any prospect of true repentance and return to the faith. (This does not mean that we are to eject the unsaved who come into the congregation and listen to the gospel, whether they receive Christ or not. This refers to those who actively espouse error and endeavor to contaminate others.) The apostle Paul indicates that we are to expect such situations, and he tells us how to act. "Now the Spirit speaketh expressly, that in the latter times some shall depart from the faith, giving heed to seducing spirits, and doctrines of devils; speaking lies in hypocrisy; having their conscience seared with a hot iron" (1 Tim. 4:1, 2).

And Peter writes, "But there were false prophets among the people, even as there shall be false teachers among you, who privily shall bring in damnable heresies, even denying the Lord that bought them, and bring upon themselves swift destruction" (2 Pet. 2:1).

On the other hand, *dichostasíai*, "divisions," can also be the works of the flesh as Paul includes them in Galatians 5:19, 20. There they are translated "seditions," but it is the same word as in 1 Corinthians 3:3. Paul condemns the Corinthians for divisions, for setting themselves apart in various parties and groups. But these divisions did not have as their basis a departure from the fundamental doctrines of the gospel—in which case they would have been spiritual not carnal acts—but they were caused by disagreements among Christians because of personalities. These groups placed one preacher above another. Those who liked Paul best became Paul's disciples. Those who liked Apollos followed him. Apparently these groups were jealous of one another and fought among themselves. Yet they were all born-again believers. That is Christian carnality. No divisions should arise in any assembly of believers because of jealousy which brings strife.

Follow the order of the words that Paul uses in 1 Corinthians 3:3: jealousy, strife, divisions. The Textus Receptus from which the King James Version was translated included this word *dichostasíai*, but in the United Bible Societies' Text used for more modern translations it is not included. Judging from the exegetical sequence, I would take the text that includes *dichostasíai*, as referring to the people standing apart in groups because of strifes that emanate from jealousy over the personalities of their leaders.

A flourishing church was once reduced to complete ineffectuality by this very sin. Sunday School had customarily been held in the afternoon. But the pastor and others in the church wanted to change it to the morning hour. They knew that the Sunday School superintendent was strongly opposed to this. Rather than face the matter openly with him, they met in secret and voted to change the hour. When he learned of it, his feelings were deeply hurt. Angry words were exchanged. People in the church began to take sides, and soon a sizable faction moved out. Bitterness quenched the work of the Spirit, and what was once a deeply spiritual and soul-winning church became a scantily attended assemblage. Lacking support, the edifice itself became shabby and unattractive, reflecting outwardly the destructive result of jealousy, that led to strife, that led to divisions.

## Lessons:

1. The spiritual Christian should be meek and duty-bound to help his carnal brother. This primarily is the result of the indwelling of the Holy Spirit. The Greek text says "be continuously filled."
2. The unconverted man is not convicted of the corruption of his nature. He thinks principally about external sins. But the carnal believer is in

a different condition; his sins are far deeper. Not until he is convicted of his carnal state and humbled can he become a spiritual Christian. It takes just one step and that step is to put everything into God's hands.

3. The Christian life is characterized by growth because the life of the Spirit indwells the believer. Such growth is not expected of the natural man because God's life is not in him.
4. You conform to the image of Christ when the Holy Spirit enters your heart and life, though some aspects of your personality do not change. You become attached to the Lord Jesus Christ, but you do not become identical to any other believer. In some ways, we are all like Christ because He dwells in us.
5. Our individuality should not cause conflicts, but occasionally there is fighting and strife among Christians. Paul calls this carnality. Jealousy or envy can be good or bad, depending on the object. A "godly jealousy" desires the godly qualities in others. An evil jealousy desires the worldly objects or status of others. A frequent cause of trouble among Christians is the attitude that says "I am better than you are."
6. It has been said, "One religion is as good as another, since we worship the same God." In Genesis 4, Cain killed Abel out of jealousy because Abel's worship was acceptable and Cain's was not. Christians are to stand apart from those who teach or embrace false doctrines. A spiritual person must be able to discern who has and who does not have the Spirit of God. No divisions should arise in any assembly of believers out of jealousy.

# 1 Cor. 3:4 — The Sin of Idolizing a Preacher

*For while one saith, I am of Paul; and another, I am of Apollos; are ye not carnal?*

Is a Christian ever justified in leaving the church of which he is a member—and if so, under what circumstances? It seems necessary for Christians to have some guidelines as to when a "party spirit" is necessary and when not. If it is necessary, it is not wrong; if it is not necessary, it is wrong.

The party spirit in Corinth at the time Paul was writing was occasioned by the admiration of some people for individual preachers, such as Paul and Apollos, both faithful to the Word of God. Paul wanted them to realize that they were not conducting themselves as spiritual men but as natural men, as people of the world.

The tragedy of this situation was that these Corinthian Christians were separatists for the wrong reason—not in defense of doctrinal truth but in defense of their preference for one man over another, elevating him to a position that only the Lord Jesus should hold. "Are ye not carnal, and walk as men?" Paul asks. The expression "as men," *katá anthrṓpon* in Greek, means "according to the manner of men," referring here, of course, to unregenerate men. You would expect such conduct from those who do not possess the indwelling Spirit of God. But when those who profess Christ exhibit such conduct, natural men will ask, "What's the difference between them and us?"

How easily we can put to shame the gospel we profess to believe by our jealousy and strife and the divisions that result from them. We need to pray as David did, "O God thou knowest my foolishness; and my sins are not hid from thee. Let not them that wait on thee, O Lord of hosts, be ashamed for my sake: let not those that seek thee be confounded for my sake [because of me], O God of Israel" (Ps. 69:5, 6). Conduct that is regarded as natural for natural men should not be the norm for spiritual men, the regenerate children of God.

Paul wanted the Corinthian Christians to understand that glorying in and glorifying men, even those as good, faithful and worthy as Apollos and himself, was in truth nothing less than dishonoring God. It showed in them a disposition more like men of the world than like those converted to the Christian faith. He gave them to understand that he and Apollos were not to be viewed in any other light than as God's ministers, through whose instrumentality they had come to believe in Christ. He clearly indicates that neither he nor Apollos did anything to bring about this party spirit among them.

Perhaps the greatest temptation that can come to a gospel preacher is to allow himself to be idolized by those to whom he ministers. Let us watch for this tendency in ourselves, fellow servants in the Lord, and do everything in our power to discourage attachment to ourselves rather than to the Lord. It is said that C. T. Studd, England's famous cricketer, who went to the heart of Africa as an ambassador for Christ, in saying goodbye to a friend at the railway station, wrote upon a card: "Take my life and let it be/A hidden cross revealing Thee."

No greater joy ever came to my heart after preaching the Word of God at a Bible conference than to have a woman say to me, "Your ministry made me love Christ more." I felt my ministry had really succeeded in what I aimed for: the glory of God. In all we do or say, Christ must have the preeminence. That does not mean we will not put our best efforts into the preparation of our sermons and ministry, but that Christ will be central. He must be preeminent.

If any preacher finds that believers want to listen to no one but him, he must beware lest he is being regarded as an idol, and must point out that those who have a tendency to idolize him are in that respect carnal. It takes courage and tact to do this. But if the Christian who attaches himself in a party spirit to any one preacher is considered carnal, how much more the preacher who allows himself to become the leader of a party or faction because he enjoys having the preeminence? As there are carnal laymen there are also carnal preachers. A preacher is carnal if he does not repudiate divisions in the church caused by adherence to him as a personality.

Do not misunderstand me. I am not saying it is wrong for Christians to esteem God's servants who minister to them and through whose ministry they are blessed. It is not wrong to think and speak well of them. But it is wrong and carnal to esteem them so highly that you treat all others as unworthy of regard. If you have no praise for anyone outside your own denomination, or other than one particular preacher, you may well come under the same condemnation as the Corinthian Christians whom Paul called carnal because of that very attitude.

We must draw a careful line of distinction here between proper esteem and idolatrous regard for God's servants. Paul commands us in 1 Thessalonians 5:12, 13, "We beseech you, brethren, to know them which labor among you, and are over you in the Lord, and admonish you; and to esteem them very highly in love for their work's sake." It is not blameworthy to prefer one man's preaching, or personality, or conduct of his ministry over another's. Some ministers may, like Paul, be more learned than others; some, like Apollos, more eloquent. But when all are servants of the same great Master, faithful to His Word, engaged in the same great work, and pursuing the same great end, then all ought to be highly esteemed. Let none of them, therefore, be spoken of with contempt, or lightly regarded. You may feel more attachment to some than to others without being culpable. But if you set up some in opposition to others, or if you disparage and despise others, you are carnal and blameworthy.

Had those who said they were "of Paul" only spoken of Paul as the minister of Christ through whom they had obtained the most spiritual benefit; or had those who said they were "of Apollos" only spoken of Apollos as the minister of Christ under whom they had made the most progress in the spiritual life, there would have been nothing wrong in their attitudes. It is certainly true that the preaching of one may be most useful to some, while the preaching of another is more useful to others. And people who attend to the one under whom they reap the most advantage are not blameworthy. Only when they cause factions by their personal attachments may they rightly be called "carnal."

### Can Any Church Save You?

When a Christian minister stands before his congregation, he does so as a representative of the truths he preaches. If he fails to live up to them, those who are weak in the faith may become disillusioned, not only with him but also with the gospel he proclaims. Losing faith in him, they may also lose faith in God. And this, not because God has failed them, but because they have set up a man in place of God and have expected of him the perfection that only God possesses.

Thus when one group of Corinthian Christians announced that they were adherents of Paul, and another group favored

Apollos, they would allow none other to be spoken of with respect. They did more than prefer one minister over another; they did more than sow the evils of discord by their partisanship. In effect they put Paul and Apollos in the place of God. Had they only esteemed such ministers of the gospel very highly in love for their work's sake; had they only esteemed them as the instrument employed in doing them good; they would have done nothing more than was really their duty. But they went too far in avowing their attachment. They ascribed too much to Paul and Apollos; and instead of acknowledging the agency of God they confined their acknowledgments to His ministers.

In this they erred; for this they were culpable. And in order to show them their error, as well as the necessity of having it corrected, the apostle Paul both asked and answered the question, "Who then is Paul, and who is Apollos?" Who are they in reality "but ministers by whom ye believed?"—merely instruments employed in bringing you to Christ, even as God commissioned and endowed them, and crowned with success their efforts to profit you. I, Paul, have introduced the gospel among you; that gospel Apollos has continued to preach; and we have done you good. But this good was not accomplished by us in ourselves. It has only and wholly been done by God through our instrumentality; and the praise should not be ascribed to us but entirely to God. I have planted, Apollos has watered, but all the increase—the genuine fruit—has been given by God. Our labors among you, had it not been for God, would never have promoted your spiritual welfare. Our endowments are of God, as well as our success. Therefore you ought to regard us as nothing in comparison to God, whom you ought to regard as all in all. "So then neither is he that planteth anything, neither he that watereth, but God that giveth the increase" (1 Cor. 3:7).

Fellow preacher, is this your attitude before God and those to whom you minister? Just one more word of caution about carnality among preachers: When you feel that nobody has written or preached anything that can be of benefit to you, then in this regard you are carnal. I have heard of a Bible teacher who publicly proclaimed that he never read any sermons or expositions of the Scriptures produced by others of the past or the present. All he claimed he needed was the Bible, dictionaries, and a concordance. But the Holy Spirit has given divine insights to others that I lack the capacity to receive directly from the Lord. I can never thank the Lord enough for the 50,000 plus volumes in my library. I stand amazed at how much the Lord has revealed to others that I have missed. The preacher who cannot learn from his fellow ministers, dead or alive, is carnal in that respect.

But to get back to the matter of when it is wrong to have a party spirit. It is carnal if your adherence to one party or another, one church or denomination, gives you the idea that this is what saves you. If the denomination or the church or the minister gives you the assurance that by being a Catholic, or a Greek Orthodox, or a Lutheran, or a Baptist, or whatever, you are automatically a Christian, you are carnal and so is the denomination or minister that tells you this. We are saved by belonging to Christ Himself, and in no other way. The Christian who puts his denomination or its founder or any saint or any preacher on the same level as Christ, or above Him, is a carnal Christian.

On the other hand, we believers are free to discern and choose the church where we feel we are best fed with the Word of God. We must be intelligently conscientious about our choice of church and preacher. But having made our choice, let us not then become religious snobs in our attitude toward other individuals and groups who love the Lord just as much as we and the group we have chosen. As Christians we must make sure that we fellowship where Christ is honored, but we must never think that Christ cannot be honored just as much elsewhere.

No party-distinction can assure any man of the favor of God or heaven. I recall in one of my trials before a criminal court in Greece, on charges of proselytizing through my gospel messages in the press, that my accuser, a high-ranking priest of the state church, claimed just that. During cross-examination one of my attorneys asked him about a young man who had cold-bloodedly killed his own mother in that same town. "He was baptized in the Greek Orthodox church. Was he a Christian? Will he be in heaven some day?" The priest's astonishing answer was that since he was baptized a Greek Orthodox he would be in heaven. That seems hard to believe, but this priest was really consistent in his party-spirit, that claims salvation for every baptized member of his church. Paul declares such claims unscriptural. No one who considered himself as belonging to Paul's party or church was necessarily a member of Christ's body. It is not membership in any church that saves, but being in Christ through personal faith in Him that warrants in any man the hope of salvation. The Scriptures are explicit on this point. Paul told the Galatians, "Neither circumcision availeth anything, nor uncircumcision, but faith which worketh by love" (Gal. 5:6). Nothing is more of a delusion than the assumption that you are a Christian—whether layman or preacher—because you belong to a particular church or denomination.

The story is told of a man who dreamed that he died and went to heaven. Whether true or not, the story points up an important truth. When this man arrived at heaven's gate, the holy watchman asked, "Whom do you want?" He replied that he belonged to a particular denomination and wished to join them in that place. "There are no such people here," was the answer. In vain he mentioned other denominations that he thought he might feel at home with, only to be given the same answer. He was just turning away in despair when, as a last resource, he said, "But I am a Christian." Immediately the gates of heaven flew open and admitted him. On no other ground will anyone be admitted to heaven than on his personal faith in Christ as his Savior and Lord.

**LESSONS:**

1. Christians who separate for reasons other than essential doctrine tend to prefer one leader over another, elevating him to a position that only the Lord Jesus should hold.
2. A gospel preacher may be tempted to allow those to whom he ministers to idolize him. And although it is not wrong for Christians to esteem God's servant when they are being blessed, it is wrong and carnal to esteem him too highly and disregard others as unworthy.
3. A church or denomination cannot save a soul. The Christian minister truly dedicated to preaching Christ is still merely an instrument to bring a soul to Christ. The good accomplished by the preaching of the Word is entirely done by God through the instrument of the Christian preacher.
4. It is carnal to adhere to one church or denomination if you believe that it will save you. As Christians we must make sure that we fellowship where Christ is honored. It is not membership in any church but being in Christ through personal faith in Him that is the hope of salvation.

# 1 Cor. 3:5 | *Is Your Job for God Important?*

*Who then is Paul, and who is Apollos, but ministers by whom ye believed, even as the Lord gave to every man?*

When people ask **who** you are, they want to know your name and what you are like. When they ask **what** you are, they want to know what kind of work you do—whether you are a doctor, a lawyer, a plumber, or whatever. Thus, when Paul addressed this question to the divisive elements in the Christian church at Corinth—"Who then is Paul, and who is Apollos?"—it would seem that he was asking them to make an assessment of their characters.

But is this really what he was asking? The King James Version, translated from the Textus Receptus, asks "Who then is Paul, and who is Apollos?" But other Greek texts use the word *tí*, "what," instead of *tís*, "who." I prefer the "what," which refers to the function they were performing rather than to their characters. There was no question of character here, but of work that Paul and Apollos performed among the Corinthians.

Paul answers the question *tí*, "what," immediately, by saying they are "ministers by whom ye believed." The word translated "ministers" in Greek is *diákonoi*, from which we derive the English word "deacons." This word best expresses the position of those who preached the Word of God to the Corinthians. The word *diákonos* probably comes from the same root that has given us the verb *diṓkō*, "to pursue, to hasten." First Corinthians 14:1 begins: *Diṓkete tḗn agapḗn*, "Pursue after love, or become the ministers of love." A deacon, *diákonos* is one who pursues a particular task. It is commonly translated in the New Testament as "minister." A minister of the gospel, *diákonos euanggelíou*, is one who hastens the gospel on to the hearts of the people. This is to be distinguished from the word *doúlos*, "bond-slave," the word the New Testament uses for those servants whom the king in the parable of Matthew 22:1–14 sent to call those invited to the wedding. But when someone was found in the house without a wedding garment, it was a *diákonos*, a deacon, not a *doúlos* or bond-slave, who was called to put him out. As Trench says:

> The bringers-in of the guests are *doúloi*, bond servants; these, the fulfillers of the King's sentence, are *diákonoi*, deacons—this distinction being a most real one, and belonging to the essentials of the parable; the *doúloi* being men, the ambassadors of Christ, who invite their fellowmen into His kingdom now, the *diákonoi* angels, who in all the judgment acts at the end of the world evermore appear as the executors of the Lord's will [Trench 1953, 32, 33].

Although Paul puts this in the form of a question, he is actually affirming here what he and Apollos and every preacher ought to consider themselves. We are voluntary executors of the Lord's will. We are servants whose aim is one: to cause those who hear us to believe on the Lord Jesus Christ and be saved. We have been nothing but the instruments in God's hands.

Observe that Paul is careful not to say "apostles," in the narrow sense of revealers of inerrant truth concerning the person of the Lord Jesus Christ. When he realized that some of the Corinthians were angry with him because of his reprimands, he asked in 1 Corinthians 9:1, 2, "Am I not an apostle? am I not free? have I not seen Jesus Christ our Lord? are not ye my work in the Lord? If I be not an apostle unto others, yet doubtless I am to you: for the seal of mine apostleship are ye in the Lord." But Apollos was not an apostle in the narrow sense of those who had seen the Lord Jesus Christ after His resurrection and who were in that small circle of the Twelve disciples. As far as the ministry was concerned, however, Paul places Apollos on a par with himself.

But deacons are not necessarily limited to any one function, such as preaching. In Luke 8:1–3 we read of some women who accompanied the Lord Jesus and His disciples on their systematic missionary outreach into the various cities and towns of Galilee. Concerned about their physical care, these women decided voluntarily to follow them in order to serve them, cook for them, wash their clothes, and do those loving offices that women are so admirably qualified to perform.

Among these women were Mary Magdalene, whom the Lord had liberated from terrible demon possession; and Joanna, the wife of Herod's chief financial officer, a man high in society. Both of these women were among those who came early in the morning to the sepulcher to see the dead body of Christ, only to find that He had risen. Those who served Him well in life loved much and expressed it on the resurrection morning. Also among the women who voluntarily served the Lord and His disciples on the evangelistic journey were an unknown Susanna and many others. Luke 8:3 says they "ministered unto them from their belongings" (new UBS text). The word translated "ministered" is the Greek *dīḗkonoun*, the verbal form of *diákonos*, "deacon," the same word Paul used to indicate his and Apollos' work among the Corinthians.

Service to Christ can take different forms. It can be preaching to intellectuals as was the case in Corinth, or it can be washing the garments of those who preach the gospel. Both are voluntary services of genuine importance. Therefore do not feel in any way inferior if the Lord has given you the responsibility of some manual physical ministry in His kingdom. In His sight it is *diakonía*, "ministry," just as important and necessary as preaching and evangelizing. Let no one look down on those who serve the Lord in any way, as though they were doing an inferior work. Do not feel bad because you cannot preach. Be glad that there are those whom God has qualified to do so. Do the job that God has fitted you for without any sense of inferiority.

On the other hand, if God has committed to you the ministry of preaching, do not feel superior to those who may simply scrub the floors in the house of God, if they are doing it as unto the Lord. Their job is a ministry unto God just as worthy in His sight as yours. Respect all who are ministering in the service of Christ, no matter what their particular task may be.

> Is your place a small place?
> Tend it with care!
> He set you there.
> Is your place a large place?
> Tend it with care!
> He set you there.
> Whate'er your place, it is
> Not yours alone, but His
> Who set you there.
>
> —John Oxenham

## Your Gift and How God Uses It

If there is one thing about the apostle Paul that stands out more than another in his letters to the churches, it is that he always spoke the truth in love. Though he never pussyfooted around when dealing with the problem of sin, neither did he castigate the sinner. His tone was one of beseeching, reasoning, persuading, rather than thundering or browbeating. He was a humble man with a grave sense of his God-given mission to preach the gospel and establish believers in the faith. Therefore it grieved him deeply when factions developed in the church at

Corinth because some felt a higher regard for Paul than Apollos, and vice versa.

"Who then is Paul, and who is Apollos, but ministers by whom ye believed, even as the Lord gave to every man?" he asks. The verb "you believed" is in the aorist tense in Greek, which refers to a time when these Corinthians made their initial decision to accept Christ and follow Him. Obviously Apollos was not responsible for that initial faith, for he followed Paul in the ministry of the gospel. Of course, some may have come to know the Lord subsequently through the preaching of Apollos, but the majority were brought into a living relationship with the Lord through Paul's preaching.

How gentle and considerate of Paul, however, not to want to take all the credit to himself. The word "we" always sounds so much gentler than the word "I." When it comes to blame, be ready with an "I," but when it comes to credit be big enough to say "we," for your success must inevitably have involved the efforts of others also. However, Paul goes on to recognize that each minister has a different contribution to make.

"[E]ven as the Lord gave to every man." Paul and Apollos each had a particular ministry among the Corinthians. But since the Lord is the giver of each and every ability, all glory ought to be ascribed to Him. Paul could not do all that Apollos could, nor could Apollos do all that Paul could. We need to realize that there is no such thing as uniformity in the gifts God bestows. 1 Corinthians 12:5 says, "There are differences of administrations [the same word used in 1 Cor. 3:5, *diakoniōn*, 'ministries'], but the same Lord."

One thing we must come to terms with, and that is to be ourselves under God as ministers of His, instead of trying to mimic others we admire for their apparent success. Be satisfied with God's gifts to you and use them as He intended you to. You may have some that others lack. Remember that no one has all the gifts God bestows. Therefore do not regard another as inferior because he may lack your particular gift, or try to make him conform to your individual pattern, as if he were no good without your distinctive endowment. Just make sure that the gift you possess has as its basic goal to bring others to faith in Jesus Christ. Make sure also that its source is none other than the Lord Himself, "even as the Lord gave to every man." As such it is a direct endowment, not acquired by your own efforts or through someone else.

We may draw certain conclusions from this verse. One is that we cannot be instruments to bring people to salvation unless the Lord endows us with the necessary ability. Another is that, although God is omnipotent, and can therefore save anyone He desires without human instrumentality, it pleases Him to use us as ministers through whom others believe. I use the word "ministers" here, not in the narrower sense of the clergy, but in the broader sense of all who serve God in whatever sphere of life He has placed them. We must be diligent in the execution of the role the Lord has assigned us. Yet we must understand that only through Him can we be effectual. We must recognize that only God has sufficient power to deliver a sinner. Sinners are spiritually dead, and only God can animate the dead. Salvation actually means the re-creation of a person, and only God has the power to create.

We conclude, therefore, that as men, no matter how great our gifts, we can do nothing independently of God. If men had a power of their own to be useful, the greatest good would assuredly be done, and universally, by those whose endowments were the most distinguished. It must be obvious, however, to the unbiased observer, that effects too wonderful to be the effects of mere human power are often produced by the ministry of the gospel; that the conversion of some, and the progress of others, make manifest the certainty of God's operations. On the other hand, those we meet in congregations who continue in their unregenerate state do not make it any more or less apparent that ministers cannot improve their condition. God is sovereign over man's salvation, and though He works through clergymen or laypeople, they cannot impart spiritual life to any man.

Scripture speaks of Lydia as a woman "whose heart the Lord opened, that she attended unto the things which were spoken of Paul" (Acts 16:14). Of the Gentiles who were saved as a result of Peter's preaching in the house of Cornelius it is said, "Then hath God also to the Gentiles granted repentance unto life" (Acts 11:18). And to the Ephesians Paul wrote, "You hath he quickened, who were dead in trespasses and sins" (Eph. 2:1). "No man can come to me," said the Savior, "except the Father which hath sent me draw him" (John 6:44). "Why look ye so earnestly on us?" said Peter and John to the wondering multitude, "as though by our own power or holiness we had made this man to walk?" (Acts 3:12). "Not I," said Paul, "but the grace of God which was with me" (1 Cor. 15:10; see Telfer 1839, 241–52).

> I tried to win a soul for Christ; how earnestly I pleaded
> That he had sinned and gone astray and Christ was all he needed.
> I begged him to forsake the world, repent and be forgiven—
> I tried to coax him to the Lord, to woo him into Heaven.
> And then I realized that Christ longed for him more than I,
> That He alone could make one care, who cared enough to die.
> Upon my knees I fought the fight. My friend was born again that night.
>
> —Barbara E. Cornet

<u>Lessons</u>:

1. Preachers should consider themselves willing executors of the Lord's will. They are servants whose aim should be to preach the Lord so that many will be saved, remembering that they are instruments in God's hands.

2. Service to Christ can take on different forms and functions. Voluntary services are of genuine importance. One should not feel inferior doing spiritual tasks which are just as important and as necessary as preaching and evangelizing. God has fitted you for some service that is worthy in His sight.
3. Do not regard another as inferior because he may lack your particular gift. Remember no one has all the gifts God bestows.
4. No matter how great our gifts are, we do nothing independently of God. God is sovereign over man's salvation, and though he works through us, we cannot impart spiritual life to anyone.

## 1 Cor. 3:6 | *The Secret of Fruitfulness*

*I have planted, Apollos watered, but God gave the increase.*

When Paul spoke of how God had used him and Apollos among the Corinthians, he illustrated it from nature. "I have planted, Apollos watered," he said, "but God gave the increase," that is, "caused the growing." Paul compared himself to a farmer who sowed seed and then left the field for someone else to care for it.

Paul was the first to preach the gospel among the Corinthians. Apollos followed him. Their ministries were distinct. "I planted," said Paul, which implies that his ministry was largely evangelistic. But when a farmer sows his fields, he cannot leave the crops unattended. If he cannot be there to cultivate, someone else must take over. And how wonderfully Apollos must have labored to cultivate the seeds planted by Paul. He watered what Paul had planted. He did not go to Corinth to do his own planting in disregard of Paul's planting. He recognized the work of his fellow minister as in need of his own labor of love and was not too proud to cultivate what another had started. We should never be so egotistical as to consider it beneath us to help someone else's work to grow and prosper.

The verbs pertaining to the work of Paul and Apollos are in the aorist tense: *ephúteusa*, "I planted [during my stay with you]," and *epótisen*, Apollos "watered [during his stay with you]," but God kept giving the increase or kept causing the growth. This last verb, *ēúxanen*, is in the imperfect tense, which indicates constant growing. In other words, Paul is saying, God continues to do His work even when Apollos and I are no longer with you.

What a wonderful lesson for us to learn—that though we should consider our ministry indispensable while God gives us the opportunity, we should recognize that God is not going to stop working when we are gone. Our labor, although necessary, is temporary, while God's is continuing.

Paul and Apollos worked in cooperation with each other, and in complete dependence upon God. We, too, need to learn to cooperate in the Lord's work. By ourselves we cannot possibly do all that needs to be done. It is impossible for anyone to know or to propagate truth exclusively. All branches of knowledge are interlinked. Agnosticism is often the effect of a solitary search for truth. The theologian and the scientist often do not trust each other, yet they desperately need each other. Think what would happen if mathematics and astronomy were divorced. Mathematics would grow lean and astronomy would stop short on the verge of its most interesting discoveries. A searcher in one realm of knowledge must depend upon searchers in other realms, for without their aid he cannot even establish the truth of his position. He will only know that he knows comparatively nothing (see Cooper 1907, 343).

The sovereignty of God has two sides to it. On the one hand God is everything, in that He provides the raw materials with which we work. I plant, but He provides the seed; you irrigate, but He gives the water. The other side is that God does certain things and works out certain purposes quite independently of man's involvement.

Whether a man believes in God or is conscious of His purpose or not is beside the point when we regard the creation and control of the heavens which declare His glory and the firmament which shows His handiwork. The sun will rise tomorrow and the planets pursue their courses despite man's unbelief or disregard.

LESSONS:

1. Paul and Apollos worked in cooperation and in complete dependence upon God. By ourselves it is impossible to do all that needs to be done.
2. All branches of knowledge are interlinked. A researcher in one field of knowledge depends upon research in other fields.
3. God provides us with the Bible (seed) and the Spirit (water) for evangelism. But He also independently opens hearts so that people will listen to us.

# 1 Cor. 3:7 | *Your Unique Task Given by God*

*So then neither is he that planteth anything, neither he that watereth, but God that giveth the increase.*

To show that without God man can do nothing, either in the physical or the spiritual realm, Paul adds in the 7th verse of 1 Corinthians 3, "So then neither is he that planteth anything, neither he that watereth, but God that giveth the increase." The participles *phuteúōn*, "planting," *potízōn*, "watering," and *auxánōn*, "giving the increase," are all in the present tense, which indicates continuous and repetitive action. We constantly plant and water, and God constantly and repeatedly gives the growth. Let us never forget that God's part is basic. He is the figure one before our zeroes; He alone gives value to our work. Unless we acknowledge this fact and keep it continually in mind, our work will bear little or no fruit.

But there is as truly a sphere of operations where God Himself intends—since He has created man in His own image—that men consciously work with Him. "Who is Paul, and who is Apollos, or what are they?" We answer this question unhesitatingly: they were ministers of God without whom certain work would not have been done. Without Paul, for instance, this letter to the Corinthians would never have been written. And just as truly there is a task which will not be done unless you do it. No one else can do what God intends you to do.

Sometimes people are looking for a great mission in life, not realizing that God has appointed a highly specialized mission for them right where they are. As one woman put it:

> I envisioned myself as one day becoming another Joan of Arc, perhaps, or another Florence Nightingale. And then one day as I was praying, it struck me that I was indeed given a unique place to fill in God's plan. I was the only one who could be a wife to my husband, a mother to my children, a daughter to my parents. No one else could serve in this capacity, and this was where God wanted me to carry out His plans; a trust He had committed to no one else. My delusions of grandeur faded, and instead came a sense of mission that has glorified the everyday tasks for me ever since.

The apostle Paul, of course, did have a wider mission, but he performed his humble duties as a tentmaker as faithfully and well, as he did his preaching and writing ministry—doing all as unto the Lord. He was a man who appeared at a critical juncture of history to spread the Christian faith throughout the world. There is a place the gospel needs to go because of your labor—beginning right where you are and spreading out wherever God gives you the opportunity. No one else can do what God expects of you. There is only one you, and only you can do the unique task for which God has qualified you.

Others might conceivably have written letters; others might conceivably have saved a difficult situation, but they would not have been Paul nor done the things Paul did. Apollos was the silver-tongued orator who by his grace and charm could inspire large congregations. Others could conceivably have done the same thing, but indisputably not in the same way.

**LESSONS:**

1. God alone gives value to our work, yet our work is unique because God makes it unique.
2. Just as Paul and Apollos were ministers without whom certain work would not have been done (e.g., Corinthians would not have been written without Paul), so no one else can do what God intends you to do.
3. Paul performed the humble duties of a tent-maker as faithfully as he did his preaching and writing ministry. There is no one as qualified as you to do that which the Lord has planned for you.

# 1 Cor. 3:8 | *Your Work for God—and Its Reward*

*Now he that planteth and he that watereth are one: and every man shall receive his own reward according to his own labor.*

Another very human trait is to consider our own work more important than that of others. He who plants may consider the planting more important than the watering. But many a promising seedling has failed to grow for lack of water. And of course the watering would be nothing if it were not for the planting. We are so often tempted to feel, "What I do is more important than what you do."

That is why Paul says in the 8th verse, "Now he that planteth and he that watereth are one: and every man shall receive his own reward according to his own labor." What does Paul mean by declaring, "He that planteth and he that watereth are one"? The Greek word translated "one" is not *heís*, which means one in a numerical sense, but *hén*, "one in quality of being." This is the same expression we find in John 10:30, where Jesus said, "I and my Father are one [*hén*]." This does not mean that the Father and Son are one person but that they are one in deity, both omnipotent and omniscient.

Paul and Apollos were two distinct persons, one a planter and one a waterer. Although these are two distinct operations, they are both human activities compared with God's divine activity. There are only two categories of labor, then—human and divine.

We can learn some fundamental lessons from this statement by Paul. The first is that our work, different though it may be from that of other human beings, ought not to be regarded as exclusive or antagonistic or even competitive, but cooperative. God needs what your brother does just as much as He needs what you do. For your work to receive God's ultimate blessing it needs to be supplemented by your brother's work. Your planting will not grow apart from your brother's watering.

A second lesson is that all of us, no matter what our work, are equally dependent upon God if our work is to bear fruit. Therefore we must never look down on anybody's work, no matter how humble it seems to us. On a railroad ticket you will sometimes see the words, "Not good if detached." So might it be said of all Christians everywhere. When we become detached from Christ and our fellow Christians, our work will soon wither and die. It is possible to serve God in isolation from our brethren, but it is not probable. If we are genuinely Christian, we will abide not only in Christ but in fellowship and cooperation with one another.

In order to encourage man to do his own God-appointed task, Paul tells the Corinthians that each one shall receive his own reward according to his own individual labor. What impresses me about this statement in verse 8 is the word *ídion*, "own," stressing the reward according to one's own particular labor. No one will be rewarded for someone else's work. It often happens that a child inherits the results of his father's hard labor. But here we have the doctrine of each one being rewarded according to his own labor.

The word translated "labor" in Greek is *kópon* (acc. of *kópos*). This word occurs some 20 times in the New Testament and refers not so much to the actual exertion a man makes as to the lassitude or weariness that follows this straining of powers to the utmost. The word designates what we are or ought to be in our labors of Christian ministry (see Trench 1953, 378).

Doing God's work in the way He wants us to do it will often make us weary. But He deserves our utmost. *Kópon* indicates that we are to give of our strength to the Lord in spite of how we shall feel afterward. Do you ever get weary and even exhausted in the Lord's service? It is according to your sense of fatigue that the Lord will reward you.

In this matter of rewards, take the time to study two parables of our Lord—that of the Talents in Matthew 25:14–30 and that of the Pounds in Luke 19:12–28. God's Word clearly teaches that our reward comes not from men but from the Lord, and it will be proportionate to the service rendered according to the opportunities He grants us. In reality God gives much more than we have any right to expect. These rewards may come either in this life or the next, or both. Ponder these verses: Matthew 16:27, "For the Son of man shall come in the glory of his Father with his angels; and then he shall reward every man according to his works"; and Luke 18:30, where Jesus says that there is no man who shall have left all for Him "who shall not receive manifold more in this present time, and in the world to come life everlasting."

> In the name of God advancing,
>   Sow thy seed at morning light;
> Cheerily the furrows turning,
>   Labor on with all thy might.
> Look not to the far-off future,
>   Do the work which nearest lies;
> Sow thou must before thou reapest;
>   Rest at last is labor's prize.

Standing still is dangerous ever,
    Toil is meant for Christians now;
Let there be, when evening cometh,
    Honest sweat upon thy brow;
And the Master shall come smiling,
    At the setting of the sun,
Saying, as he pays thy wages,
    "Good and faithful one, well
done!"
—author unknown

LESSONS:

1. Your work, though different from your brother's, should be cooperative, not exclusive, antagonistic, or competitive. God decrees the increase of what your brother does as much as He determines the success of what you do.
2. We are all equally dependent upon God if our work is to bear fruit. If we are genuinely Christians, we will abide in Christ and in fellowship and cooperation with one another.
3. Each one will be rewarded according to his own labor. Although we may grow weary doing God's work, He deserves our utmost and will reward us in proportion to our sense of fatigue.

# 1 Cor. 3:9 | God's Responsibility and Yours

*For we are laborers together with God: ye are God's husbandry, ye are God's building.*

One of life's great mysteries is what part God plays in the affairs of men and the measure of each man's responsibility in the ultimate aim and result. Is God responsible for what I am, or do I share in that responsibility? Is the world as God planned it, or is it the mess or the wonder that man has made it?

Where God's planning and sovereignty end and man's work and responsibility begin is admittedly a problem that can never be resolved by our finite minds. We can turn to God and say, "I am what I am because that's the way You made me," and to a certain degree that is true. A child does not bear the entire responsibility for being what he is. The parents must share in that responsibility. But since God is the sovereign dispenser of His life and grace, as well as the sovereign judge of what we are and do, His judgment of our state and life cannot but be guided by His sovereign dispensing of grace and opportunity. If He has given us but one talent, He will not demand an accounting for five in that day when we stand before Him to be judged.

In cultivating a field or doing the work of a preacher, man sows. That is his responsibility. Man waters. But neither the seed nor the water are of his own making. The ingredients and the environment are of God. That is why, after stating that he sowed the seed of the gospel in Corinth and Apollos watered it, Paul adds, "but the important consideration is the God who causes growth."

There are two basic principles Paul wants us to understand as we labor in this world of ours—whether our labor be physical or spiritual. The first is that nothing grows simply because man does his assigned part, but that God's intervention is needful at all times to complete man's labor and bring it to fruition. The first principle to which we must assent, then, is that God's sovereignty must never be disputed by an individual because of the partnership God permits him to have in the accomplishment of His foreordained will.

Spurgeon told of "the petty sovereign of an insignificant tribe . . . who every morning stalks out of his hovel, bids the sun good morrow, and points out to him with his finger the course he is to take for the day. Is this arrogance more contemptible than ours," Spurgeon asks, "when we would dictate to God the course of His providence, and summon Him to our bar for His dealings with us? How ridiculous does man appear when he attempts to argue with his God!" And we might add, how ridiculous is that Christian who takes credit, not just for the work he does, but for the end result. You may have planted and watered, and God will recognize and reward your faithfulness in doing these things, but He alone can provide the seed and water, and then make the seed germinate and bear fruit.

One of the most humbling truths man must perceive and acknowledge is that in most instances **GOD WORKS ALONE**. He created the universe without man's assistance. That is indisputable proof of His omnipotence. When God does not do what we in our faulty wisdom seem to think He should do, we must never conclude that it is because He is unable to. Whenever God does not act, or remains seemingly impassive, it is because in His infinite wisdom and understanding He chooses such a course. There is a marvelous, mysterious interaction between God's omnipotence and His wisdom. All that God asks of us in this matter is to recognize, not that He is going to do what we ask or expect, but that He is able to.

Take the two blind men who came to the Lord Jesus to ask that He restore their sight. The Lord could have done this without pursuing the matter further. But He asked them, "Believe ye that I am able to do this?" (Matt. 9:28). Notice that the question was not "Do you expect me to do this, or do you think I am going to?" The Lord does not expect you to know what He is going to do, but He expects you to believe that He is able to do what His sovereignty chooses to do. Those blanket promises that indicate we will receive whatever we ask must always be modified by the other Scriptures that teach that our petitions must always be according to God's will in order to be answered.

Not only did God create the universe by Himself because He chose to, but He also sustains the world without our help. His providence is a result of His own omnipotent choice. Although there are some realms in which we can be considered God's helpers, as in planting and watering, it is God Himself who is the first and ultimate provider. We treat symptoms as far as our knowledge of the function of the body carries us, but God is ultimately the healer and sustainer of life. A doctor may operate on two individuals suffering from exactly the same ailment. One recovers and the other does not. Who or what makes the difference? It is God who is the sustainer and provider of life.

God will also act alone in the final judgment. When He comes to judge you and me, it will be according to His sovereign grace. In the judgment you cannot influence Him to show leniency or stringency toward anyone. His decisions are His, and they will be final. He will judge us not only according to our actions and our appearance but also according to our motives, which are an open book to Him. The Scriptures teach that believers will judge the world—even angels— but we will not judge ourselves.

The laws that govern the world and our lives have been instituted by God without our help. We are bound by them, but we had no say in making them. God did not consult us when He made the law of gravitation. He alone is responsible for the law of metabolism. In the same manner He is responsible for instituting the law of cause and effect, both in the physical and spiritual realms.

Take the example the apostle Paul gives us of the man who plants and the man who waters. They have to do these things in order to secure the fruit they desire. But actually they had nothing to do with the origin and functioning of the mystery of life by which the plant grows. That was and is exclusively God's work. Man is called upon to be God's co-worker but not to take credit that does not belong to him.

A young woman who won a coveted award smiled when her mother said, "I was praying you would get it." "Well, thank you," she replied "but I earned this by my own hard work." Some people feel so sure of their self-sufficiency that they resent any implication that they owe God a word of thanks for the good things that come their way. Such an attitude could be justified only if a person were able to say, "I brought myself into the world, I endowed myself with all my talents and abilities, I raised myself, taught myself all I know, and control my present and future." If life ended for you tonight, would you dare to face God with your little handful of achievements and boast, "I did it all myself"?

### The Interaction of God and Man in Salvation

When the apostle Paul tells Christian believers that they are laborers together with God, what does he actually mean to convey? Certainly not that we have any part in God's work of creation or of sustaining the universe. There is only one department of God's activities in which it has pleased Him to take man into association with Himself, and that is in the plan of man's salvation. God does not save man from sin without saving his will. If that were the case, all men everywhere and at all times would be saved willingly or unwillingly, and none would be lost.

Yet even in God's plan of salvation for man there are aspects of it in which He acted alone without man's prior knowledge or consent. First of all, He alone devised the plan of salvation and its execution. God decided to act in mercy toward man, not because man asked for or deserved mercy, but as an absolute act of His sovereign grace in its initial concept and execution.

Second, God acted alone in making the atonement that was necessary to accomplish His purpose. He did not ask for the sacrifice of anyone from among the ranks of humans. Instead, the eternal and infinite Logos, the Word who always had been with the Father, became flesh so that He could die for man's sin. "For God so loved the world that he gave his only begotten Son": that was God acting entirely on His own in loving and giving. But in the second part of John 3:16, "that whosoever believeth in him should not perish, but have everlasting life"—which speaks of the effective impartation of God's life, eternal life, to man—we see that God chose to ask for man's faith, his consent.

Third, it is also true that in the transformation of the human soul man plays no part. It is purely and singly a divine accomplishment—the work of the Holy Spirit. If we as humans could accomplish it, would we not have done so long ago? Who does not want to change a debased drunkard or addict or profligate? But we stand helpless in the face of men's spiritual weaknesses and needs. The only thing we can do is to pray for them and point them to Christ, who alone can save them, radically transform them, and make new creatures of them.

When Paul tells us in 1 Corinthians 3:9 that we are God's co-workers, he is not pointing out God's weakness but His condescension. God has not chosen any individual, either for salvation or service because He has need of him. It is always because that individual needs God.

It is interesting to note that the word "God" in this verse (*Theoú*, in the gen.) is not preceded by the definite article. This does not mean that the word God can be modified by the indefinite article in English, so that it reads "a God." We are not co-workers with "a God" or a divinity. That is what the ancient Greeks believed—that there were so many gods that a man could take his choice of the divinity with whom he wanted to cooperate. The seaman could choose Poseidon, god of the sea; the farmer, Demetra, goddess of earth, and so on.

It is absurd to add the indefinite article "a" whenever the definite article is missing in the Greek, as the Jehovah's Witnesses do in some instances in order to rob Christ of His deity. In John 1:1, for instance—"And God was the Word"—they say that *Theós ḗn hó Lógos* should read "And a god was the Word," as if there were many gods. The same construction appears in John 1:18, "God no one has ever seen." It would be absurd to translate *Theoú* as "a god," as if the New Testament were introducing polytheism. Evidently Jehovah's Witnesses are not consistent, since they do not include an indefinite article before God in the 18th verse.

As we stated in our study of John 1:1–18, in our book *Was Christ God?*, whenever the definite article is missing before God or any other proper or common noun, it is for the purpose of predicating deity to the person or thing spoken about (see Robertson 1923, 794). Deity includes omnipotence, omniscience, holiness, timelessness, and so forth, all the very special and unique characteristics of God. By contrast, we are subordinate to space and time. But God is spaceless and timeless, transcending both forms of creation. The most difficult thing anyone to recognize is that in all actions and accomplishments God is present. We cannot see Him but we can know his presence and activity by His revelation to us in the Word of God.

> I cannot row it myself,
> My boat on the raging sea;
> But beside me sits Another
> Who pulls or steers with me,
> And I know that we two
> Shall come safe into port—
> His child and He.
>
> Coward and wayward and weak,
> I change with the changing sky;
> Today so eager and brave,
> Tomorrow not caring to try;
> But He never gives in,
> So we two shall win—
> Jesus and I.
>
> Strong and tender and true,
> Crucified once for me!
> He will not change, I know,
> Whatever I may be.
> But all He says I must do,
> Ever from sin to keep free.
> We shall finish our course
> And reach home at last—
> His child and He.
>
> —T. G. Selby

Yes, He is Spirit, but He is right there with you. As Paul pointed out in the second chapter of this great epistle, spiritual truths are perceived and understood only by the spirit of man. "But God hath revealed them unto us by his Spirit: for the Spirit searcheth all things, yea, the deep things of God. For what man knoweth the things of a man, save the spirit of man which is in him? even so the things of God knoweth no man, but the Spirit of God" (1 Cor. 2:10, 11).

## How to Make a Success of Your Life

Because man and God are constituted so differently, the Christian believer finds it hard to comprehend that God works all things. A relationship exists, not because man has taken God into cooperation with himself, but because God has graciously taken man.

Once you realize this, you will never be tempted to take any glory for the accomplishments God enables you to achieve. Physician, realize that you are not the healer, but that God has shown you how He made the human body so that you can help to treat others. Preacher, do not become puffed up when God uses you to win souls to Himself. You only proclaim the life-giving message of the gospel; God alone awakens dead souls to life.

Whatever your vocation or role in life, Deuteronomy 32:39 will put your work in perspective. "See now that I, even I, am he, and there is no god with me: I kill, and make alive; I wound, and I heal: neither is there any that can deliver out of my hand." Another good verse to paste on your mirror is 1 Corinthians 4:7: "For who maketh thee to differ from another? and what hast thou that thou didst not receive? now if thou didst receive it, why dost thou glory, as if thou hadst not received it?" And another is Psalm 57:2, "God . . . performeth all things for me."

In our previous study we saw that the definite article was omitted before the word "God," *Theoú*, in 1 Corinthians 3:9. According to that eminent grammarian of the Greek language, William Edward Jelf, "The effect of the omission of the article is frequently that the absence of any particular definition or limitation of the notion brings forward its general character" (Jelf 1861, 124). The general character of God is His omnipotent love. And that is exactly what Paul wanted us human beings to realize—that it is "of God" (*theoú)* that we (e.g., Paul and Apollos) are "fellow-workers" (*sunergoí*).

This ought to dispel all fear and discouragement as we undertake to serve Him either in the physical or spiritual realm. True, you and I are temporal and finite in our abilities, but God under whom we labor together is eternal and infinite. Paul's stress here is not so much on the fact that we are coworkers with God but that God hammers believers together as fellow-workers (*sunergoí*). This assures us success. All the power and wisdom of heaven are on our side. We are never alone. The eternal and infinite God is constantly with us.

In verses 6 and 7, you remember, Paul told the Corinthians, "I have planted, Apollos watered, but God gave the increase. So then neither is he that planteth anything, neither he that watereth, but God that giveth the increase." In other words, the workmen are nothing without their Master. All the laborers on a farm could not manage it properly if they had no one at their head. And all the preachers and other Christian workers in the world can do nothing unless God is with them. We are called upon to remember that every laborer in God's vineyard has derived all his qualifications from God. All good seed comes out of God's granary; and all rain comes from heaven.

Now let us look at verse 8, "Every man shall receive his own reward according to his own labor." But why should God reward us if we are nothing? Actually, though in comparison with God we are nothing, He regards us as something. What that is, is found in verse 9: "We are laborers together with God," we are His co-workers. The nothing becomes something worthy of reward because God becomes our partner. Our willingness to be used is the first step in the obtaining of that reward. And our reward is not so much proportionate to our success as to our labor. No labor in which God is our Senior Partner is ever a failure. "But God giveth the increase." In other words, whatever we do is all in vain unless God makes it grow.

However, we must not overlook the truth that when Paul planted and Apollos watered, God did give the increase. Verses 6 and 7 tell us that God makes the difference. And verse 9 tells us that He who makes the difference is our co-worker, and therefore we cannot fail. "But let him that glorieth glory in this, that he understandeth and knoweth me, that I am the Lord" (Jer. 9:24).

One day at Perth, England, Bishop Wilkinson noticed a thin-faced boy looking at him intently. He went up to him and asked if the boy wished to speak to him. "No, sir," said the lad, "only I sing in the same choir as you are in." The bishop's friends laughed at the boy's idea of his association with the bishop in the church, but the bishop did not laugh. It was precisely that spirit of partnership in God's work that he wished to encourage. Similarly what a wonderful sense of satisfaction a Christian has when he can look at an infinite and eternal God and say, "Lord, I am your co-worker." That is the most rewarding and unique privilege we can have.

A gardener expressed the same idea when he said, "I feel when I am growing the flowers or rearing the vegetables that I am having a share in creation." And when a mother says to a little child who carries some small item into another room for her, "You are helping me," what stature it gives to that child and what a sense of dignity and place in life's affairs.

This ought to take away your sense of the worthlessness of the countless small tasks you perform day by day. Look beyond the temporal and limited as you work in partnership with God. Your attitude will determine your sense of satisfaction with your task. Take those three men who were working on the construction of a great cathedral. When asked what they were doing, one man said, "I am mixing mortar." Another said, "I am working for so many dollars per day." But the third man said, "I am building a great cathedral where men may come and worship God."

Without the vision of God as our unfailing partner, we will be tempted to limit the scope of what we can do, instead of seeing it in its larger implications. Mother, you may be discouraged as you cook, and mend, and scrub. When asked what you are doing, do not simply say, "Just the same old round of housework," but "I'm helping to clean the world, to keep my family and humanity healthy, to raise children who may change the course of the world for the better."

You will no longer think small when you realize that God, the eternal and infinite one, is your co-worker. If you want to make a success of your life, link it up with God in all its endeavors and aspirations.

### Fellow Laborers with God

How proud some people are when they become associated with big, rich, powerful companies. They feel secure and confident that their work is worth something. How much more should we as Christians rejoice when we are associated in partnership with Almighty God. That is the highest association possible. In what areas does God work with man to accomplish His purposes? First of all:

### On the Physical Plane

God permits man to become almost a co-creator with Him on this earth. We cannot help admiring man in his accomplishments. God made textile fibers, but He left it to man to weave them into a piece of cloth. God made a silkworm, but man made silk of it. God made iron, but man fashioned it into a tool. Man has made the desert wastes to blossom by his marvelous system of irrigation. Holland is a beautiful country, but it is man who made out of the watery waste a fitting habitation for humans. God supplies us with food, but He does not cook it for us. God like a wise parent has not chosen to do everything for His children but has been helping them to help themselves.

The person who works in harmony with God and His law in the material universe can really accomplish something worthwhile. Man takes the forces of electricity, harnesses them, and gets things moving. Electricity, however, has always been around. God has put rich soil upon the earth, but He leaves it up to man to cultivate it. He puts coal in the depths of the earth, but He leaves it up to man to find it and dig it out. Radio waves have been here since Adam, but God left it up to man to tune in to these waves. The component parts of the airplane in their elementary form have always been here, but God left it up to man to invent this flying miracle. We have always had the atom, but only in recent years have men worked with God in such a way as to find and harness the power wrapped up in the atom (see Ford 1961, 111–12).

But let us not take more credit to ourselves than we deserve. As someone has said, "It is a curious thing that, as soon as men find out how anything is done, they should immediately rush to the conclusion that God did not do it." Think of the flowers in the garden. In order to produce them, two persons have been at work. The first is God. Without Him the flowers could not be. He has endowed the seeds with life; He sends the rain to water them, the air to feed them, and the sun to quicken them. But God also enters into partnership with man for their creation. And so man has to sow the seed, to graft one plant into another, to dig, to prune, to irrigate. Thus, because God and man are fellow workers, these flowers that delight the eye are found in our gardens and on our tables.

A householder left a patch of land completely unattended. On returning from a journey he found it full of stones, old bottles, and other rubbish. Though he had never attempted to garden before, he got hold of a spade and began to dig up the ground and clear away the debris. Then he sowed a few seeds. With tremendous excitement he watched his garden patch. When at last he saw little shoots pushing up through the ground, he was almost in ecstasy. Gradually the plants grew and at last the flowers appeared. To him it looked beautiful. One day his pastor stopped by. He could not get the pastor excited about his garden. Finally the pastor said, "Yes, it is wonderful what Almighty God does with a patch of ground like that." "Oh, it is," said the man, "but I wish you had seen this place when the Almighty had it all to Himself!" Unfortunately, the man failed to acknowledge that it was man's fault the patch of ground was such an eyesore in the first place. But, with the exception of Eden, it is true that God does not choose to make a garden without a gardener. This does not mean that the wild and rugged beauties of nature do not often surpass man's best efforts. If you have ever seen a field of wildflowers in bloom, you will know what I mean. But in most instances God commits the raw elements to man and allows him to bring beauty, order, and usefulness out of them.

## All Labor Is for God

How different our work would seem if we fully understood our partnership with God—the God of the physical as well as the spiritual world. Then what we do would not seem so aimless but would have meaning. Let us not be so ready to divide life into the secular and the religious. It is all God's gift and we are partners with God in all things. If you are an engineer, a doctor, a truck driver, an office worker, or a housewife, stop to think of the high privilege of being a co-laborer with God. It is God who provides the materials with which you work. The end results are His, but they are yours too. Do not shut God out from whatever you do. We are all too prone to put God in a compartment of

His own where He operates independently from us, and to feel that we must shoulder the whole burden of doing our own work in our own compartment. If we fail to see God as the Masterbuilder of everything around us, we will also fail to recognize Him as a miracle worker, and as the one who can work the miracle of regeneration in our own hearts.

Visit a factory where thousands of persons are employed. There is the manager sitting in his central office where he directs all the operations of the factory. Everyone is doing his or her separate job. But they are all fellow laborers with the manager; they are all necessary. Not one could do without the other. If one does his work badly, the whole organization suffers. If one does his work well, they all benefit. Some feel they have important work, some less important. But there is not one who is unimportant in the eyes of that man who is sitting in the general manager's office.

It is the same with this great workshop called the world. God has His purposes for it, and He does not carry them through without us. Not one of us is unimportant, not one can be done without. If we are selfish, then we are holding up that work. But if we are faithful, then we are helping it go forward. As we go back to our daily work, however exalted or humble our position may be, what a splendid thing to remember, that we are fellow laborers with God. We may be unimportant in our own eyes, or in the eyes of others, but we are not unimportant to God because our work is necessary for the task He wants to accomplish.

If only we could get hold of this truth, our work would take on new dignity, and life would take on new meaning and become worthier than it is. It does not matter whether we are famous or unknown, high or low, there are no such distinctions with God. We are all fellow laborers with Him.

## Man's Redemption, the Exclusive Work of God

Did you ever stop to think that every scientist, whether he acknowledges or is aware of it or not, is a co-laborer with God? A scientist ceases to be worthy of the name the moment he ceases to cooperate with the God-ordained laws of nature. A scientist is an observer of the way God works even through man's cooperation—but he is not always an interpreter, an exegete, of what he observes and discovers. He bows down to the way things work, without always understanding the how and why of it.

We can never cause a single blade of grass to grow. All we can do is obey the laws and conform to the conditions for growth by getting the soil ready and putting in the seed. God sees to the rest. That mysterious remainder which God reserves for Himself always eludes us.

That is exactly what happens in the spiritual world. As God's minister I preach the gospel. I tell you on the authority of God's Word that you are a sinner, that Christ died for you, that you can receive the benefits of His death for your sin. But that is as far as I can go. God alone, through His Spirit, can take that Word—just as He takes the seed—and cause new life to spring up within you, make you a new creation in Christ. If you can explain how a blade of grass grows, I will explain how a sinner is born-again and becomes a saint.

There is a fascination about the certainty of God's work. Every time we put a seed in the ground, we confidently expect God to bring up the corresponding plant—as long as we obey the laws He has prescribed. There is a charm about the inevitableness of all God does, which makes cooperation with Him one of the greatest delights of life. Buck God in your work and you come up against a stone wall. You will be frustrated; you will fail. But cooperate with God, and the end results cannot help but be good. Human partnership can be good, bad, or indifferent. But to be admitted to partnership with God, to be consciously working in the same direction with Him, is the highest guarantee of character as well as of the greatest joy and peace that life can afford.

It is a commonplace of biological truth that "the higher we ascend in the scale of being, the more does nature need assistance in carrying out her designs." It is thus man's dignity as God's highest creation that makes him a worker at all. The animal is not God's fellow worker. God does all. The instinct of the animal is all-sufficient. But God has issued His invitation to man to assist Him. God always succeeds in the animal. But in man's seeming imperfection lies man's superiority. He comes into the world helpless—unshod, unclad, unarmed. The germ of all possibility lies in him. But he can only realize his full potential as he fits into God's plan and will, and works in harmony with His natural and spiritual laws (see Cooper 1907, 343).

The same principle holds in the higher sphere of mind and spirit. The artist sees reality and beholds its beauty, but it is he who sees it. God does not give us the masterpieces of art or the strains of music without the artists and the musicians. It is not otherwise in the spiritual realm. The Bible did not drop from heaven *en bloc.* The revelation within sacred script came from God through men. And in particular there is one department of God's activities in which it has pleased Him to associate men and that is the work of salvation. Yet even in this there are certain elements in which God acts alone.

He planned His scheme of mercy all by Himself. When God loved the world enough to die for it, He did not ask anybody. There was no prior consultation with man to find out whether such an expression of love and mercy would be ultimately acceptable to him. God did not ask man whether he thought such mercifulness wise or foolish. He did not take sinful man into partnership in the matter because He knew man's judgment was corrupt. As sinful man now considers the cross of Christ foolishness, so would he have done had he been consulted before the plan was conceived and executed.

That is Paul's argument right along in this Corinthian epistle. God's wisdom is foolishness to man; and man's wisdom is foolishness to God. Therefore it would have been foolish of God, knowing man's foolishness, to ask for his advice and consent in the matter of man's redemption. God planned your salvation and mine without consulting us, and it was a good thing He did.

Even in making the atonement that was necessary for carrying out His plan, God acted alone. How many times the disciples tried to hinder the Lord Jesus from going to Jerusalem to die on the cross. They could not understand it. In Mark 8:31–33 we read: "And he began to teach them, that the Son of man must suffer many things . . . and be killed, and after three days rise again. . . . And Peter took him, and began to rebuke him. But when he had turned about and looked on his disciples, he rebuked Peter, saying, Get thee behind me, Satan. . . ." In Luke 9:51 we read, "He steadfastly set his face to go to Jerusalem." It does not say that He and His disciples did this. The cross was His own choice, and He marched to it alone. There were no coworkers in the atonement itself. Christ was not a mere martyr at the hands of men. The very purpose for which He came to the world was to die for man's redemption. It was not a fate He had to suffer but a work He had to do; and not only did He plan it alone, but He also executed it alone.

There are no co-redemptors or co-redemptresses. It is completely unscriptural to call even His dear mother His co-redemptress. Christ as God eternal and infinite in His preincarnate state planned His birth as man in order to die, and He died alone for man.

And finally in His exclusive work of redemption God made possible and actual the transformation of man's character through His sacrifice on the cross. That is what is called conversion. When a man or woman is converted, that person is a new creation. It is God through the Holy Spirit who performs this miracle. You and I cannot claim any part of it, and we cannot help Him in making it effectual in individual lives.

> It was alone the Savior prayed
> In dark Gethsemane;
> Alone He drained the bitter cup,
> And suffered there for me.
> Alone, alone, He bore it all alone;
> He gave His life to save His own—
> He suffered, bled, and died alone, alone.

## Life's Greatest Privilege

No one can save your soul but God—no church, no evangelist, no priest or layman. God alone can bring about this miracle of the new birth in your heart and life.

But having said that, I would add that there are departments in the enterprise of salvation in which God has been pleased to employ men. He prepared the world for the reception of the coming Messiah through specially appointed men. These were the prophets and priests who foretold His advent and mission. The world was not left in ignorance. God gave His Ten Commandments through Moses. He foretold of the suffering Savior through Isaiah. From the very beginning it pleased Him to use men.

Then, when the fullness of time came, and the babe of Bethlehem was born, the Lord used the shepherds to carry the announcement He sent from heaven. Christ Himself employed common men as His co-laborers. Disciples were with Him all through His earthly ministry. And just before the Ascension they received from Him the great commission to spread the gospel throughout the world. Again, on the day of Pentecost, they received the power to carry out this commission by going forth to preach the gospel that had been committed to them. In every step of the introduction and inauguration of Christ's work, God employed human instrumentality.

No doubt Christ could have saved the world without the help of man, but He chose not to do so. He chose Twelve disciples and at the end sent them out into the world to continue His work. He risked everything upon their love and loyalty.

The same thing holds true today. The world will never become better of itself. The nations will not hear the gospel unless we who love the Lord preach it to them. It is very easy to say, "Yes, I believe that Christ can save the world," but can He—without you, without me, without men and women who are prepared to sacrifice for Him and in the last extremity to give their lives for Him? Not in His providence and plan of operation—for He has asked us to labor with Him in this great task.

What a distinct privilege this is! It seems to be a rule of the divine procedure to work for man through man—not through angels or the direct intervention of heaven itself. Angels seem almost to be warned off from, rather than commissioned for, man's salvation. An angel was sent to Cornelius, not to preach the gospel to him but to tell him where he could find a man to do it.

It surprises us that this most important of all God's activities should be entrusted to us fallible followers of Christ—not just to ministers but to all believers. Upon the persecution that arose about Stephen, all the church was "scattered abroad" from Jerusalem "except the apostles." While these apostles remained behind, "they that were scattered abroad went everywhere preaching the word" (Acts 8:1, 4).

That last chapter of Paul's letter to the Romans is not a dry list of salutation but is full of revelation as to the fellowship of the early church. Honorable names of men and women are given as "fellow-laborers" with the apostles; so that we may paraphrase Scripture to say to all who have received Christ as their Savior, "Ye are laborers together with God. . . . A dispensation of the gospel is committed unto you; a necessity is laid upon you; woe is unto you if ye preach not the gospel" (1 Cor. 3:9; 9:17, 16).

Remember that God gives you the privilege of calling His work yours. You are missing the greatest joy of service if you fail to realize that God is following your labor of love for Him as closely as if He were in your shoes. Even the pagans could teach us a lesson in this respect. It is said that when Phidias was preparing the figures for the Acropolis in Greece, the work was perfect in even the smallest details, although these figures were to stand upon a background so high that nobody could see them. A sculptor was working on the hair of one of them with minute fidelity when someone said to him, "What is the use of that expenditure of time and labor? Nobody will ever see your work." The craftsman replied, "Yes, the gods will see it."

God makes you His instrument. No miracle of Christ is more expressive of God's desire to have us work with Him than the feeding of the 5,000. This was a type of giving the gospel to hungry hearts. Christ could have fed the multitudes without human cooperation, yet He gave the opportunity to a little boy to contribute his lunch of five small loaves and two fishes. Instead of multiplying this boy's offering, our Lord could have created food out of nothing, as in the original creation when He acted alone. But in this instance He chose to use what a little boy had, small and insignificant though it was. Then He chose to distribute the multiplied loaves and fishes through His disciples, though He could have made them appear before each person instead of using distributing agents. Christ can save multitudes without preachers or witnesses, but He chooses to use them.

The Lord did not really have to ask Philip, "Whence shall we buy bread, that these may eat?" (John 6:5) because as we read in the next verse, He already knew what He would do. The same holds true when God asks our opinion, or when He tells us to bring our needs to Him in prayer. He knows all things. And yet He condescends to use our cooperation. What is really arresting in the Lord's question to Philip is the plural pronoun. The Lord did not say, "Where will you buy bread?" or "Where will I buy bread?" but "Whence shall we buy bread"—you and I together?

Have you ever thought of the Lord as being with you in such earthly concerns as going shopping? Perhaps if we thought about it, we would be more careful of our purchases, less self-indulgent with luxury items. A spiritual Christian says, "We buy"; a carnal Christian says, "I buy"—without regard to what Christ may think about it. Christ did not really need to buy anything, and He knew that Philip did not have enough money to feed the 5,000. But there is a sufficiency in the "we" of Christ and the individual, in spite of his individual insufficiency.

The Lord did not consider it beneath His dignity to have Philip and the other disciples as His co-workers. With the Lord as our co-worker, any problem can be solved. But we notice that it is the Lord who says "we," not Philip. The initiative of cooperation between God and man is always taken by God, and we respond to this initiative. Philip was indeed a true co-worker with God—in finding Nathanael and bringing him to the Lord; or in company with Andrew finding the lad with the loaves and fishes and bringing him to Jesus; and again with Andrew in finding the Greeks and bringing them to the Lord. May God help us to have a like spirit of selfless cooperation with Him.

## The Only Thing You Can Do to Save Yourself

In the gospel account of the feeding of the 5,000, the Lord did not hesitate to use a little boy's willingly surrendered lunch. We do not have to possess much for the Lord to consider it worthwhile for His purposes. The important thing is to place in His hand all we have. When this lad showed the Lord his five loaves and two fishes, he did not say, "I'll keep a loaf and fish for myself." He was not afraid that giving all he had would leave him with nothing.

Look at the end of the story. Thousands—all that were there—were fed; and there were twelve baskets full left over. I have no doubt this boy went home with much more than he came with. If you have never attempted such partnership with God, try it, and you will find this to be His method of accounting: when you give all, you are always left with more than you have given.

You will find this principle of God's partnership with man in other miracles recorded in John's gospel. In the second chapter the Lord changed the water into wine. But He used the servants present at the wedding feast as helpers. In the 4th chapter (vv. 46–54) we find that the Lord healed a nobleman's son. But it was because the father was concerned enough to go to the Lord with his plea for help. And in the raising of Lazarus (John 11) the Lord again asked for human cooperation in locating the tomb and in removing the stone. He did not have to ask, "Where have you laid him?" of course. He already knew, being God. Therefore these requests for help are not to be considered indications of His ignorance or impotence, but are rather proofs of His condescension in taking into His intimacy and cooperation human beings like us.

On the other hand, you will find some miracles in John's gospel that show us we are utterly hopeless and helpless without Christ's personal intervention. Take the impotent man at the pool of Bethesda (John 5:1–15). For 38 years no one had helped him until the Lord Jesus came along. And then in John 6:16–21 we see how incapable the disciples were of coping with the storm on the Sea of Galilee until the Lord appeared to them walking on the water. He did not need anyone's help then, nor did He ask for it.

Exactly whom did Paul mean when he said, "We are God's co-workers"? He meant himself, Apollos, and all other believers. He did not include unbelievers. Before anyone can be God's co-worker, he must first be God's workmanship. He must submit to God, being born from above. As a baby does nothing to bring himself into the world, so also a man can do nothing to regenerate himself and thus be born into the spiritual world. Before he can live spiritually, he must be given life from above. As Paul says in Ephesians 2:10, "For we are his [God's] workmanship, created in Christ Jesus unto good works, which God hath before ordained that we should walk in them."

The Greek word translated "workmanship" is *poíēma*, which basically means "something made," in this case that which is made by God, the result of His work. Paul indicates that God made us what we are as believers. This refers to a reshaping from our sinful state to the state of being indwelt by God. This new state can be achieved only through Jesus Christ. Observe how Paul expresses it in Ephesians 2:10, "created in Christ Jesus." The word for "created" in Greek is *ktisthéntes*. This differs in meaning from the previous substantive, *poíēma*. *Poíēma*, "something made," and in later Greek "a poem," denotes the result, the object, the end of an act (see Trench 1953, 361). The participle *ktisthéntes* (2 aor.), "having been created," refers to God's creative activity. It denotes His singular and miraculous work upon us, in transforming us from natural to spiritual men, from sinners to saints. It is the divine transfer of man from the sphere of Satan to the sphere of Christ.

Again we note an expression that occurs repeatedly in 1 Corinthians, *én Christṓ*, "in Christ." We are His workmanship (*poíēma,* something made, i.e. by Him), having been created (*ktisthéntes*) "in Christ Jesus." Paul stresses both the end result of God's activity and the actual work of making us what we are. And this activity results in our being "in Christ Jesus." We had nothing to do with it. We should never take any credit for being in Christ. No one can ever move himself from the sphere of Satan to the sphere of Christ. It is the almighty and gracious hand of God that picks up a sinner and brings him there. All you and I could contribute is our willingness to be acted upon by God. That is an absolute prerequisite for our becoming co-workers with God.

Observe again what Ephesians 2:10 says, "We are his workmanship [the result of His work, having been created by Him]" and now we are "in Christ Jesus." Is that the end of the matter? Can we now lie idle and enjoy our salvation? No, we are "created unto good works." And the Greek word for "works" is basically the same as that in 1 Corinthians 3:9, "For we are laborers together with God"—God's co-workers—*sunergoí*, a word derived from the conjunction *sún*, "together," and *ergázomai*, "work," workers together with God. But this is only after we have become the workmanship, the creation, of God.

Ephesians 4:24 says basically the same thing. A literal translation from the Greek text would be, "And put on the new transformed man, having been created [*ktisthénta*, exactly the same verb found in Eph. 2:10] in righteousness and holiness of truth." And in 2 Corinthians 5:17 we read, "Therefore, if anyone in Christ [no verb is given, so that this could apply to people of the past, pres., and fut.], a new [*kainḗ*, as in Eph. 4:24] *ktísis*, creation. The old things passed away, behold, all things have become new."

There is therefore a distinct and different kind of cooperation that God asks of sinful man with regard to his soul. It is that cooperation of faith, belief, reliance, submission. But that can hardly be considered in the same category as the partnership of the believer with God in good works. It is the same kind of cooperation and assistance a drowning man gives to a lifeguard. It is letting the one who comes to save you do everything to accomplish his lifesaving mission. If you resist and fight him, he cannot rescue you. Submissiveness is the extent of your being a co-worker with your Savior in His work of regenerating, saving, you. And this comes about through your realization that there is nothing you can do to save yourself except to be willing. Never make the mistake of thinking that by some miracle wrought independent of your own will you will ever be found "in Christ." God will not force Himself upon you. He is there to save you, but you must let Him.

### Working with God in His Field

Most of us have heard John 3:16 so often that it conveys no fresh message to us. As Sunday School children we may have rattled it off by heart: "For God so loved the world, that he gave his only begotten Son, that whosoever believeth in him should not perish, but have everlasting life." Yet this verse contains the message of salvation to man in a nutshell. Add to it Christ's words in John 6:37, "Him that cometh to me I will in no wise cast out," and you will know all that anyone can do to cooperate with God in the matter of his own salvation.

God invites, but He will not force His way into the citadel of your heart. He never uses force as a weapon to coerce the human spirit into receiving Christ as Savior and Lord. "Work out your own salvation with fear and trembling," was Paul's admonition to the Philippian church. That is your part. "For it is God which worketh in you both to will and to do of his good pleasure" (Phil. 2:12, 13). There you have God's co-partnership. "Behold, I stand at the door, and knock," says Christ. "If any man hear my voice, and open the door, I will come in to him, and will sup with him, and he with me" (Rev. 3:20). If you stop your ears and refuse to open the door, Christ will stand outside to all eternity. You must do your part; you must heed His call; you must fling the door open; you must admit Him. Then your life will become new and meaningful. You will be a new creature—His creation (see Burns 1938, 25–26; DeHaan n.d., 24–30; Janes 1957, 230, 231).

What does Paul mean by calling us God's co-workers? He gives himself and Apollos as examples of laborers together with God in His field. It is as if he were saying, "We are a couple of gardeners. One of us did the planting and the other the watering. But when you come right down to it, neither of us had anything to do with originating the mystery of the life by which the plant grew. That was God's work, and we who planted and watered were nothing. So what is the use of fighting over which of the two nothings is the greater?

"But that is not the whole story," Paul seems to say in 1 Corinthians 3:9. "That is not all the truth. The gardeners do not communicate life, but they do provide for its nourishment. Man has his own distinct function of assisting God to accomplish His purpose."

Each man has his own work to do. There is no reason why one should be considered more important than the other. Planting without watering would not produce the result God intended when He created the seed; and watering the ground before the seed has been planted would be fruitless labor.

Again I want to emphasize that the work of laborers in God's field ought not to be exclusive but complementary. "We are laborers together." The word is one in Greek, *sunergoí*, made up of the conjunction *sún*, "together," and the substantive *ergoí*, "workers," from *ergázomai*, "to labor." The word is a very ancient one from the time of Homer and Hesiod. Both *érgon*, "work," and *ergázomai*, "to work," are used repeatedly in the New Testament. They both denote action or active zeal in contrast to idleness (*aergía* or *argía*), or useful activity in contrast to useless busyness (*periergázesthai* in 2 Thess. 3:11, or *períergos* in Acts 19:19 and 1 Tim. 5:13).

What Paul refers to is any active work that may help God to accomplish His eternal purposes for man. We must always bear in mind, of course, that this does not reflect any weakness on God's part, but is only indicative that in His wisdom He has chosen that part of His work of salvation to be done by humans (see Kittel 1964, 635).

We may learn certain lessons from Paul's statement here. First, both the planter and the waterer need the ground, and the ground is the Lord's. In this case, the ground, of course, is a metaphor for the soul of man. Solomon likens the soul to a garden (Song 4:12; 5:1; 6:2). Isaiah likens it to a vineyard (Is. 5:1–7). And Paul compares it to a cultivated field (1 Cor. 3:9): "Ye are God's husbandry."

The Greek word translated "husbandry" is *geṓrgion*, a compound made up of *gḗ*, which means "land, ground," and *ṓrgion*, derived from *ergṓ*, which means "to do, to work." This is the only place in the New Testament that this metaphor is used. It denotes, not just a field, *agrós* (as in Matt. 13:24; Luke 14:18), but a piece of ground that needs cultivating, since from this same word we get *geṓrgos*, "farmer." *Geṓrgion*, then, is the field that needs a farmer. It is land that needs to be worked on, tilled, cultivated. The farmer or husbandman in Modern Greek is still called *geṓrgos*—literally "George." In fact, this very expression, some think, accounted for the popularity of the name George in the early days of Christianity.

The thing Paul wanted to stress in writing to the Corinthians is that they were a farmland that needed to be cultivated by him and others who were serving Christ. We are God's coworkers, *sunergoí*. Observe that the same basic word, *ergoí*, from *ergṓ*, "to work," is in "co-workers" as in *geṓrgion* (*ṓrgion*, also from *ergṓ*). We are the tillers together with God in the field of souls.

Observe also that when Paul refers to co-workers he says "we are," and when he refers to the field, land, or garden, he says "you are." We are the farmers; you are the farm on which we must work. Paul does not say, "You are our field," in spite of the fact that both he and Apollos had worked on it. They recognized that it was God's field, not theirs.

How glibly, almost boastfully, we speak of "my field, my church," as if we had any claim to ownership. Paul and Apollos may have sowed a great deal of seed, but they never made the seed. And the ground on which they planted and watered these seeds was not theirs but God's. "Ye are God's field," not ours. We would do well to remember with the Psalmist, "The earth is the Lord's, and the fulness thereof; the world, and they that dwell therein" (Ps. 24:1).

## Do Not Wall Yourself In and Others Out

We have been considering in these studies how God and man can cooperate in man's salvation. In Scripture we have found that man's soul is like a field or garden plot in need of cultivation. But why is this so? How did it all come about?

When God first created man and placed him in Eden, both Adam and the earth were blessed together. God created a paradise, but man's sin and disobedience caused it to become a common ground that needs cultivation. In consequence, Adam and the earth were cursed at the same time, from the same cause, and in a similar way. The word of the Lord to Adam after he had sinned was, "Cursed is the ground for thy sake; in sorrow shalt thou eat of it all the days of thy life" (Gen. 3:17). God then went on to tell Adam of the labor necessitated by the curse: "Thorns also and thistles shall it bring forth to thee; and thou shalt eat the herb of the field; in the sweat of thy face shalt thou eat bread, till thou return unto the ground; for out of it wast thou taken: for dust thou art, and unto dust shalt thou return"

(Gen. 3:18, 19). There you have the whole picture. The ground is the Lord's. It was defiled by man. God cursed it. It will not bring forth fruit unless man cultivates it with sweat and toil. But that does not mean man can claim ownership of the ground he tills.

In the same manner the souls of men are the Lord's They are soil that needs cultivating if they are to bring forth fruit. But when the fruit does come in other lives because of our labors, that does not mean the fruitful ground is yours or mine because we planted God's seed and irrigated it with God's water. None of us has the right to claim the souls of converted men. They are God's workmanship.

Unregenerate man is a rebel in relation to God. "My life is my own, and nobody has any right to interfere with it" is his conscious or unconscious assumption. He resents God's attempts to break through his "No Trespassing" sign by sending His redeemed people to sow His seed and water the ground of the sinner's heart.

In olden times gardens used to be enclosed. In Palestine every garden was enclosed by a wall—as was Gethsemane—or by a prickly hedge. "A garden inclosed is my sister, my spouse" (Song 4:12). To separate one's garden plot from the open field, and shield it from harm, was always the gardener's first care. Man in his sinful condition also shuts himself up. He discourages others from entering his property. He is afraid they will harm him. But Christ has commissioned His followers to plant the seed of the gospel and to water it in the hearts of men.

However, this proclivity toward self-determination is not confined merely to the unregenerate. There seems to be a remnant of Adamic sinfulness remaining with us even after our souls become the cultivated field of the Lord. We tend to claim our lives as our own, and even claim the souls of others as if they were ours because we worked in them.

> We are a garden walled around,
> Chosen and made peculiar ground,
> A little spot enclosed by grace,
> Out of the world's wide wilderness.

An excellent illustration of man's tendency to claim ownership of what does not belong to him is the parable of the wicked husbandmen recorded in Matthew 21:33ff.; Mark 12:1ff.; and Luke 20:9ff. The owner of a vineyard sent three servants, one after another, to collect the fruit that belonged to their master, but they were all refused and beaten. Finally, when the owner's son was sent, they killed him. Their claim was, "Since we cultivated the field, both the fruit and the land are ours." "Do not ever be like that," Paul warns us, even as he speaks of the unique privilege God gives us to be His co-workers. But that is always a temptation.

Or take the risen Christ's conversation with Peter in John 21:15ff. Notice the pronoun in His command to Peter: "Feed my lambs" (v. 15), "Feed my sheep" (v. 16). And again in the 17th verse, "Feed my sheep." Undoubtedly these referred to some of the souls Peter would be winning to Christ when he preached at Pentecost. Christ stresses the fact that Peter dare not call them his sheep, though they would be won through Peter's preaching, and fed through Peter's shepherding. They are my sheep, first, last, and always, Christ insisted.

We preachers must never refer to God's people as though they were our exclusive property simply because we preached the gospel to them, led them to Christ, and fed them spiritually. What we must remember, preachers and laymen alike in God's field, is that the hope of any garden lies not within its walls but in the overshadowing heaven that pours its bounties down.

A philosopher was asked by a friend to show him the splendid garden of which he was always boasting. He led him to a bare rocky space behind his house. "Where is your garden?"

the friend asked. "Look up," said the philosopher; "heaven is a part of my garden." Every good gift in the garden really comes from above; for should God command the clouds to send no rain, the earth would soon be like iron. Heaven shields, broods over, and enriches every fruitful plot of ground. Turn, then, your whole being fairly toward the sunshine of God's grace, and pray that the garden of your soul may always be as ready to receive heavenly blessing as is the garden around your dwelling. And when by God's enablement you become a planter, remember that the seed is God-made, and when you become a waterer, remember that the water is also God-made.

Every soul redeemed by Christ is a cultivated garden. Somebody entered in and broke up the stony ground, planted the seed and watered it. If you are Christ's, you now live in a virtual paradise. But are you not disturbed by all the land you see around you that has not been cultivated for the Lord? There used to be a famed spot in Norway called Gudvangen, that is, God's Garden or Field. It was a little patch of life and fertility in a district that ruin has claimed for its own, and it is enclosed with awful rocks that seem to fill the earth and reach to the skies. You are a little paradise, a little patch of fertile ground in the midst of the desolation around you. Do not let the walls you have built around your beautiful garden keep you from seeing the desolation outside. Get on the spiritual bulldozer; break up the rocky ground; plant the seed of God's Word, and water it. Your own garden ought to give you the hope that this desolation can be transformed by the power of the same God who transformed you. What happened to you should be an inspiration as to what can happen to others through you.

### Cooperation among Christians

Workers for God may be compared to candle-bearers, who are to shed the light of the gospel wherever God calls them. But in the sunlight of His presence, how foolish to compare one candle with another, or to boast that one gives a better light than another. As Joseph Parker says,

> If there were no sun, it would be interesting to compare one artificial light with another, and to say, I prefer this to that, but when the sun has risen and claims the whole firmament for his dominion, then all our little sparks must vanish. It is because there is a Christ in the church that there must be no Paul in it, no Apollos, except in a secondary and subservient and collateral sense, helping, assisting, contributing to the general smooth ongoing of the household, but nothing more.

Of course, Paul did not mean that anyone's work in partnership with God should be ignored. He reminded the Corinthian church that he had indeed contributed something: "I have planted." And he admonished the Thessalonian Christians, "We beseech you, brethren, to know them which labor among you, and are over you in the Lord, and admonish you; and to esteem them very highly in love for their work's sake" (1 Thess. 5:12, 13). He also tells Timothy, "Let the elders that rule well be counted worthy of double honor, especially they who labor in the word and doctrine" (1 Tim. 5:17). He also wants them to remember Apollos as well as himself, and to thank God equally for the services of each, without drawing comparisons. That may be hard to do, but we must remember that God is one and we are the other part of the partnership. I without my fellow workers cannot possibly constitute that "other part." Paul worked with Apollos, without any thought of rivalry. Labor in cooperation with others in partnership with God, and your life will be far more effective for Him.

Solomon led the people in building a great temple for God. We call it Solomon's Temple, but he could not have done it alone. With him were 70,000 who carried the materials. And far away, hewing the stones from the mountains, were another 80,000. These never came near the temple. Hundreds of skillful men worked with gold and silver and brass to contribute to the beauty and usefulness of the whole.

The Lord did not send His disciples out one by one but two by two. There is great joy in working harmoniously with others when all are working for God on the plan that He Himself instituted. We read in Luke 10:17, after Christ had sent out the 70 two by two: "And the seventy returned again with joy, saying, Lord, even the devils are subject unto us through thy name."

We also read in Scripture that when the Holy Spirit came upon the Christian church at Pentecost the disciples and others "were all with one accord in one place" (Acts 2:1). The trouble with us as Christian workers today is that too often we are all in discord in one place. No wonder the Holy Spirit's power fails to come upon us. We need accord; we need to work together for God. The "loner" in God's service tends to become the victim of spiritual pride. He feels, No one is so close to God as I am in the work I am doing; therefore no one can work in partnership with me. This very spirit of exclusiveness may be the reason the fruit of his work is so meager.

A man who was visiting a mental institution asked a guard, "Aren't you afraid these people will unite and overpower you and others?" The guard replied, "Mentally ill people never unite on anything." Is the Christian church full of spiritually unbalanced "loners"? If so, that may be one reason so little is being accomplished.

As you look outside on a snowy day and admire the beauty of the landscape, you may recall that no two snowflakes have ever been found to be alike. Yet each individual snowflake is nothing as it falls to earth. But many snowflakes together cover the ground and can change the course of things and persons. When you do your best, and join that best with the efforts of other Christians, you will be amazed at what God can do with your combined "bests."

When a missionary had finished speaking at a meeting, the ushers took up an offering. A girl of sixteen who sat in the front of the church had no money to give. She had been paralyzed for ten years. Not having anything else, she tried to place her crutches on the offering plate. "Sell them," she said, "and give the money to missions. I'll just not walk again, so that others may have a taste of life that is more abundant."

A young man following the scene rose to his feet and volunteered for missionary service. Another man rose to pledge his financial support so that he might be well-trained and sped on his way to the mission field. Then it was suggested that a new offering be taken. It was a big one. And the inspiration for all this was a crippled girl who was willing to give her crutches—all that she had.

Who knows what God can do through all that you have, small and insignificant though it may seem from the human standpoint? When you can say with Frances Ridley Havergal, "Take my life, and let it be consecrated, Lord, to Thee," and are willing to work in even the humblest capacity with others, then God can use you more fully. There is a division of labor in the church, and it is God who divides up the work to be done. He equips each one accordingly. And it is not according to the greatness of our labor that we shall be rewarded, but according to the faithfulness with which we do our part—small or large as the task may be.

Read the 12th chapter of 1 Corinthians to see that there is room for great diversification in God's vineyard. But though there are "diversities of operations . . . it is the same God which worketh all in all" (v. 6). No one has all the gifts, and even the humblest of us has some gift to dedicate to His service. As there is an acknowledgment of God-given tasks, so there must be unity of purpose. How wonderful to take the attitude, "I can only achieve my best because of all that everybody else is doing and as God blesses our work together as a whole." We are partners together—all of us together constituting one part, with God the other part without which ours would be of no avail. To each of us Christ says,

> "I gave my life for thee,
> My precious blood I shed;
> That thou mightest ransomed be
> And quickened from the dead.
> I gave, I gave it all for thee;
> What wilt thou give for Me?"

### A Difficult Lesson to Learn

A Sunday School teacher was endeavoring to impress upon his class of teenagers the desirability of having right attitudes toward others. He said, "If we let the Bible criticize our thoughts, we will have the right attitude toward everybody. It will help us to act as Christians should act in all their relationships with others. Do you understand the truth I'm trying to put across to you?"

"I think I do," said a seventeen-year-old girl. "Before I knew the Lord Jesus as my personal Savior, I used to single out certain people to be nice to. In my thoughts they were more important than others. But now I know that, as a Christian, God expects me to be courteous to everybody." How difficult it is for us to learn this lesson.

When the apostle Paul spoke of himself and Apollos as coworkers with God, and of the souls of the Corinthians as being God's field in which they were called to work, it is interesting to note that he did not say, "Ye are God's *fields.*" True, those among whom they worked were many. It would have been feasible for Paul to use the plural *geṓrgia,* "Ye [pl.] are God's fields," instead of "field." But he used the singular to indicate that all the souls of men are one field. There is to be no discrimination. All the souls of men are to be looked upon by Christian workers and witnesses as one great field in need of cultivation.

It is partisanship that Paul is trying to remedy in this third chapter of 1 Corinthians. To be willing to accept that the souls of men everywhere are God's field and therefore our proper sphere of labor is a difficult lesson we must all learn.

On one occasion a prime minister of France summoned an eminent surgeon to perform a very serious operation upon him. "You must not expect to treat me in the same rough manner that you treat your poor miserable wretches at your hospital," said the prime minister. "My Lord," replied the surgeon with great dignity, "every one of those miserable wretches, as you are pleased to call them, is a prime minister in my eyes." How important it is for us to realize that the soul of a rich, famous, or highly educated person is not more precious in the sight of God than that of an ignorant beggar. We are all God's field. There is not a soul on earth to whom we ought to give anything but our best in cultivating it and making it what God originally meant it to be. Let us look upon the whole of humanity as God's own field deserving of our best service.

A businessman on his way to prayer meeting saw a stranger looking in the door of the church. He invited him to come inside with him. "All right," said the stranger. That was the beginning of a Christian life for him and his family. He afterward told the man who invited him, "I lived in the city for seven years before I met you. No one had ever asked me to go to church. I was not here three days before the grocer, the dairy man, the insurance man, and the politician called on me. You are the first one to invite me to church." And it took seven years! Do not wait to pick and choose among the souls of men, but consider anybody you bump against as God's field for you to work on.

Paul moves from the metaphor of a field to that of a house. "Ye are God's field, ye are God's house." From agriculture he passes on to architecture. Food is essential, but so is shelter. Paul uses the commonest and most necessary elements of physical life to teach spiritual truths. Our Lord Himself brought out the numerous parallels between the physical world and the spiritual realm.

The Greek word for "house" is *oikodomḗ,* a word unknown in classic Greek up to the time of Aristotle. The same word is used in 2 Corinthians 5:1, "We have a house from God," meaning built by God. The word is used in 1 Corinthians 3:9 rather in the sense of a building still in the course of construction, even as the field is still in the process of cultivation. *Oikodomḗ* here, then, has the meaning of *oikodomḗsis,* "a building under construction," rather than *oikodomḗma,* which would refer to a completed building (see Edwards 1855, 76; Godet 1957, 178).

The Corinthians were babes in Christ, carnal in their attitudes and actions, yet they prided themselves on some gifts that are never mentioned as existing among Christians of other local churches. They thought they were a field whose cultivation was completed, a building that was finished. Paul wanted to correct this misconception. "You are a field under cultivation, a building under construction," he told them in effect. Growth is never complete in a Christian, nor can workers for God ever feel that there is nothing left for them to do in God's field.

LESSONS:

1. Two basic principles to remember as we labor are that God's sovereignty must never be disputed by an individual because of the partnership God permits him and that there is a wonderful interaction between God's omnipotence and His wisdom. We are to recognize not that God is going to do what we ask or expect, but that He is able to.
2. There is only one area of God's activities in which it has pleased Him to associate Himself with man and that is in the plan of man's salvation. God does not save man from sin without changing man's will. God's plan of salvation was devised and executed alone in mercy toward

man and not because man asked for or deserved mercy. God chose to require faith.

3. The Christian finds it hard to comprehend that in all things he is God's co-worker, a relationship that exists because God graciously chose to take man as His partner. Christian workers can do nothing unless God is with them.
4. God planned and carried out His plan for our salvation without consulting us. Although even the disciples tried to hinder Him from the cross, the very purpose for which He came into the world was to die for man's redemption. The actual transformation of man's character through His sacrifice on the cross is called conversion, and God through the Holy Spirit performs this miracle.
5. Only God can perform the miracle of new birth in a man's heart and life. Even so, God was pleased to appoint prophets, priests and shepherds to prepare the reception of the coming Messiah. Christ also chose Twelve disciples and sent them into the world to continue His work.
6. God involves men in His work. For instance, He used a lad's lunch to feed 5,000 people. He also tells us to bring our needs to Him in prayer even though He knows all things and thus our needs before we ask Him.

# 1 Cor. 3:10 — *Why All Men Are Not Equally Gifted*

> *According to the grace of God which is given unto me, as a wise masterbuilder, I have laid the foundation, and another buildeth thereon. But let every man take heed how he buildeth thereupon.*

The Bible says that every born-again believer in Jesus Christ is a house built by God in which He Himself dwells. God made our bodies to be the dwelling place of our spirits. And as our own spirit dwells in our own body, so He who is Spirit also dwells in our body. This is what the apostle Paul tells us in 1 Corinthians 3:9.

Furthermore, each believer is joined to other believers to form yet another body, the body of Christ, His church: "The church, which is his body, the fullness of him that filleth all in all" (Eph. 1:22, 23). "For as the body is one, and hath many members, and all the members of that one body, being many are one body: so also is Christ. For by one Spirit are we all baptized into one body, whether we be Jews or Gentiles, whether we be bond or free; and have been all made to drink into one Spirit. For the body is not one member, but many" (1 Cor. 12:12–14). Paul calls this body of Christ the building of God—the building that is being erected by God and which therefore belongs to God.

In verse 10 Paul proceeds to remind the Corinthians again that, although they are God's building, it took man's cooperation to erect that building. "According to the grace of God which is given unto me, as a wise masterbuilder, I have laid the foundation, and another buildeth thereon." This whole matter of the part man plays in what God builds brings to mind Psalm 127:1, "Except the Lord build the house, they labor in vain that build it." This does not mean that human effort is set aside in God's program. It presupposes man's best—his early rising and late toiling, the keenest exercise of eye and ear and intelligence. But, even when the builders and watchmen have done their best, there is an unknown element—a force as unavoidable as gravitation and as insistent as the laws of architecture—there is God, and to ignore Him is to build a castle of air on a foundation of sand.

What Paul was afraid of was that the Corinthians, and by extension all people, might face the temptation to forget the Senior Partner on the one hand and on the other might expect Him to do all—even the part that belongs to them. The first temptation comes from the quiet, unobtrusive, silent way God shares in the building process. God is always building. God is always keeping watch. God is always helping. But we do not always recognize it. We need to wake up and realize the predominant share God has in our lives.

We could call the discovery and recognition of our Unseen Partner and Helper "faith." "For by grace are ye saved through faith" (Eph. 2:8). "By grace," that is, by the help of God. "Through faith," that is, through becoming aware of God's grace in its immediacy, and then working in cooperation with His purposes and plans. "According to the grace of God which is given unto me," Paul says. He played his part in order to bring the Holy Spirit into the hearts of individuals in Corinth. He was the first to preach the gospel to them. But this he did only by the help of God.

It is true that Paul started God's work in Corinth. He laid the foundation. That is the first step in erecting a building. But he is careful to give God the credit for enabling him to do that much, "according to the grace of God which is given unto me." We could paraphrase the Greek work *katá,* translated "according," as "in the measure." In other words, Paul recognizes that the work he was able to do in Corinth was according to the measure of God's grace given for the task. God knew what Paul needed to do, and He enabled him to do it.

We need to recognize certain things about the grace of God. The first is that it is freely given. This is implicit in the Greek word for "grace," *cháris.* It is also clearly brought out in Romans 3:24: "Justified freely [without having to pay for it] by his grace." God's enablement to lay the foundation of the Christian church in Corinth was not deserved by Paul, nor was it gained by any natural capacity.

The second thing we must recognize is that God distributes His grace at will in whatever measure He deems wise. In 1 Corinthians chapter 12 we have a discussion about God's free gifts to men, which in Greek are called *charísmata* (sing., *chárisma*), "gifts," akin to *cháris,* "grace." Paul is still addressing the same people here as he did in chapter 3. "Now," he says, "there are diversities of gifts, but the same Spirit" (1 Cor. 12:4). The Greek word translated "diversities" is diaíreseis (pl. of *diaíresis*), "division." The Holy Spirit divides up His gifts to people, not only by quality but also by quantity.

Notice 1 Corinthians 12:11, "But all these worketh that one and the selfsame Spirit, dividing [*diairō̃n* (from *diaireō̃*), the same word translated 'diversities' in v. 4] to every man severally as he will." God exercises His sovereign will as He divides up His gifts qualitatively and quantitatively. Of one thing we can be sure, however—that what and how much He gives each one of us is enough to accomplish His purposes through us. Let us stick to what He has enabled us to do, realizing that He gives specific gifts to specific individuals for specific purposes. Not all of us can do the same thing. Nor can someone else do what God has gifted us to do as individuals in the circumstances in which He has placed us. Nor can we do that which God has specifically gifted others to do in their circumstances. That is all included in Paul's phrase, "according to the grace of God which is given unto me."

Men's gifts vary because their God-appointed tasks are unalike. What God asks of Christian people is not brilliance of accomplishment, but fidelity in their appointed sphere and in the use of their ordained equipment, along with the recognition that all enablement comes from Him.

A woman doctor on the mission field restored to health the greatly loved child of a native. In gratitude he knelt at her feet and not only thanked her but worshipped her as a god. She remonstrated, saying that she was a mortal like himself and worship belonged only to God. He replied that no one but a god could have saved the child's life. "Whom would you thank and praise," the missionary replied, "for a princely gift sent by the hand of a messenger—the servant or his generous master, the giver? I am but God's servant by whose hand He has been pleased to send you this great gift of healing." May a like humility and faithfulness possess us as we use our gifts, small or great, in the service of our Lord and among those in the sphere where He has placed us.

### Laying a Proper Foundation for Life

A minister preaching from the text, "I will run in the way of thy commandments when thou shalt enlarge my heart" (Ps. 119:32), imagined the following dialogue between himself and the author of this verse:

"Well, David, what is your first remark?"
"I will run."
"Run away, David! What hinders you? What is your next word?"
"In the way of thy commandments."
"Better yet, David. And what next?"
"When thou shalt enlarge my heart."
"No thanks to you, David. We could all run as well as you with such help."

When God gives the command to "run," to do some particular task He has in mind for us, He always supplies the needed grace, the help to do it. This is what the apostle Paul acknowledged, when reminding the Corinthians that he had laid the foundation for the church in Corinth. To make sure that there would be no misunderstanding as to whether this ability or grace or gift was acquired or granted, Paul added the participle *tḗn dotheisán* (*dídōmi*), "which is given unto me." Actually this participle is in the second aorist tense, passive voice, indicating that this grace or enablement was given to Paul some time in the past for the purpose of accomplishing a specific task that is now completed, and so it should be translated, "which was given unto me."

When Paul went to Corinth, he had to lay the foundation for a Christian church. He had to preach Christ and Him crucified as the only means of salvation. This ability to lay a foundation was given to him by God, as indicated by the passive voice, and it was granted him for the purpose that was at hand. God gives certain grace to accomplish certain tasks. The grace of God does not fill us once and for all, for all future tasks. He gives us further and different grace to accomplish other tasks at other times and in different places.

I have been impressed by the number of times it is said of the various disciples that they were filled with the Holy Spirit. There are some who would ask, "Have you been filled with the

Holy Spirit?" Before I can intelligently answer that question in the light of biblical teaching, I must ask, "When and for what purpose?" The Holy Spirit does not fill us in a vacuum. There is always a purpose for filling, and although every believer has received the Holy Spirit initially there is no once-and-for-all filling for every purpose of life.

In Acts 2 we read of the descent of the Holy Spirit upon the disciples at Pentecost. Peter was there and quite obviously was filled. Acts 2:4 confirms this: "And they were all filled with Holy Spirit." (The definite article is missing from the Greek text, emphasizing here the Holy Spirit's characteristics and qualities of working.) Because of this filling, Peter was able to preach, and souls were saved. That was the laying of the foundation of the Christian church. Yet later on in Acts 4, when Peter and John were brought before the Council for discipline because of their preaching, we read in verse 8: "Then Peter having been filled with Holy Spirit [again no definite article] said unto them. . . ." But had he not already been filled at Pentecost? Apparently he needed a fresh filling for a new task, a new defense of the gospel. It is interesting to note that only Peter, the speaker on this occasion, is said to have received this filling, and not John, who apparently remained silent. The Spirit fills us every time we are called upon to do something for God; and if we are to remain silent we may have no need of His filling.

This same truth can be illustrated from the life of Paul. After he was saved by encountering the risen Christ on the road to Damascus, Ananias came to him and said, "Brother Saul, the Lord, even Jesus, that appeared unto thee in the way as thou camest, hath sent me, that thou mightest receive thy sight, and be filled with the Holy Ghost" (Acts 9:17). Paul surely must have been filled with the Holy Spirit at that time. But a little later we find him in Cyprus confronted by the need to handle a false prophet by the name of Bar-jesus and a sorcerer called Elymas. Acts 13:9 tells us, "Then Saul, (who also is called Paul,) filled with the Holy Ghost, set his eyes on him." The previously filled Paul is filled again to face a new situation.

So it was in Corinth. When Paul came there he wanted to lead souls to Christ, thus establishing a Christian church. Therefore he had to preach the fundamental doctrine of Christ and Him crucified. For this he received the grace of God. Who can say, however, that this was the only doctrine Paul ever preached there or to others? He taught almost every conceivable doctrine pertaining to Christ and the Christian life. Just read his epistles to know what a multi-talented man he was.

But in Corinth he did the thing that was needed—he laid the foundation. When you preach the gospel to people for the first time you do not teach secondary or peripheral doctrines but the one central doctrine, the cross of Christ, by which they can be saved. If you hear anyone teaching or preaching anything else to unbelievers, you know he is emphasizing the wrong things, right though the teaching may be for maturing believers. If the foundation has not been securely laid, any teaching about how to live the Christian life will crumble and fall when put to the test by an unsaved person.

Tourists stand in wondering admiration before some of the palaces of the old world that have endured for more than a thousand years without a crack or seam. The Pantheon at Rome stands just as it did well over two thousand years ago. This would be impossible had not its foundations been right. The Rialto Bridge that spans the Grand Canal in Venice was erected in 1588. It has stood as it now stands for nearly four centuries, but that bridge rests on 12,000 piles driven deeply into the soil. What is true of buildings is also true of life. God cannot and will not build the Christian virtues into your life, or fill you with the Holy Spirit for His service, until the proper foundation of receiving Christ and Him crucified as your Savior and Lord has been laid.

## Building a Good Life

The story is told of two famous enemies of Christianity who were talking of a plan for the reconstruction of religion. They wanted to build a temple that would express man's religious impulse yet glorify this present life. In talking over a program of marvelous music, forever in the major key, they admitted that something was lacking. "I know what it is," finally declared one. "It's that hymn, 'O Sacred Head Now Wounded.' Without that there is a fatal lack of beauty and of power."

The compelling beauty of Christianity is in its doctrine of Christ's sacrifice to save sinners. Without making that the foundation of our lives, whatever superstructure we raise will never stand the test of time or of eternity.

The apostle Paul called himself a wise architect. That is the literal translation of the Greek in 1 Corinthians 3:10: "As a wise architect I laid foundation." His wisdom lay in the fact that he laid the necessary foundation for the Christian church in Corinth so that others could build on it. The Greek word translated "masterbuilder" in this verse is *architéctōn*, from which we get our English word "architect." It is a compound of *archḗ*, "ruler, beginning," and *téknōn*, "an artificer, a craftsman." In the narrower sense it means a carpenter, and this is what Joseph was called, *téknōn*, in Matthew 13:55 and Mark 6:3.

An architect is a masterbuilder. He conceives of a building in its totality. He realizes however that his first consideration must be the ground on which it is to stand; it must have a solid foundation. Of course, no one can live in a house that consists only of its foundation. A superstructure is needed. But without a proper foundation the superstructure will not stand.

Because Paul was the first Christian leader to come to Corinth, he realized that the laying of a proper foundation for the church must come first. Perhaps he would have preferred to teach the deeper things of the faith to the Corinthians, but he chose the part of wisdom in doing, not what he would have liked best but what was most needed. Preacher, teacher, is that the first consideration in your ministry?

How it must have hurt Paul to have to say to the Corinthians, "And I, brethren, could not speak unto you as unto spiritual [i.e., mature Christians], but as unto carnal, even as unto babes in Christ" (1 Cor. 3:1). But he did what was necessary, laid a foundation, and in that he proved wise. "For I determined not to know anything among you, save Jesus Christ, and him crucified" (1 Cor. 2:2).

It may be that Paul's Corinthian critics thought that laying the foundation was a comparatively easy matter, which need not have taken so long or required the services of a masterbuilder. It took Paul actually a year and a half to lay the foundation. They would have liked to see him get on with the building.

Paul did not underrate the importance of the structure. He did not think that the foundation was the house. He did not believe that the whole task of Christian ministers was to lay foundations. On the contrary, he maintained that it is a disgrace to a Christian community when all they are ever capable of assimilating are the simplest elements of the Christian faith, over and over again. He chided the Corinthians because when they ought to have been mature men and women in Christ they still had to be given baby food, still needed to be taught the first principles of the oracles of God.

Paul did not find fault with those who came to Corinth after him for building instead of laying a foundation. He claimed only to have done wisely when he laid a foundation upon which any man could build a structure that would stand, "Jesus Christ and him crucified." He felt that all the time he had spent on that was none too much, that he had no need to be ashamed of having occupied himself so earnestly and so long with such an unostentatious but infinitely important work.

Observe the two tenses of the verbs Paul uses in 1 Corinthians 3:10. "As a wise masterbuilder I *laid* a foundation." The verb "laid" in the Greek text is *éthēka* (*títhēmi*), which is in the second aorist tense, referring to an accomplished task in the past. He is finished with it now. In fact he was finished with it when he left Corinth after his year-and-a-half stay. The verb referring to the rearing of the superstructure by others, however, *epoikodomeí* (*épi*, meaning "upon;" *oikodomeí* [*oikodoméō*, "builds"), is in the present tense, indicating that the work of building on the foundation he had laid still continues and will continue as long as believers are alive. This means that the Christian must never cease to grow and that Christian ministers must recognize this and contribute what they can toward that goal.

"But another buildeth thereon." This does not mean that this other person need be basically different from the one who laid the foundation. The word translated "another" is *állos* in the Greek text, meaning another in a numerical sense, as contrasted to *héteros*, which means another of a different quality. This indicates that Paul could have been the one to build the superstructure if that was what was needed, and also that another servant of Christ could have been the one to do what Paul did in laying the foundation, had that confronted him as the need of the hour. The basic precept, then, is "Do that which is needed, whether it be laying a foundation or building a superstructure."

And Paul finally adds this admonition: "But let each one see how he builds thereon." "Each one" is *hékastos* in Greek. It is an individual responsibility—not only of the Christian minister who instructs others, but also of each Christian believer—to take care how he builds on that one foundation, which is Jesus

Christ. A man may have a wonderful foundation but a poor and shoddy superstructure. The discovery of a good foundation does not exempt a man from the necessity of building his house. To build up our lives into temples of God is the grandest of all work, one which needs our best thought and effort. It takes self-denial and toil. It demands a constant putting on of what is solid and true, and a constant casting out of what is hollow and false.

Day after day, year in year out, we must keep adding to our lives more knowledge, more self-control, more diligent practice of good and conquest of evil. We must keep casting out indolence, self-indulgence, pride, lack of love to man and neglect of God. Only then will we become fit temples of the Holy Spirit, to the glory of God.

Lessons:

1. God made our bodies a dwelling place for our spirits, so He who is Spirit also dwells in our body. By one Spirit we all are baptized into one body. The body is not one member but many.
2. We must recognize that the grace of God is freely given and that God distributes His grace at will in whatever measure He deems wise.
3. When God gives a particular task, He always supplies the needed grace for us to do it. He also gives further and different grace to accomplish other tasks at different times.
4. The Holy Spirit does not fill us for no reason. There is always a purpose for filling, although every believer has received the Holy Spirit initially.
5. We must rest upon the foundation of Christ, continually building our lives which, together, are His temple. This is the greatest work of all; and it needs our best thought and effort.

# 1 Cor. 3:11 | No Other Foundation

*For other foundation can no man lay than that is laid, which is Jesus Christ.*

In a city like the Corinth of Paul's day—cosmopolitan, advanced, highly literate and sophisticated, as well as wicked and corrupt—there were many different and dangerous foundations on which men could build their lives. Then, as now, the selection of ground that would give way was quite unlimited.

To those whom the god of this world, Satan, has blinded, it is foolishness to be told that there is only one true foundation on which a man may wisely rest all his confidence for time and eternity. Yet God's Word plainly declares, "Other foundation can no man lay than that is laid, which is Jesus Christ."

The apostle Paul had just been speaking in the previous verse as if he had laid the foundation of the church in Corinth. Now, in 1 Corinthians 3:11, he seems to half retract that statement. It was true in substance, but not sufficiently precise. Paul felt that, strictly speaking, he had not and could not lay the foundation, so here he says it "is laid," intimating that no one but God really put it there. This is exactly what is meant by the last part of the verse, "that which is laid." In the Greek text it is *tón keímenon* (*keímai*)—intimating that Christ, the foundation of our faith, had been there for all time eternally, in fact—and was not placed there by man.

The participle *keímenon*, "laid," is different from the verbs used in verses 10 and 11 referring to the laying of the foundation by Paul or any other human agency. As Kittel says, the verb *keímai*, from which the participle *keímenon* (laid) is derived, "can either denote the fact as such or the results" (see Kittel, vol. 3, 1965, 654). Here we believe Paul does not refer so much to the fact of Christ becoming the foundation as to the result—that He is such, and that He is responsible for any change that occurs in the heart of a believing person

The Greek word for "lay" as a transitive verb is *títhēmi*, "to place down." It involves a subject, someone who does the placing or laying down. It is equivalent to "to bring to a place, to establish" (Op.cit., vol. 8, 152). The participle *keímenon*, "that is laid," is in the present tense which indicates that it lies there permanently. There is no subject to indicate by whom it was laid. Paul does not say anything about who laid this universal foundation or how it was laid. He wants to make it absolutely clear that the foundation he brought to Corinth was exactly the same as that eternally laid by God Himself.

Paul calls himself a wise architect because the foundation he laid was not different from the one eternally laid. How foolish an architect would be if he refused to follow the laws of nature and civil engineering, which are actually the laws of God. You, too, are unwise if you diverge from the church's one foundation, "Jesus Christ, and Him crucified," laid down by God from the beginning.

"According to the grace of God which is given unto me, as a wise masterbuilder, I laid [*éthēka*, 2 aor. of the verb *títhēmi*] a foundation." Paul, as a second cause, did this by preaching Christ crucified. But actually, as to primary causality, says Paul in verse 11, this is not true, for Christ was not laid down by any human agency. He has always been there. He placed Himself there as the eternal God and Redeemer of mankind. He is *keímenon* (neut., referring to the foundation), "lying there"—an entirely different word from *tethḗmenon*, "placed or laid by someone else." Paul wants the Corinthians to know that his part was merely to bring the already universally laid foundation to a particular place, Corinth.

This recalls the assertion Christ made to the Jews when He told them that He knew Abraham. Astonished and infuriated they asked how He, who was not yet 50 years old, could have seen Abraham who lived hundreds of years before. You remember the Lord's answer: "Verily, verily, I say unto you, Before Abraham came to being [lit. translation], I am" (John 8:58). In other words, No one put Me there; I have always been. This is exactly the idea conveyed by the expression *tón keímenon*, "the one [foundation] lying there—that has always been."

Paul does not say, "For no other foundation has anyone laid," but "No other foundation can anyone lay." It is a mere impossibility. He is not stating a historical fact but an impossible situation. Observe that in referring to another foundation it is the Greek word *állon*, meaning another numerically, and not *héteron*, another of a different quality. Oh, yes, men have been able to lay down foundations of different qualities, but never one of the same quality as the Lord Jesus. There is no other like Him; He is unique.

Of course, there are others who are qualitatively different, but they can never do for you what the Lord Jesus can. There is no other who can forgive your sins, or recreate you into a new person. Many religious leaders have formed the foundations of religions and systems of thought, but they cannot save you from sin or give you victory over your lower nature.

Everyone else has a beginning and an end. But Christ has neither beginning nor end. He Himself is the beginning and the end. He has the keys of death and hades (Rev. 1:18). He is the beginning—not the passive beginning, not the effect, not the result of someone else's creative power, but the active cause of the creation of God (Rev. 3:14). There is no one who can lay such a foundation. The word translated "no man" in Greek is *oudeís*, which refers not only to man but also to any other created being—not (*oú*) *heís*, a single one. He has been there eternally.

How careful we should be not to ascribe a beginning to the Lord Jesus Christ. Sometimes we preach as though the gospel itself were an innovation, yet it has always been there. Though it has found its greatest exposition and unfolding in the New Testament era, it was there for the people of the Old Testament. Abraham found it lying there as the foundation stone of his acceptance with God, and so did everybody else. It is by His grace that He permits us to preach the gospel and become workers together with Him in laying the foundation in the lives of others But let us not take more credit for Christ being born in the hearts of those to whom we witness than is really our due. It is God Himself who has laid the foundation. Isaiah knew about it in his day when he wrote, "Thus saith the Lord God, Behold, I lay in Zion for a foundation a stone, a tried stone, a precious corner stone, a sure foundation" (Is. 28:16). All that we can say to others is, "There it is." All we can do is to recognize it.

But let us remember that it will not avail us that a foundation has already been laid, or that it has already been pointed out to us, unless we desire and choose it and use it as the foundation upon which we build our lives and our eternal salvation.

### "All Other Ground Is Sinking Sand"

Many people are puzzled as to what someone means when he says, "I am a Christian." Is he the genuine article, or is he merely giving lip-service to what he thinks is expected of him? Is Christ the foundation on which he is building his life, or is he trusting in his own merit and good works for acceptance with God?

The apostle Paul says, “Other foundation can no man lay than that is laid, which is Jesus Christ.” It is to be feared that many who profess to be Christians are only lying around about the foundation, so to speak, like the broken and useless stones that may be seen lying in heaps around a house that is in the process of building, but which are never fitted into it. To those who truly believe in Christ, He is the chief cornerstone, elect and precious; to those who do not, or who merely give lip-service to such belief, He is a stone of stumbling and a rock of offense.

But why is this? Is it because Christ has not been laid as the sure foundation for every soul? Is it because, while laid for salvation for some, He has been laid for destruction to others? Not at all. It is only because some will not be saved by Him, will, in spite of His invitation to build their lives on Him, stumble and fall on Him, will in spite of all the lessons of God’s providence, and all the warnings of God’s Word, and all the strivings of God’s Spirit, refuse to be truly united to Him, or will even dash themselves against Him with insane hostility, although it can only be to be broken, to be destroyed.

This truth is clearly stated as the application of the parable of the wicked husbandmen, which we considered in an earlier study. When the farmers who were hired to cultivate a vineyard would not pay the owner what was due him, and persecuted the servants he sent to collect the money, the owner sent his son. The wicked husbandmen killed him, thinking that in this way they could eliminate him and thus any claim he had to the field. At the conclusion of this parable, the Lord said, “The stone which the builders rejected, the same is become the head of the corner” (Luke 20:17). In other words, without Christ, the Son of God sent by the Father, no building, no superstructure can stand. And then Christ adds, “Whosoever shall fall upon that stone shall be broken, but on whomsoever it shall fall, it will grind him to powder" (Luke 20:18).

The word "stone" in Greek is *líthon*, which is used here to mean the foundation. In fact, sometimes the word "foundation" in Greek is the masculine *themélios*, which implies the word *líthos* (masc. nom.), the "foundation stone" (*themélios líthos*). Either word can be used to include the other (Luke 20:17, 18; Rev. 21:14, 19). The foundation is a stone, not sand, upon which man is called to build if he wants an edifice—a life—that will stand. If he refuses to build on the foundation God has laid in Christ, then one of two things will happen according to Luke 20:18: either he will fall upon the "stone" and be broken, or the "stone" will fall upon him and pulverize him.

If you attack Christ, it is you who will be shattered, not He. The day is also coming when He, the stone or foundation, will fall on unbelievers and will pulverize them. These are serious words concerning Christ, the one eternally laid for our redemption or destruction, whether as individuals or nations. Either opposition or indifference to the gospel of the crucified Christ will prove fatal. You will perish unless you repent and come to Christ for salvation—that Rock of Ages who is the foundation eternally laid for your salvation for time and eternity.

Paul declares that this foundation stone "is Jesus Christ," in the present tense. Though the Lord was already gone from the earth when Paul wrote these words, he does not hesitate to use the historic present of perpetual existence, encompassing all time. It fully agrees with the participle *keímenon*, "lying," referring to the foundation that is eternally laid. Christ was, is, and ever shall be the foundation stone of every individual believer, of every Christian church locally, and of the Christian church universally. No other can be equal to Him or do what He can do for you personally as well as for the world.

What Paul also brings out here is that Christianity is not a mere system of doctrine, not a mere ethical code—although it includes these elements in their highest form—but it involves a Person primarily and centrally. And that Person is not only historical, as indicated by His name "Jesus," but is also redemptive, as shown by His name "Christ," the anointed one for the purpose of performing a mission.

Other religions are based on teachings and on keeping the precepts prescribed by their leaders, the following of which causes you to belong to them. Not so with Jesus Christ. You cannot be accounted a Christian merely by accepting Christ's ethical teachings. As a building must be joined to the foundation, so must you be united to Jesus Christ as a Person. When you become a Christian, you do not merely acquire a philosophy of life but you become a new creation. You are joined to Christ even as the superstructure is joined to the foundation.

Paul was partly contemporary with Jesus. He was converted shortly after the death of Christ. He wrote his first letter to the churches within 25 years of Christ's death. He wrote the whole of his letters within 38 years of Christ's death. Paul then was speaking of Jesus Christ as a historical reality not as a myth. Jesus was of Paul's time. He had walked and talked in Paul's Jerusalem. He had been crucified there within Paul's memory only a year or two ago. We are forced to face the facts of primitive contemporary beliefs about Jesus. Paul was among His contemporaries. With these historical occurrences vivid in his mind, what has Paul to tell us about Jesus?

Paul's experience had proved to him that Christ was a living Savior. So many today are willing to concede that Jesus was an actual historical personage. They may also concede that His teachings have done much good in the world. Some even profess to be His followers in much the same sense that certain people are followers of Ghandi, although they know he is no longer living. They venerate his memory and strive to follow his teachings. But only those who are built upon the foundation of a living Christ can truly be called Christians in Paul's meaning of the word, or of what the other New Testament writers believed and taught. Anything else is a watering down, a dilution of the gospel. "All other ground is sinking sand."

### Does the Bible Teach That Christ Was God?

Homes Dudden gives an extended answer to this question that is well worth quoting:

> . . . if you open your Bible to [Paul's] very first letter—the first to the Thessalonians—and turn to the very first chapter and the very first verse, you will find an astonishing sentence:—"Grace be unto you, and peace, from God our Father, and the Lord Jesus Christ." How remarkable this is! We modern men are so accustomed to the formula and the doctrine it implies, that we fail, perhaps, to realise the wonder of it and the novelty. But with what a thrill of horror would an orthodox Hebrew of the Apostle's age have read these words!
>
> Remember that the reference is to One who in living memory died, so to speak, on the scaffold; remember the common belief that "cursed," not by man only but also by God, "is every one that hangeth on a tree"[Gal. 3:13]; remember, moreover, that the title "Lord." here most emphatically ascribed to Jesus is the very word which is used by the Greek translators of the Old Testament to render the Hebrew Jehovah; and then conceive the feelings of the Jewish monotheist when he heard of this crucified Sufferer being crowned with the Divine name, and positively linked, as the Giver of grace and peace, with the One and Only God, the God of Israel, the Almighty!
>
> . . . . He was . . . . God's "own Son," in whom "dwelleth all the fullness of the Godhead" [Col. 2:9], essentially Divine. To Him Paul prays; for Him Paul gives his life; in Him hereafter Paul expects to see his Judge; to Him Paul finally assigns the incommunicable name: He "is over all, God blessed forever" [Rom. 9:5]. Could any creed, I say, be more explicit? Could any loftier claims be made for Jesus than these which were actually made within forty years of His death? Here surely is a notable fact with which we are compelled to reckon. For the first generation of believers, as for the later Church, the system of Christianity is grounded

upon a Person, a Being at once human and superhuman, truly man yet no less truly more-than-man, the "God-Man," Jesus Christ.

. . . . Now if you and I had had the privilege of sitting at the feet of Jesus, we should at once have been struck, I think, by one thing—by a strange characteristic undertone of greatness, which runs throughout His discourse. It is only an undertone because it is more overheard than heard. For Jesus does not dilate upon His glories. . . . He undoubtedly betrays the self-consciousness of a Being immeasurably exalted above the level of mankind. He speaks as Someone from another sphere, whose home is far away.

. . . . Listen, then, attentively, and mark what unprecedented claims he makes. He says He is greater than Jonas [Matt. 12:41], greater than Solomon [Luke 11:31], greater even than the sacred temple [Matt. 12:6]. The prophets, kings, and saints of olden time—He stands above them all. Over the very angels He exalts Himself; they are His ministers, subject to His bidding. Towards His disciples His imperiousness is unbounded. He demands, as though it were the most natural thing in the world, that they should live for Him alone, that they should give up all in life that they love for Him—father and mother, children, and home, and wife.

With God, again, He claims a unique relation. He says without any attempt at justification: "All things are delivered unto me of my Father: and no man knoweth. . . the Father save the Son, and he to whomsoever the Son will reveal him" [Matt. 11:27]. The sublimity of the sage, the speculation of the sophist, the awful wisdom of the anointed priest—all this He sweeps aside, proclaiming that He alone of men can fathom the abysses of the Infinite.

So too this youthful Galilean carpenter ascribes to Himself an ecumenical importance. He looks on the seething turmoil of nations, races, peoples, and He calls them to His heart, crying, "Come unto me, and I will give you rest" [Matt. 11:28]. The whole great world may come like a little child and nestle at His bosom. He looks again into the distant future and sees the nations gathered at His judgment-seat. The dead come up and the living come up, while He sits majestic on the throne of the Almighty and utters the final, dreadful words of life and death.

How startling, how utterly astonishing, is this self-consciousness of Jesus! Surely no thoughts or visions such as these ever found entrance into merely human mind. . . . The very idea of being the one and only Mediator of God! No moral teacher or enraptured prophet ever conceived of himself in a character so sublime. Yet this was the character that Jesus, as a matter of historical fact, not only conceived but consistently sustained.

....when we listen to Jesus, so imperious yet so tender, bidding men love Him, live for Him, die for Him; calling Himself Master, calling Himself Lord, calling Himself Shepherd, calling Himself Judge; claiming to interpret God to men, claiming to be the only source of joy and rest for human souls; we are amazed at the consciousness of greatness which His words express. And when we go on to compare His utterance with His character, when we think of His nobility, His sanity, His unexplainable originality, His unconsciousness of sin, so astounding in a man who was really good, why we feel—do we not—that here is One who is quite outside the measure of our little earthly standards. It is no mere man, though unmistakably man, that comes to meet us here. We are constrained to bow in worship [see also Flint 1889, 329–32]

.... On every sphere of our life He has left His mark. To the politician He has given a law, to the thinker a philosophy, to the poet a song, to the saint a passion.... He has set up a throne in the universal human heart, and millions of every age and race and class and character have yielded to His sway. Tired men, wearied with the frets of life, have found in Jesus rest and full refreshment. Bad men, smirched and polluted with the soil of sin, have come to Jesus and have been made clean, ... Timid men, trembling on the edge of life, and shivering at the dark unknown that lies before them, have looked to Jesus and dismissed their fears.

For great results there must be cause proportionate. is a proportionate cause.... Could any mere man have done this? My brethren, the experience of the race says No (Dudden, 1910, 20-27).

## LESSONS:

1. The foundation Paul brought to Corinth was the same foundation God the Father eternally laid— Christ crucified.
2. Many religious leaders have attempted to lay other foundations, but none of these can save men from sin. By His grace God leads us to preach the gospel as the only foundation of faith.
3. We must build upon the foundation of Christ by continually preaching His Name, which alone can save others.
4. Those who oppose the gospel of Christ will die in their sins.

5. Jesus Christ stands above all prophets, kings, and saints. He was exalted above angels. He sits majestically on the throne of the Almighty. Intensely compelling, Jesus bids men to love Him, live for Him, die for Him. We are constrained to bow in worship before Him; He is our hope; He is the unique foundation.

# 1 Cor. 3:12, 13 | *Building or Rebuilding Your Life*

*Now if any man build upon this foundation gold, silver, precious stones, wood, hay, stubble; every man's work shall be made manifest: for the day shall declare it because it shall be revealed by fire; and the fire shall try every man's work of what sort it is.*

What good is a foundation unless you erect a building on it? What good does it do to say you accept Christ as your Savior unless you build your life upon Him? Christ had no use for those who merely gave lip-service to Him when He was on earth. His invitation to men and women to come to Him included taking His yoke upon them, to be linked up with Him and travel the same road He did, even as two oxen joined by a common yoke must always go in the same direction.

When Paul declared Jesus Christ to be the only foundation for the individual and for the church, in 1 Corinthians 3:11, he was carrying out his metaphor of the Christian's life being a building in verse 9. Now, in verses 12 and 13, he proceeds to call our attention to the importance of choosing the right materials with which to build on that foundation.

Six kinds of materials are mentioned in verse 12, but they may be reduced to two—good materials and bad, those that will stand the fire and those that will not. Gold, silver, precious stones—the fire will not readily consume these. Wood, hay, stubble—these will easily go up in smoke.

The various good materials may be of different degrees of goodness. Silver is not as valuable as gold; gold is not as valuable as certain precious stones. But they are all good and capable of enduring the fiery ordeals of life. The various bad materials are not all equally bad. A fairly durable house may be made out of wood, but not even a tolerable hut can be made out of hay and stubble. Yet all are bad, for even wood can be reduced to ashes by a conflagration.

All this can be applied to our own lives. The materials out of which we may construct our lives seem at first sight to be infinite in number, yet there are really only two great kinds. These are the right and the wrong—those that are in accordance with God's will and those that are opposed to it; those that are prompted by the Holy Spirit and those that are prompted by our carnal hearts.

Thus Paul envisions two builders on the one foundation, Jesus Christ. The one builds a palace, the other a shack. No doubt in Corinth, as in other ancient cities, side by side with the temples shining in marble and brass were the huts of the poor and the slaves, built of flimsy materials such as Paul mentions. He envisions a sudden flame playing around these buildings, the fire of the Lord coming to judgment. The marble gleams whiter, the silver and gold and jewels more resplendently, while the tongues of light leap about the palace. But the straw hut goes up in a flare. The two builders stand before God, the ultimate Paymaster. The one man gets wages for work that lasts; the other gets no pay for what perishes.

There is only one foundation, but there can be two kinds of builders who erect a superstructure upon it. Paul called himself a wise masterbuilder because he had laid a good foundation in proclaiming Christ and Him crucified, and had proceeded to build the church in Corinth out of lasting material. Thus we see that the materials here primarily symbolize the teaching brought by Christian ministers and teachers. Since both the builders to whom Paul refers in verses 12 and 13 build on the same foundation, Jesus Christ, there can be no doubt that both are truly born-again. But the structures of these two believers can vary greatly in quality and value. The one represents solid teaching of the Word of God, and the other flimsy teaching. The responsibility lies squarely not only on those who teach but also on those who listen.

What kind of preacher or teacher are you? What kind of preacher or teacher do you listen to? Are you mainly interested in the external and trivial things of Christianity or the solid material of the Word of God? Do you come under Paul's condemnation of the Corinthians because you constantly demand to be fed with milk like a baby, or are you able to sink your teeth into a spiritual steak? Does your preacher regale you with pretty little stories and humorous anecdotes? These will not see you through the fire that is sure to come. Is the cross of Christ central in your preaching or in the preaching you hear? Is Christ presented as the only foundation for your life? Are you taught from God's Word how to build on that foundation so that your works will be acceptable to God? On the same foundation some Christians build a fortress and others build a shack of straw. The latter will be saved as by fire, but what a poor testimony and what regret when all is said and done in life!

The life of a Christian is represented in many places in Scripture as a building, suggesting not only the idea of the whole life resting upon Christ as the foundation but also the thought of slow, continuous progress, stone by stone, layer by layer; and in addition implying that the result is a homogeneous whole.

Of course, Paul is presenting two extreme cases here for the sake of illustrating a principle. But although few Christians would be found at either extreme, we know only too well from our own experience and observation of the life of the average Christian that many a true follower of Jesus Christ may pile much upon the foundation that is unworthy of it. We build inconsistently, and in our own persons often combine these two builders. We lay one course of precious stones and the next of straw. How carefully we need to examine our life structure to see if some demolition is needed and some rebuilding. Yes, it can be done, as the poet once said:

> Oh, to go back across the years long vanished,
> To have the words unsaid, the deeds undone,
> The errors canceled, the deep shadows banished,
> In the glad sense of a new world begun;
> To be a little child whose page of story
> Is yet undimmed, unblotted by a stain,
> And in the sunrise of primeval glory
> To know that life has had its start again!
>
> I may go back across the years long vanished;
> I may resume my childhood, Lord, in Thee,
> When in the shadow of Thy cross are banished
> All other shadows that encompass me;
> And o'er the road that now is dark and dreary
> This soul, made buoyant by the strength of rest,
> Shall walk untired, shall run and not be weary
> To hear the blessing that has made it blest.
>
> —author unknown

## Making the Right Choices in Life

Everybody wants freedom, but not everybody is willing to accept the responsibility that goes along with freedom. God has given us freedom of choice in certain areas and not in others. We cannot choose whether or not we shall be born or who our parents shall be. We cannot choose the mental and physical makeup we are born with. But in 1 Corinthians 3:12 the apostle Paul makes it clear that we *can* choose what we shall do with them. And the most basic choice we have to make is whether or not we will accept the Lord Jesus Christ as the one foundation on which to build our lives.

But even after choosing Him as Savior and Lord, we are confronted with the choice of what materials we shall use to build on that foundation. We can select precious materials of lasting value, such as "gold, silver, precious stones," or we can choose cheap and shoddy material that will only serve temporarily. But in writing to the Christians of the Corinthian church Paul makes it very clear that when the fire comes, as it must some day, we will have no choice as to what will become of our building. Either it will survive the judgment of fire or it will be reduced to ashes.

Shoddy material is cheap; lasting material is costly and requires hard work to come by. But you get what you pay for, both in material and spiritual things. The same God who made the inexorable laws of the material universe also made the laws of the spiritual world, and they are just as inexorable. Both kinds of material are available. Your choice will depend on your sense of values and your wisdom in building for the future as well as for the present. The wise Christian builds his life with eternal values in view and selects his building materials accordingly.

Paul speaks of these materials as precious stones and metals, in contrast to wood, hay, and stubble. Yet God made both kinds. In each He placed intrinsic value, but it is up to you to discern and evaluate their relative worth. God has a purpose for each thing He has created. If you choose the wrong ones, do not blame God for having made them. The possibility of choice is one of God's greatest gifts to you. If you stop to think about it, I am sure you would not have it otherwise. Nobody wants to be a robot.

You may fool men into believing you are building a worthy superstructure of Christian character on the foundation of your faith in Christ. But you cannot fool God. The precious gold and gems that He has made available to you are yours if you work hard enough for them. Do not gold-plate your life. Let it be solid. Do not be satisfied just to keep up outward appearances, but let your Christian life and character be genuine through and through.

Ruskin told of visiting a famous cathedral in which there are a number of colossal figures high up among the heavy timbers that support the roof. From the pavement these statues have the appearance of great beauty. Curious to examine them, Ruskin climbed to the roof and stood close beside them. He was disappointed to find that only the parts of the figures that could be seen from the pavement were finished. The backs were rough and unsightly.

It is not enough to make our lives true only so far as men can see them. They must be true through and through. A little flaw, made by a bubble of air in the casting, has caused a great girder to collapse years afterward, bringing down the immense bridge whose weight rested upon it.

Again, we see that each of us must make his own building. "If any man build upon this foundation. . . ." Each of us builds his own house and lives in it and will be responsible for what ultimately happens to it. Others may help lift the blocks into place, but we must lay them on the wall. Our own hands give the touches of beauty or ugliness, whatever other hands hold the brushes or mix the colors for us. If the building is marred and unsightly when finished, we cannot lay the blame on someone else.

Others may have sinned and passed on consequences to you. Others may have deeply wronged you, and the hurt stays with you. You may never be what you might have become in this world because of this wounding. But you are not responsible for these marrings of your character that were wrought by other hands. Still, you are the builder—you and God. You can take even the broken fragments of what seems a ruin and, through God's grace, make a noble edifice. It is strange how many of earth's beautiful lives have grown up out of what seemed defeat and failure. Indeed, God seems to love to build spiritual beauty out of cast-away fragments of lives, even out of sin's debris.

In a great cathedral I have heard that there is a window made by an apprentice out of the bits of stained glass that were thrown away as worthless refuse when the other windows were made—and this is the most beautiful window of all. You can build a noble character for yourself, in spite of all the hurts and injuries done you, wittingly or unwittingly by others, with the fragments of the broken hopes and joys and the lost opportunities that lie strewn about your feet. No others, no matter how badly they have hurt and marred you, can prevent you from building a beautiful character for yourself. And conversely, no others by their best work can cause you to build a beautiful character. The fine character of your father or mother is not yours; you have to build your own.

There is much truth in saying that every man is the architect of his own fate. Your choices affect your destiny. Out of a rough block of stone one man may make a beautiful statue, another gravel. Both products are good and useful under certain conditions. But a statue can be immoral in conception, and gravel can be the grudging and punitive work of a condemned criminal. The point is that, whether you are a gifted artist or a competent gravel maker, you can choose whether to use your abilities worthily or unworthily. In building a Christian life you have the same choice.

## God Has a Plan for Your Life

We have seen in a previous study that you and I as Christians can select good or bad materials with which to build on the foundation of our faith in Christ. We have also recognized that God made both kinds of materials but left the choice, and the responsibility for the choice, up to us. And we have seen that we cannot fool God if we build a shoddy life house or character, no matter how good a front we may put up before men. We have also learned that, in dependence on God, each of us must make his own building; we cannot live in the life house of another but must build our own worthy edifice, no matter what adverse circumstances seem to militate against it.

Now we come to another basic lesson, and that is that the plan of your life and mine is not actually left to us to figure out. The same architect who lays the foundation is the best one to plan the superstructure. Otherwise there may be conflict and disagreement between us. Since the only foundation has been laid there by God Himself, it is only logical to believe that He also has a specific plan for each superstructure. What we build must be according to a plan that will fit the foundation or it will collapse.

Do you realize that God has a plan for every life, including yours? The Creator never brings a human soul into being and starts it on its immortal destiny without knowing precisely what place He means it to fill in this world, what work He means it to do, and what He means it to become. The plan is not the same for any two lives. The superstructures may vary greatly. There is a beautiful variety in God's building of Christian lives. It is not up to us to tell others to build their houses to conform to our pattern. God may have a different plan for our friends. Conversely, we should not attempt to copy someone else's lifestyle. We reach our highest success in life, and do the best work possible for us as individuals, when we discover what God's will is for us and try our best to work it out. God's basic plan for you is knowable. Find out what it is. God is not an unreasonable taskmaster who requires certain things of us without letting us know what they are.

No mere builder would throw aside the plan of a wise architect and substitute his own poor judgment instead. Where can you find God's plan for your life? In His Word. Study it. Imagine a builder working away on an edifice day by day without referring to the architect's drawings—just building haphazardly as his fancy struck him. What a struggling, shapeless, mongrel pile the house would be! The same thing would be true of your life if you fail to study the Bible to find there the Lord's pattern for your life.

But you may object, "The Bible doesn't tell me what business or calling to choose." True, it does not spell out the details, but it lays down principles by which you can make proper judgments each step of the way. No one need ever take a step in the dark. Of course, we are not to expect to be led and shown the way and told what to do as if we had no brains. God gave us our intelligence so that we would use it. He wants us to think for ourselves, to inquire and judge and choose a plan. He guides us most frequently through our judgment as illuminated by His Word. We are to pray for light and then think for ourselves and act—doing what seems to us to be the right thing, taking what appears to be God's way. We may sometimes make mistakes, for we are not infallible. But we learn by our mistakes and grow wiser as we go on (see Maclaren 1886, 157–61; Miller n.d., 8–14; Miller 1914, 54–62).

One further lesson may be drawn from what Paul says about the variety of superstructures built on one and the same foundation, Jesus Christ. That is, that neither the preachers nor the converts of early Christianity were faultless. Paul recognized a situation among the Corinthian believers and tried to correct it by reminding them of the day of judgment. He saw folly and wisdom dwelling side by side in every man. And he declared that only what was true and stable would survive.

And since individual believers were not perfect, neither was the local church. Just as every Christian's work is going to be tried by fire, and worthless works cease to be, so it will be with Christ's church, local and universal. Our work—and the church's work—on earth will be done one of these days. The church as it is on earth is a temporary structure, a temple reared for earthly needs, and as God's witness on earth, an organization that will perish in this respect when the need for it has passed. The one imperishable thing about it is Jesus Christ, the true and one foundation.

Hasn't the entire history of the church been filled with such imperfections as the apostle Paul describes? Do we not have a proliferation of denominations today, each thinking they have a structure built entirely of gold, silver, and precious stones? Let us be frank and honest about the wood, hay, and stubble in the structure of our churches. It may be well hidden behind the gold and silver. It may be in between the precious stones. But it is there. On the other hand, let us be honest and discerning enough to see some precious stones in those churches that differ from ours in denominational practices and beliefs.

Can you find a saint in the Old Testament or the New that we do not have to apologize for on some point? Has Christianity produced a single leader since then who can escape censure? Even Paul and Peter had their quarrel. "There is no perfect church and no perfect preacher. . . . Paul saw the gold and stubble side by side in the work of the best men" (Dawson, 1894, 269, 70). But he saw something far more important—that, imperfect as they were, by God's grace they strove to build to the measure of their power on the foundation stone of Jesus Christ.

As we look at our own stubble mixed with our gold, we must learn charity toward even the unworthiest builders. But at the same time, knowing of the coming trial by fire, we should show no leniency toward our own imperfections. "Thus the St. Paul who can acknowledge the better side of imperfect men can only speak of himself as the chief of sinners" (Dawson 1894, 270; see 1 Tim. 1:15).

LESSONS:

1. Jesus Christ is the only foundation. It is vital to build upon this with the right materials—those recorded by the Holy Spirit, not those prompted by our carnal hearts.
2. The structures of two believers can vary in quality and value. A believer filled with the Spirit builds his structure from the solid teaching of the Word of God, whereas the carnal believer builds on other, flimsy, teaching. The responsibility to have a good structure lies not only with those who teach but also with those who listen. How do you preach; how do you listen?
3. The basic choice we have is whether or not we accept the Lord Jesus Christ as the foundation on which to build our lives. Our choice of building materials depends on our sense of values and our wisdom concerning the future. Will our choice be precious lasting materials or cheap and shoddy ones?
4. Every Christian's work is going to be tried by fire. Gold and stubble are side by side in the best of men. Knowing of the coming trial by fire, we must learn charity toward all believers.

# 1 Cor. 3:13 | *Will Christians Face Judgment?*

*For every man's work shall be made manifest: for the day shall declare it because it shall be revealed by fire; and the fire shall try every man's work of what sort it is.*

C. S. Lewis once said, "Human beings judge one another by their external actions. God judges them by their moral choices." The apostle Paul tells us in 1 Corinthians 3:13 that a day is coming when the work of each Christian believer will be judged: "Every man's work shall be made manifest: for the day shall declare it because it shall be revealed by fire; and the fire shall try every man's work of what sort it is."

What Paul implies is that the whole truth about people's character and work is not known here and now. They may be thought great and mighty, but time may prove them otherwise. There is truly a day coming when the secrets of all hearts will be revealed. We can see only the works; we can only guess at the motives. These may have an annulling effect. What we now admire as gold may turn out to be stubble because of its motivation. What glitters now may not stand the test of time. Justice and truth, virtue and principle, alone insure final success.

"If the thing is unjust," said Thomas Carlyle, "thou hast not succeeded: no, not though bonfires blazed from north to south, and bells rang, and editors wrote leading articles, and the just thing lay trampled out of sight, to all mortal eyes an abolished and annihilated thing." The most admired person may turn out to be but stubble, and the most obscure servant of God may one day shine as the brightest star in the heavens.

If it seemed necessary for St. Paul to review his own work with the searching and critical eye of one who dared not spare himself by any plausible deceit of simulated success, how much more it becomes us to review our character, our life, our work. Let us judge ourselves before we are judged. There is an hour of testing that will reveal the quality of our life and work. Let us pause and take stock now. Let us survey our building.

The work of each of us will become visible, clear, plainly to be seen, open. That is the meaning of the word *phanerón*, "manifest," in the Greek text. It implies that the work of each one may go on for a long time without being openly apparent to others or to oneself. A person may easily be self-deceived, thinking that he is doing a great work, while it is very small in God's sight.

The word *phanerón* comes from the verb *phaínō*, which means "to shine forth" when it is used intransitively. It is the same root from which we derive *epipháneia*, one of the three words used in the New Testament to denote the appearing of the Lord Jesus Christ to meet His saints (1 Tim. 6:14, 2 Tim. 4:18). When the Lord appears, there will be a light (*phṓs*, "light," akin to *pháō*, "to give light or shine") that will fall on every individual, making manifest, apparent, visible, his entire life before all. We sense here a subtle suggestion that this is not so now. People's works can be pretty well hidden from sight. We manage to conceal a great deal about ourselves now. But we will not be able to do it forever. The work of each one will one day become evident.

To some people this may be a source of great joy, but to others it is a very sobering thought. Those who have worked faithfully for God and others, not for the sake of public applause, will have their day of full recognition. Those who have merely pretended to be faithful but have done a great deal of their work for worldly acclaim or other selfish motives will be in for a disappointing revelation. The work of each one will become (*genē̃setai*) what it is not now. That means that the future estimate of it may be entirely different from its present status in the eyes of the world and even our own eyes.

Robert Browning tells of a famous musician who, under financial pressure and the influence of popular demand, lowered his standards and produced some inferior works that brought in ready cash and a measure of success. One evening as he stood on the platform enjoying the applause of the audience, he happened to glance at a private box and see the master, Rossini. His eyes fell and his color rose. The mob applauded, but he knew that the master condemned the cheap and unworthy work.

Observe that Paul does not speak of "works" but of "work" (*érgon*, sing.). Your whole life will be made manifest—though not necessarily every act and thought so much as the appraisal of the whole building of life. There will be an averaging of all that you do and say, just as a student's average is taken in school to find his standing. The use of the word *érgon,* "work," refers, of course, to the building spoken of previously. The building we erect upon the foundation of Christ is our work of faith of which Paul spoke in 1 Thessalonians 1:3. It is the sum total of our earthly behavior after our salvation through Christ. The real value of our Christian edifice will be appraised.

James 2:12, 13 speaks eloquently of the judge's attitude toward two classes of believers, the unmerciful ones (those who have been building with wood, hay and stubble) and the merciful ones (those who have been building with gold, silver, and precious stones). Let me paraphrase these two important verses from the Greek text: "Thus speak and thus do [work] as if you were going to be judged by a law of liberality." In other words, the judge, Jesus Christ, will want to be liberal toward His own.

But His liberality will be in proportion to our own talk and walk being filled with mercy.

See what James 2:13 says: "For he shall have judgment without mercy, that hath shewed no mercy; and mercy [your own mercifulness while here on earth] rejoiceth against judgment [i.e., is not afraid of judgment]." This is a definite law with regard to the judgment of the believer, just as the Lord taught in the Beatitude, "Blessed the merciful ones: for they shall obtain mercy" (Matt. 5:7). Therefore each of us should get busy and build our reservoir of mercy, erect our edifice of gold, silver, and precious stones, that the fire of judgment will not burn up like the cheap and worthless wood, hay, and stubble. Let us pray as the poet did:

> Teach us to build; upon the solid rock
> We set the dream that hardens into deed,
> Ribbed with the metal time and change doth mock,
> The unfailing purpose of our noblest creed;
> Teach us to build, O Master, lend us sight
> To see the towers gleaming in the light.

## Heavenly Fire Insurance

The judgment of believers has absolutely nothing to do with their salvation, the fruit of which is eternal life. But I am convinced there will be degrees of enjoyment in heaven as well as degrees of punishment in hell. The basic joy of heaven will be the portion of all who have received Christ as their Savior. But there is much more than that for some—the "rewards" of which Scripture speaks.

The Lord Himself said in Matthew 16:27: "For the Son of man shall come in the glory of his Father with his angels; and then he shall reward every man according to his works." And Paul says in 2 Corinthians 9:6, "He which soweth sparingly shall reap also sparingly; and he which soweth bountifully shall reap also bountifully." "And whosoever shall give to drink unto one of these little ones a cup of cold water only in the name of a disciple, verily I say unto you, he shall in no wise lose his reward" (Matt. 10:42). "That thine alms may be in secret: and thy Father which seeth in secret himself shall reward thee openly" (Matt. 6:4).

Paul says in 1 Corinthians 9:17, "For if I do this thing willingly, I have a reward: but if against my will, a dispensation of the gospel is committed unto me." "The Lord . . . will bring to light the hidden things of darkness, and will make manifest the counsels of the hearts; and then shall every man have his praise of God" (1 Cor. 4:5 RSV).

So the judgment of the believers will be for our work of faith, not of how it appeared but what its permanent value has been. The "counsels of the hearts" of 1 Corinthians 4:5 would indicate also how this work was done and why. Malachi 3:16, 17 says, "They that feared the Lord spake often one to another: and the Lord hearkened, and heard it, and a book of remembrance was written before him for them that feared the Lord, and that thought upon his name."

So our "work" includes our words, as James 2:12, 13 mentions that we shall be judged for both. Matthew 12:36 tells us that we must give account of "every idle word." But every time we speak of the Lord He makes a note of it that He may reward us by and by. "And they shall be mine, saith the Lord of hosts, in that day when I make up my jewels; and I will spare them" (Mal. 3:17).

Thoughts and desires that we were never able to put into action will be reckoned as done. "For if there be first a willing mind, it is accepted according to that a man hath, and not according to that he hath not" (1 Cor. 8:12). In 2 Chronicles 6:8, 9 we have an example of this with the Lord saying to David, "Forasmuch as it was in thine heart to build a house for my name [the temple], thou didst well in that it was in thine heart: notwithstanding thou shalt not build the house, but thy son which shall come forth out of thy loins, he shall build the house for my name." And Solomon did indeed build the temple, but God gave credit to David for simply desiring and purposing to do it.

How often we have mourned over the things we wanted to do and could not, and have looked upon the thinking as of no use, but our God does not regard it that way. He treasures up the wish, and counts it for the deed, if He sees we do not have the power to carry it out.

On the other hand, how much we shall lose by the fact that some of what we considered our best work has been rendered unacceptable because of the poor motives from which it has sprung: "to be seen of men" (Matt. 23:5); "that they may have glory of men" (Matt. 6:2); "for they loved the praise of men more than the praise of God" (John 12:43). Though these verses refer primarily to the unsaved, such unworthy motives may exist to a degree even in believers because of our present imperfections. God grant us the honesty and clarity of vision to test our work by the standards by which He will test it.

Who is Paul speaking about when he says, "Every man's work"? The Greek word is *hekástou*, which means "each one separately." This indicates that people are not going to be lumped together in groups and judged as such but as individuals. Each one separately is going to have the searchlight of Christ focused upon him or her. Can you stand the thought of such a judgment? How carefully we must watch our step in view of what is coming.

The "each one" here refers only to believers, those who have built upon the one foundation, Jesus Christ (vv. 11, 12). Verse 9 tells us that we are God's building, which means that before starting our work as builders we have first been made part of that building of which the great Master-Builder is God Himself. Peter also says, "Ye . . . as lively [living] stones, are built up a spiritual house" (1 Pet. 2:5). Ephesians 2:21, 22 refers to Christians as "a holy temple in the Lord . . . a habitation of God through the Spirit."

Every living stone in God's corporate house, the church universal, becomes in turn a builder of his own individual house, which he spends his life in rearing. Therefore it is evident that this particular judgment has nothing to do with those who are not stones in God's building. They, too, are builders, but not on the foundation stone, Jesus Christ. They are the "foolish" ones, who "without a foundation" are building their houses on the sand, which, when the storm breaks, will fall, and their ruin will be great (Luke 6:49).

Many years ago a man named Simpson built a house on the Canford Cliffs, near Bournemouth, England. Friends and neighbors tried to warn him he had chosen a site much too near the edge of the cliff, that landslides frequently occurred along the coast, and that the very weight of the house would be likely to precipitate such a catastrophe. But Mr. Simpson would not listen. He built a very beautiful house there and for a time all went well. Then the inevitable happened, and the ominous warnings all came true. All that remains of his house is a heap of ruins on the beach known as "Simpson's Folly."

You say hardly anybody would be that foolish. But when you come to look at the end result of all your building, when you stand before God and show Him your life house, what will His judgment be? Will you be able to tell Him you built your house according to His plan, out of good sturdy materials; or must you confess that you chose whatever material suited your fancy, whether it would stand the scrutiny of His Word or not? They alone are wise who build their characters and hopes alike on the one Foundation planned and laid by the heavenly Architect, out of the gold, silver, and precious stones of obedience and good works performed, not for glory but out of love for God and neighbor.

### The Fire of Judgment for Christians

You have heard preachers speak of Judgment Day. But did you know that the Bible tells of four divine judgments that will take place? These are

1) The judgment of Christians, to receive their rewards for deeds done in the body (1 Cor. 3:8–15; 2 Cor. 5:9, 10; Rev. 11:18).

2) The judgment of nations, for reward or punishment (Zech. 14; Joel 3; Matt. 25:31–46; etc.).

3) The judgment of Satan and his allies, for condemnation (Rev. 20:10).

4) The judgment of the Great White Throne, for condemnation (Rev. 20:11–15).

"For the day shall declare it," that is, the work of each individual believer, says Paul in 1 Corinthians 3:9. What day is he referring to? Paul does not have to specify it. The Corinthians knew what he meant. It is the day of Christ referred to in 1 Corinthians 5:5; 2 Corinthians 1:14; Philippians 1:6, 10; 2:16; 1 Thessalonians 4:16—5:2. The work of each believer then will be made evident on that day when Christ comes for His saints. "For the day shall declare it."

The verb "declare" is *dēlṓsei* in Greek, which means "to make plain" (the same word as used in 1 Cor. 1:11 and Col. 1:8). There is no doubt that these two events are coincidental.

In the word "manifest" (*phanerón*), Paul gave us the implied symbol of light. Now he gives us a second symbol, that of fire. Thus we have light to show the work of each believer, and fire to test the work or the building of each one. This fire is to see whether the building is made of gold, silver, and precious stones, or of wood, hay, and stubble. "Because it shall be revealed by fire."

The Greek verb translated "shall be revealed" is *apokalúptetai*, which is another of the three words used in relation to the coming of the Lord: *apokálupsis* (1 Cor. 1:7; 2 Thess. 1:7; 1 Pet. 1:7, 13; 4:13); *epipháneia*, akin to *phanerón*, used in the expression "every man's work shall be made manifest" (and occurring in 2 Thess. 2:8; 1 Tim. 6:14; 2 Tim. 1:10; 4:18; Titus 2:13); and *parousía* (Matt. 24:3, etc.).

What is this fire? Is it literal? Is the light implicit in *phanerón*, "manifest," a literal light? Whether they are or are not literal is not as important as the purpose they accomplish. And that is that the work of each believer becomes clear to all and that it be tested as to whether it is of permanent or temporary value, or of no value at all.

Fire in the Old and New Testaments is often used to indicate the revealed presence of God. How did the angel of the Lord appear to Moses? We read in Exodus 3:2–4, "And the angel of the Lord appeared unto him in a flame of fire out of the midst of a bush. . . . And Moses said, I will now turn aside, and see this great sight, why the bush is not burnt. And when the Lord saw that he turned aside to see, God called to him out of the midst of the bush." This was real, literal fire.

When Moses brought forth the Israelites out of the camp to meet with God, they stood at the foot of Mt. Sinai. We read in Exodus 19:18, "And mount Sinai was altogether on a smoke because the Lord descended upon it in fire"—again God's presence in fire.

While John was in exile on Patmos he had a vision of the Lord, who appeared to him "as a flame of fire" (Rev. 1:14) that caused even the beloved disciple to fall at His feet as dead. "Our God is a consuming fire" (Heb. 12:29); therefore "let us have grace, whereby we may serve God acceptably with reverence and godly fear" (Heb. 12:28). The fire to come, which is symbolic of the presence of God, has a salutary effect on our present lives.

But why does Paul use the symbolism of fire in addition to light? Because light merely shows what is on the outside, while fire puts something to the real test and discovers secrets. A wooden beam may be all unsuspected, high up in a stone chimney, but some windy night the house may go up in flames because the fire has discovered the wood. Much that has passed for gold will prove to be only gilded wood when the fire lays hold of it. Luke 8:17 declares, "For nothing is secret, that shall not be made manifest; neither anything hid, that shall not be known and come abroad."

Pompeii in Italy and St. Pierre in Martinique can both teach us a lesson. On both of these fire caused by a volcano brought unprecedented destruction. The museums that contain relics of these catastrophes display nothing that was made of wood. All that survived the fire were metallic objects. In Pompeii the petrified body of a woman was found whose hands were filled with jewelry. The bracelets, necklaces, and other ornaments survived the fire because they were composed of gold, silver, and precious stones. But no remains of wood, hay, and stubble have ever been discovered, for these things were completely destroyed in the heat of the catastrophe.

In such a way, when the believer in Christ stands before the *Bḗma*, the judgment seat or tribunal of Christ, to receive the things done in the body (2 Cor. 5:10), that is, his actions since he received Christ as his Savior, his work will be made manifest in two ways—by light and by fire. If it is found to be of gold, silver, or precious stones, the testing fire will not consume it but will rather purify it. But if it is found to be of wood, hay, or stubble, it will be burned and nothing will be left of the work. In such a case, the believer will indeed be saved, but so as by fire and without any reward (see *Our Hope* Nov. 1957, 265, 266).

How will you meet the Lord, Christian—saved so as by fire, or by good works in His name will you have laid up "treasures in heaven"?

## The Purpose of Judgment for Christians

Do you consider yourself a good judge of character? Can you tell an honest man from a dishonest one at a glance? Not always. But Someone can. First Samuel 16:7 tells us, "The Lord seeth not as man seeth; for man looketh on the outward appearance, but the Lord looketh on the heart."

Even born-again Christians can put up a false front, seeming to be more righteous than they actually are. Into each life built on the foundation of Jesus Christ there is some admixture of good and bad material. That is why even Christians must face a judgment, not as to whether they were saved—that was settled when they received Christ as the propitiation for their sins—but as to the value of their works thereafter.

The illuminating fire of the day of Christ will reveal unholy secrets and holy ones. How much hidden work for God that was never known, perhaps even by those nearest to the "builder," will be manifested in that day—often to the surprise of the worker himself. Read Matthew 25:37–39 and you will see how the day of judgment is coupled with the element of surprise. This passage predicts that those who thought they did a great deal worthy of reward will finally discover it was not as great as they thought; and those who felt they did little may receive great rewards, to their utter surprise. Much that has been despised by men will have "praise of God," and much that has been glorified by men will turn out to be "loss," which will burn before the builder like wood, hay, and stubble, and be utterly consumed.

In view of all this, how carefully we should examine our earthly building and settle matters on the way to the Judge, rather than wait till we stand before His judgment seat. Failure and shortcomings confessed now and put away here will not be mentioned there. Much of the wood, hay, and stubble can be burnt up now in the presence of the Lord, instead of standing to witness against us in that day. "If we would judge ourselves, we should not be judged" (1 Cor. 11:31). Let us examine ourselves, repent, and build more worthily now while we have the opportunity.

What is the purpose of this testing as by fire? The last part of 1 Corinthians 3:13 states the reason clearly: "and the fire shall try every man's work of what sort it is." The intriguing word here is *dokimásei* (pres. indic. of *dokimázō*), which is translated "try." The verb is in the future tense, referring to a specific day that is coming—the day of Christ—in which the fire, which is God's presence, will try each believer's work to see whether it is of lasting value or not.

As serious students of God's Word, we need to differentiate between two Greek words referring to how God "tries" men, if we are not to be misled by some of the statements in our English Bible about God. How many times I have been asked about that sentence in the Lord's Prayer, "And lead us not into temptation [*peirasmós*]" (Matt. 6:13). Is it conceivable that the Lord would tempt anyone? Let us examine that Greek word, along with the word *dokimázō* that occurs in 1 Corinthians 3:13.

Sometimes these two words occur together, as in 2 Corinthians 13:5, "Examine yourselves [*peirázete: peirázō* in the pres. indic., the same verb from which we get *peirasmós*, "temptation"], whether ye be in the faith; prove [*dokimázete: dokimázō* in the pres. indic., as used in 1 Cor. 3:13] your own selves."

These are the two perplexing words we need to examine, *peirázō* (to examine, to tempt) and *dokimázō* (to try, to prove). These two words are used together also in Hebrews 3:9, *epeírasan* (verb), and *dokimasía* (noun). "When your fathers tempted me, proved me" (Ps. 95:9). The words *peirázō*, "tempt," and *dokimázō*, "try or prove," are translated into English by any number of words. Both are translated as "prove" in John 6:6 and Luke 14:19; as "try" in Revelation 2:2 and 1 Corinthians 3:13, and as "examine" in 1 Corinthians 11:28 and 2 Corinthians 13:5. But although the translators made them synonymous, they are not perfectly so.

*Dokimázō*, "try," the word used in 1 Corinthians 3:13, is also rendered by four other English words: "discern" in Luke 12:56, "like" in Romans 1:28, "approve" in Romans 2:18, and "allow" in Romans 14:22. In this word there always lies the notion of proving whether a thing is worthy to be received or not. It is interesting to note that the Naval Academy of Greece is called the School of *Dokimoí* (*Navtikḗ Scholḗ Dokimṓn*), that is, the school of those who have been accepted or proven worthy or able. A man has to be tested and tried in order to be declared *dokimós*, "approved or accepted."

But the word *dokimázō* almost always implies that the one who is tried is proven worthy, as if the one who did the trying knew ahead of time that what *is proved* is going to be *approved.* When we are being tested, it is to prove that we are genuine, as is indicated by the usage of 2 Corinthians 8:8; 1 Thessalonians 2:4; and 1 Timothy 3:10. God tries us, not to disprove our genuineness but to prove it.

Now see how beautifully this blends with what Paul declares in 1 Corinthians 3:13, "Every man's work [i.e., every believer's work] shall be made manifest: for the day shall declare it because it shall be revealed by fire; and the fire shall try [shall test and prove genuine] every man's work of what sort it is." Will any believer be found unworthy of heaven? No. It is just like taking an examination—and for the same purpose that tests are given in our schools—not in order that those who do not satisfy the examiners may be punished or degraded, but to give honor and promotion to those who succeed.

## Tested or Tempted—Which?

When we as Christians stand before the Lord for judgment in the day of Christ, and our works are tried as by fire, the primary purpose will not be that our unfaithfulness may be punished or even primarily that it may be exposed to ourselves, much less to others. We are passing on as saved ones to a great examination day for our rewards.

This trial of testing (*dokimasía* in Gr.) not only implies for the most part a victorious coming out of the trial but also that the trial was made in the expectation and hope that it would turn out that way. We are put to such trials (*dokimasías*) in this life as believers, not that the Lord may find that we are pure gold (for He knows that we are never that), but to make us such, to purge out our dross, never to make evident that we are all dross.

We have said before that a believer has both good and bad material in his building on the foundation, Jesus Christ. The Lord tries in this life to separate the two elements, the precious and the worthless, but He does not complete the process here because of our bodily imperfections that militate against it. However, what He does not accomplish in us down here He will accomplish in the day of Christ, when He shall refine (try, *dokimásei*) the work of each, the make-up of each, to find out how much is gold, silver, and precious stones, that He desires to reward. The discarding or burning of the wood, hay, and stubble is incidental to the refining process.

Now the other word, *peirázō*, which is sometimes translated as though it were synonymous with *dokimázō*, "try," has this basic difference: it refers in certain passages to the solicitation of Satan (Matt. 4:1; 1 Cor. 7:5; Rev. 2:10) leading us into an experience for the purpose of entangling us in sin. This is never the meaning of the word *dokimázō.* That is why James 1:13 says, "Let no man say when he is tempted, I am tempted [*peirázomai*] of

God: for God cannot be tempted [*apeírastos*, from the privative alpha, *á*, and *peirastós*, possible to be tempted] with evil, neither tempteth he any man [*peirázei*]."

There you have the difference. God does *dokimázei*, "try," us, as 1 Thessalonians 2:4 clearly indicates: "But as we were allowed of God to be put in trust [exactly this same word *dokimázō* in different form, *dedokimásmetha*] with the gospel, even so we speak." In other words, God tried us and found us worthy to proclaim the gospel. "Not as pleasing men, but God, which trieth [*dokimázonti*] our hearts." You see, God tries our hearts with the expectation of finding them pleasing to Him. But He does not tempt them (*peirázei*), for God would never lead us into an experience with the intention of entangling us in sin.

Satan is never said to *dokimázei* the believer because that would mean the believer would come out approved and victorious. Satan always tempts in the sense of *peirázei*, in the hope and expectation that we will sin.

Since God *dokimázei*, "tries," us to show us approved, but never tempts us with the intention of making us sin, why did the Lord teach us as believers to pray, "Lead us not into temptation [*peirasmós*]"? Better still, the word *eisenéngēs* (from *eisphérō*, "to bring in") should not be translated "lead us not," but "do not bring us into" temptation—any experience that purports to make us sin. It is this that we should fear—the experiences that may result in sin—and not the trials of our faith (*dokimasías*), which always result in triumph.

Of one thing we may be fully persuaded, and that is that the petition in the Lord's Prayer asking Him not to bring us into an experience in which He intends us to sin does not imply the possibility that the Lord does sometimes lead us into such an experience. James clearly states, "Let no man say when he is tempted [the same word *peirázō* (*peirazómenos*) as used in the Lord's Prayer], I am tempted [*peirázō* (*peirázomai*)] of God:

for God cannot be tempted [again the word *peirázō* (*apeírastos*)] with evil, neither tempteth he any man [*peirázō* (*peirázei*)]." The Lord tests us to prove us genuine, not that we may sin.

When therefore the Lord taught us to pray that our heavenly Father would not lead us or place us in an experience of temptation, He meant the attempt that Satan makes to lead us into sin. That this is the meaning of this seemingly perplexing request of the Lord's Prayer is clearly shown by the request that follows, "but deliver us from evil," the evil that Satan intends.

So God's temptings or testings are experiences that always result in our good or victory, while Satan's temptings are designed to lead us into sin. "And lead us not into temptation," therefore, means "Do not allow us to be tempted as Satan tempts, but deliver us from the evil he hopes to make us fall into."

Christ Himself had passed through the flame of being tempted by Satan, and He knew we might not be able to bear it. Only pure gold can abide the fierceness of that heat, and mere men have so many flammable natures (see Trench 1953, 278–81).

LESSONS:

1. A day is coming when the work of each Christian believer will be made visible and judged. Let us pause and take stock before that hour of testing that will reveal the quality of our life and work.
2. Believers will be judged on the basis of their working faith, not on their appearance before men. Good and bad motives both put and not put into action will be judged.
3. Each believer will be judged separately before the Lord
4. The work of each believer will be made manifest (known) in two ways—by light and by fire. The believer whose works are burned by fire will be saved without reward.
5. Christians must face a judgment on the value of their works. We have to be tested and tried in order to be declared "approved" (accepted). Gold, silver, and precious metals will survive and be purified and rewarded; wood, hay, and stubble will be consumed.

# 1 Cor. 3:14 | *Working Toward a Goal*

*If any man's work abide which he hath built thereupon, he shall receive a reward.*

Some people seem to think that Christians should work for the sheer joy of accomplishment, without looking for praise or other forms of reward. Yet we reward our children for good behavior; we hold out prizes and scholarships as rewards for getting good grades in school; and we offer incentives for good work in the business world.

True, the person who works merely for the sake of reward is not as highly motivated as the one whose work is a labor of love. Nevertheless, even to such individuals, reward can be a source of gratification as a recognition of work well done.

Therefore it should not surprise us that God Himself often stresses reward as an incentive to the Christian. In 1 Corinthians 3:14 the apostle Paul, in explaining the reason for the Christian's final judgment, says, "If any man's work abide which he hath built thereupon [i.e., on the foundation of Jesus Christ], he shall receive a reward." The purpose of this judgment, then, is not punishment, in spite of the fact that the symbolism of fire may cause some to jump to that conclusion. It is what stands the test that counts, not what is destroyed by fire. Whatever deed is done worthily, even though imperfectly, will be counted as pure gold upon which the fire of God will have no power. As we saw in the previous verse, that is what the word *dokimázō* (*dokimásei*) means, the testing for approval not disapproval, the examination for the sake of a just reward.

God will make no mistakes in the judgment of Christians. Perfect justice will prevail. Why be concerned? It will be a wonderful day, when the flame shall deliver us from what spoiled our lives, and all that was of Christ will abide. The flame is terrible only to impurity and hypocrisy, but it cannot harm those works done in the purity and sincerity of obedience to Christ.

What our concern and prayer should be is that an earlier flame of testing, of whatever kind, rather than the flame of the last judgment, may find and purify us. At the judgment there will be no opportunity for rectification. Now there is. Therefore let any form of discipline that may seem good to God, as we are able to bear it, test our character, that its imperfect elements may be purged away and only the pure gold be left. Let our prayer be,

> One thing I of the Lord desire,
> For all my way hath miry been;
> Be it by water or by fire,
> Oh, make me clean!
>
> So wash Thou me without, within,
> Or purge with fire, if that must be:
> No matter how, if only sin
> Die out in me.
> [see Dawson 1894, 271–75].

In verse 14 Paul speaks of the work that remains. Here again he says "work" (*érgon*), not "works." It is a whole life, a field, a building, a character that he is referring to. Paul here is concerned about the entirety of our life, although he is fully aware that the whole is made up of particulars. Our lifetime consists of years, months, weeks, days, hours, minutes, and seconds. Every particular act is a brick or a bit of mortar that makes up the walls of our building. When we speak of our works of faith, it is hard to pinpoint just where our strong and weak points lie.

A physician once said, "One of my ideals is to do the day's work well and not bother about the next day. I owe whatever success I have had to settling down to that day's work and trying to do the best I can, and letting the future take care of itself."

It is necessary to examine the "works" if we are going to have a "work" that will stand. So many Christians think that talk is work. But Paul is not necessarily referring just to witnessing for Christ, essential and primary though that may be. Work here means that which results in actual accomplishment, not necessarily the effort, whether that effort be spiritual or physical. "Work," declared Thomas Alva Edison, "is measured not by hours but by what is accomplished." This entails the setting of a goal and making every effort to reach that goal. And the goal for the Christian worker is winning souls to Christ, and helping them to be conformed to His glorious image.

Many Christians are very busy at this and that, but seem to accomplish little. It is like watching people scurry about in a factory but seeing no end product as a result of their activity. The excuse is sometimes put forth that what the Lord really looks for is our faithfulness—as if that meant working without accomplishment. None of us would be pleased with puttering around that never produced anything. The work, the actual labor, should be viewed only as a means to an end. If it is not accomplishing that end, then we should seriously examine the means to see whether what we are doing is actually the work of Him that sent us or mere ineffectual activity—a waste of time.

> We are building every day
>    In a good or evil way,
> And the structure as it grows
>    Will our inmost self disclose.

Build it well, whate'er you do,
Build it straight, and strong, and true,
Build it clean, and high, and broad,
Build it for the eye of God.
—I. E. Dickenza

## Is Your Work for God Bearing Fruit?

A farmer was showing his fine orchard to a friend, who admired its neat and regular appearance. "But," said the friend, pointing to a peculiarly shaped tree, "if that were my tree I would root it up, to preserve the uniformity of the orchard."

The farmer smiled and said that he was more interested in the fruit than in the form. "This tree," he said, "has yielded me more fruit than any of those trees that conform to a more regular pattern." Sometimes Christian workers may become so accustomed to doing things in what they consider the traditional or time-honored way that they forget to evaluate its productivity.

One of the most fruitful methods of evangelism I have used in my ministry around the world is the placing of gospel messages as paid ads in secular national magazines and newspapers. In fact, in Ceylon, just four two-inch ads offering Christian literature, and costing twenty dollars, brought over a thousand responses in one month. These came mostly from Buddhists who had never read anything about Christ before.

The full-length gospel messages placed in the newspapers and magazines in many lands and languages are producing marvelous results in bringing thousands to the Savior. Yet when I have sought the cooperation of fellow missionaries to help inaugurate this method of evangelism in the countries in which they work, a disappointingly large number of them reply, "We're too busy with what we're doing already" (this in spite of the fact that we offer to pay the cost of the ads). I feel the right attitude in view of what Paul is saying in 1 Corinthians 3:14 would be to ask: "Is what I am so busy doing producing results; is it leading souls to Christ; is it accomplishing the purpose for which I am here? If not, then shouldn't I get busy with something that may be more productive?"

Being busy for the Lord is not an end in itself. Fruitbearing is. The Word of God says, "He that goeth forth and weepeth, bearing precious seed, shall doubtless come again with rejoicing, bringing his sheaves with him" (Ps. 126:6). Sheaves are the end results for a farmer. If his labor does not produce results, he will re-examine his seed to see if it is the right kind, or his field, or his method of planting. But no farmer will continue to work day after day, year after year, without harvesting a crop. He cannot afford to. He must have sheaves as a result of his labor, or else that labor is vain.

Of course, each person has an individual calling from God which he must fulfill. Some are called to work in difficult areas of the world and some in more responsive ones. God does not intend that all should concentrate on the fertile areas to the neglect of the more difficult ones. But within the framework of one's calling he should examine his methods and weigh his work in view of the accomplishments desired. What is your aim? See it through. Let your goal of winning souls to Christ and building them up in the faith be fixed but the means flexible.

"If any man's work abide which he hath built. . . ." The verb "abide" in Greek is *menei*, which can be considered present tense if accented on the *me*, or future tense if accented on the *nei*. I believe it should be regarded as future (*meneí*), since the reward is future, expressed by the verb *lḗmpsetai* (*lambánō*), "he shall receive a reward."

The whole argument here is about the future judgment of the Christian's work. Actually it is only in that day that we shall find out how much of what we have done was worthwhile and will count for eternity. All we can do now is try to follow certain criteria. Our Lord and the disciples did not give us a set of do's and don'ts, telling us what professions or vocations we should follow. Each of us must follow God's guidance and will. Whether we have made the right choice and performed well must be left for the future finally to evaluate.

But we have a few yardsticks by which we can judge our lives now in view of the final future judgment. Paul says in 2 Corinthians 13:5, "Examine yourselves, whether ye be in the faith; prove your own selves." A good criterion for examining ourselves is to see what Scripture says about what God will reward the believers for on that day, and to see whether we measure up to the requirements.

First of all, we read that a reward will be given for a steady, unswerving Christian life, such as Paul referred to when he said, "I have fought a good fight, I have finished my course, I have kept the faith" (2 Tim. 4:7). How did he do this? In 1 Corinthians 9:26, 27 he tells us: "I therefore run, not as uncertainly; so fight I, not as one that beateth the air: but I keep under my body, and bring it into subjection: lest that by any means, when I have preached to others, I myself should be a castaway" (see also Phil. 3:7–16). The word "castaway" in Greek is *adókimos*, meaning "not accepted for a prize." It does not in any way involve the loss of one's salvation or entrance into heaven.

Other qualities that will be rewarded are boldness and patience. In Hebrews 10:35–37 we read: "Cast not away therefore your confidence [*parrēsían*, boldness], which hath great recompense of reward. For ye have need of patience, that, after ye have done the will of God, ye might receive the promise."

### Those Whom God Will Reward

The work for which God promises to reward believers is not necessarily full-time service for Him, as we usually speak of it, but the faithful execution of whatever task confronts them day by day. In Colossians 3:22–24 Paul addresses Christians who were slaves and therefore had no choice as to their work. "Servants, obey in all things your masters according to the flesh," he tells them, "not with eyeservice, as menpleasers, but in singleness of heart, fearing God: and whatsoever ye do, do it heartily, as to the Lord, and not unto men; knowing that of the Lord ye shall receive the reward of the inheritance: for ye serve the Lord Christ."

And to the Ephesians Paul writes, "Whatsoever good thing any man doeth, the same shall he receive of the Lord, whether he be bond or free" (Eph. 6:8). In other words, the Lord will make allowance for our circumstances, whether we are at liberty to choose the work we want to do for Him or not. What a comfort this is for those who live under systems that suppress the freedom of the individual. A person living under communism, for instance, does not have the opportunities of a person living in a free country. God rewards each one, therefore, according to his faithfulness in living up to the opportunities he possesses.

If you are a Christian, it should show in whatever you do. A girl who worked in a chocolate factory had a genuine conversion experience. Sometime afterward a friend said to her, "Tell me the difference your conversion has made in regard to your work." The girl replied, "Formerly I made chocolates for my employer. Now I make them for God and my employer." Is that your attitude?

How aptly it has been said, "Between the great things we cannot do and the little things we will not do, we are in danger of doing nothing." The rewards God gives are for doing something—it makes no difference whether great or small as long as it is done for Him. It is not the quantity of our work regardless of quality, but the quality of it in whatever quantity we have the opportunity of doing that counts.

"I am only one person but I am one person. I cannot do everything but I can do something. What I can do I ought to do, and what I ought to do by the grace of God I will do." And determine to do it well!

Rewards are also promised for our compassion on the poor. To a rich man the Lord said, "When thou makest a feast, call the poor, the maimed, the lame, the blind: and thou shalt be blessed; for they cannot recompense thee: for thou shalt be recompensed at the resurrection of the just" (Luke 14:13, 14). Of course, even the poor can usually find someone poorer to help, and for this, too, there is a recompense. There are few who cannot give something, even if it is only a cup of water. Our Lord promises, "Whosoever shall give you a cup of water to drink in my name because ye belong to Christ, verily I say unto you, he shall not lose his reward" (Mark 9:41).

Of course, the rich man often receives public recognition for his help to the poor, while the poor man who helps another is unnoticed except by the recipient. But in both cases the Lord will repay those who help others in His name especially where the kindness cannot be repaid by the recipients.

Have you understood what is really involved in the "cup of cold water," as Matthew 10:42 calls it? There is more to it than appears on the surface. In Eastern lands the water is drawn up from a well in the court or else fetched from a distance. The housewife brings in a supply in the morning and lets it stand ready for use. As the day goes on the water gets warm. It would be easy for her to give a cup of this water to a thirsty friend or stranger, but a "cup of cold water" implies the kindly thought that would lead her to take the trouble to draw it or fetch it straight from the well, perhaps in the heat of the day. So often we give what amounts to tepid water to save ourselves extra work. But I believe it is the "cup of *cold* water" that shall in no wise lose its reward. The principle would seem to be that going out of our way, making sacrifices to help the poor, will have a sure reward.

There is also a promise of reward for spiritual ministry. The Corinthian believers were the result of Paul's work among them. In 2 Corinthians 1:14 Paul says to them, "We are your rejoicing, even as ye also are ours in the day of the Lord Jesus," that is, the day of judgment. In 1 Peter 5:2–4 we find two important additional facts:

1) The reward will depend on the motive of spiritual service. "Feed the flock of God which is among you, taking the oversight thereof, not by constraint, but willingly; not for filthy lucre, but of a ready mind." If you are serving the Lord reluctantly, or for the money there is in it, you will receive no reward, even though you may be rendering spiritual service.

2) The reward will also depend on what kind of example you set. "Neither as being lords over God's heritage, but being ensamples to the flock." The special reward mentioned here is "a crown of glory that fadeth not away." This is in contrast to the corruptible crown referred to in 1 Corinthians 9:25, which, being made of leaves, soon withered. In 1 Thessalonians 2:19 Paul speaks of his future crown as consisting of the souls won and blessed through his ministry. He calls it his "crown of rejoicing." In writing to the Philippians he calls them "my joy and crown." The souls that you and I win to Christ will be our reward in that day when we stand before our Lord for judgment.

### Rewards Promised for Loving Your Enemies and Enduring Trials

Whenever God commands us to do something, there is always an implied or explicit penalty for failure to do it, as well as a reward for obedience. We have seen in previous studies that, when Christians stand before Christ for judgment at His Second Coming, it will not be to determine whether they are saved or not. That matter was settled once for all when they received

Him into their hearts by faith, being born anew by the grace of God through the Holy Spirit.

However, the works they did thereafter will undergo the fire of judgment at the Second Coming of Christ, either to consume those works that were unworthy or to prove the imperishable nature of those that God deems worthy. We have seen that Christ will reward the believer for faithfulness in living up to the opportunities he possesses. We have also seen that rewards were promised for helping the poor and for spiritual service through witness and example.

Another area of service for which a reward is promised in Scripture is love and practical kindness shown to enemies. Our Lord said, "Love ye your enemies, and do good, and lend, hoping for nothing again; and your reward shall be great" (Luke 6:35). However, we must be careful not to construe "love" as permissiveness in regard to the evil our enemies may be doing. That would mean being an accomplice in evil. The word love (*agapáō*) does not imply that you are to make him your friend (*philéō*) in the sense of having the same interests and goals as he, but that you are to befriend him by seeking to change him from his evil ways. Sometimes this can only be done through punishment; at others, acts of kindness may move him. Whatever you do to change your enemy and bring him to Christ is truly loving him.

A father who chastises his child for disobedience, or deprives him of what he wants that could harm himself and others, is not acting out of hate but love—the same love that provides for his legitimate needs.

Perhaps no command of Christ has been as misunderstood as this one to His disciples: "Love ye your enemies." The word love here (*agapáō*) is the same as that used in Luke 6:35 and John 3:16. "For God so [thus] loved that he gave." What did He give? Not indulgence toward sin, permitting the sinner to continue in evil-doing, but His only begotten Son to die on the cross so that the sinner who hates God might be changed. Loving your enemy, therefore, has an eternal reward, for, when you do what is needed to change him, you are acting in a Christlike manner.

During the Turkish atrocities against the Armenians in Asia Minor, a young woman and her brother were pursued by a Turkish soldier. The brother was brutally murdered. The sister escaped. Later she became a nurse in an army hospital. One day a critically ill Turkish soldier was brought in whom she recognized as the one who had slain her brother. Any slight inattention would have meant his death. However, as a Christian, she tenderly cared for him.

When the soldier convalesced, he recognized the young woman. In amazement he asked, "How could you care for me so kindly and nurse me back to health? Why did you not get revenge for the merciless slaying of your brother and let me die?" She replied, "I am a follower of Christ, who said, 'Love your enemies and do good to them.' " For a moment the soldier was speechless. Then he exclaimed, "I never knew there was such a religion! Tell me more about it. I want it!"

I myself vividly remember an incident that took place at our Greek Keswick in Macedonia one year. The Lord had just opened the door for a special ministry among the Turks. After I announced it, a devout Christian woman came up to me, placed some Greek currency in my hand, and said, "I want this used to win Turks to Christ. They killed my brother." There will be a special reward for that woman at the day of judgment for believers.

A special reward is also promised to those Christians who endure trials and conflicts. Several Scripture passages attest this fact. In 2 Corinthians 4:17, 18 we read: "Our light affliction, which is but for a moment, worketh for us a far more exceeding and eternal weight of glory [recognition in heaven of our real worth in view of our acceptance of suffering for Christ's sake]; while we look not at the things which are seen, but at the things which are not seen."

And Peter encourages us by saying, "Now for a season, if need be, ye are in heaviness through manifold temptations: that the trial of your faith, being much more precious than of gold that perisheth, though it be tried with fire, might be found unto praise and honor and glory at the appearing of Jesus Christ" (1 Pet. 1:6, 7).

Or again, in 2 Thessalonians 1:6, 7, Paul says, "It is a righteous thing with God to recompense tribulation to them that trouble you; and to you who are troubled rest with us, when the Lord Jesus shall be revealed from heaven."

While James tells us, "Blessed is the man that endureth temptation: for when he hath been approved, he shall receive the crown of life, which the Lord hath promised to them that love him" (James 1:12, RSV). Revelation 2:10 promises, "Be thou faithful unto death, and I will give thee a crown of life." And the Lord Jesus said, "Blessed are ye, when men shall revile you, and persecute you. . . . For great is your reward in heaven" (Matt. 5:11, 12). Lastly, in Revelation 3:21 we read, "To him that overcometh will I grant to sit with me in my throne."

### The Reward for Those Who Love Christ's Appearing

We usually think of rewards as recompense for work well done. But did you ever think that you would be rewarded for merely looking forward to something with keen anticipation? God's Word promises a special reward to those who love the Lord's appearing. In 2 Timothy 4:8 we read: "There is laid up . . . a crown of righteousness, which the Lord, the righteous judge, shall give . . . at that day . . . unto all them . . . that love his appearing."

How wonderful that the Lord Jesus Christ should care so much about our wanting to see Him, and to behold that glory which He is so set upon our seeing and sharing, that He has actually prepared and laid up a special honor and dignity for all who have this desire! And how sad that so many will miss it! This special reward is in addition to the rewards that will be given to believers on that day when they shall stand before Him to receive the rewards of faithfulness and service. Consider these wonderful verses:

"As ye also are ours [our rejoicing, i.e. because it will be acknowledged that we won you to Christ] in the day of the Lord Jesus" (2 Cor. 1:14). "For what is our hope, or joy, or crown of rejoicing? Are not even ye in the presence of our Lord Jesus Christ at his coming?" (1 Thess. 2:19).

"And when the chief Shepherd shall appear, ye shall receive a crown of glory that fadeth not away" (1 Pet. 5:4). "That the trial of your faith, being much more precious than of gold that perisheth, though it be tried with fire, might be found unto praise and honor and glory at the appearing of Jesus Christ" (1 Pet. 1:7).

"And they shall be mine, saith the Lord of hosts, in that day when I make up my jewels; and I will spare them, as a man spareth his own son that serveth him" (Mal. 3:17). "For thou shalt be recompensed at the resurrection of the just" (Luke 14:14). "And to you who are troubled [God will recompense] rest with us, when the Lord Jesus shall be revealed from heaven with his mighty angels" (2 Thess. 1:7).

It is clear from all these passages that the judgment for the distribution of these rewards will take place after the rapture of the saints (see 1 Thess. 4:13–17), and the manifestation of their glory will be simultaneous with the manifestation of Christ's. "If so be that we suffer with him, that we may be also glorified together" (Rom. 8:17). "Beloved, now are we the sons of God, and it doth not yet appear what we shall be: but we know that, when he shall appear, we shall be like him; for we shall see him as he is" (1 John 3:2).

"When Christ, who is our life, shall appear, then shall ye also appear with him in glory" (Col. 3:4). "And the nations were angry, and thy wrath is come, and the time of the dead, that they should be judged, and that thou shouldest give reward unto thy servants the prophets, and to the saints, and them that fear thy name, small and great; and shouldest destroy them which destroy the earth" (Rev. 11:18).

But when the Lord and the Scriptures speak of reward, what are we to understand by that term? The Greek text of 1 Corinthians 3:14 says, "If anyone's work shall abide which he built up, he shall receive wages." The word translated "reward" in our English Bible is *misthós* in Greek, which primarily means "wages." That is what you get at the end of the week or the month for the work you do. The verb *misthóō* means "to hire or let for payment," and is used exactly in this sense today in Modern Greek.

We must not make the mistake, however, of taking this word in its literal sense as "pay for hire or work," and conclude that the Christian is to work for the sake of the pay he will receive. *Misthós*, "wages," bears the connotation of worth, of merit, and therefore of rightful demand by the worker. This notion is entirely absent from both the Lord's teaching and that of Paul and the other apostles. No Christian is asked to do—nor should he do— anything merely for the sake of reward. No Christian worker should have his eyes fixed solely or primarily upon the recompense at the end of the way. There is enough recompense and joy now in what he does for the Lord. The pay is really incidental. That is why our Lord never bargained with His disciples when He called them to follow Him. He made no promise that He would pay them a specified amount of money, food, fame, or the like. His call to follow Him was unconditional.

One result of this unconditional following of Christ is a transforming relationship. This is clearly brought out in Luke 6:35: "But love ye your enemies, and do good, and lend, hoping for nothing again; and your reward shall be great." What is this reward—so much money, so many friends, so much acclaim? No, the reward is not things, not a paycheck in your hands, but a relationship unknown and unknowable to those who hate their enemies and return evil for evil.

A Christian barber habitually handed out gospel literature to his clients as naturally as others might hand out the day's newspaper or the latest magazine. On being asked when he took his vacation he answered, "I haven't really had one in twenty years. I don't need one. Oh, I get away for a few days now and then, but my work is my life. I enjoy it. I love people. When I finish at the shop at the end of the day, I am as fresh as when I started. All my children, now grown up, love the Lord and are serving Him in whatever they do. That makes me happy." Loving the Lord and serving Him in whatever we do will make us truly happy also.

## Serving God with the Right Motive

Work well done can be a great source of satisfaction. I feel sorry for that man or woman whose sole reward for labor is a paycheck. A root cause of our labor troubles is that the worker often has no interest in his job apart from the pay, and the employer often has no interest in the worker other than to get his dollar's worth of work out of him. If each says, "I'll get everything I can out of you," the country is in for constant labor-management conflict.

The dedicated Christian does not serve God in order to get as much as he can from Him. Nor does God exploit His servants merely for His own gratification. His concern is that their service will also benefit them. There is intrinsic value in labor for

God. The pay comes to His servants as a result of God's faithfulness, never in response to the meritorious demands of those who serve Him.

The paycheck should never be the be-all and end-all, either in secular employment or Christian service. The compensations of knowledge, skill, and constructive participation in life should always take precedence over material rewards. If a man works only for money, a time will come when no amount of it will be adequate or will satisfy him.

A friend was invited to a Scotsman's home for dinner. When tea was served, the guest asked if he might have some sugar. "Man, the sugar is already in the cup of tea," said the host. "Stir it up, my friend." Maybe you're saying, "My job is not my cup of tea." Perhaps you have missed stirring up the sugar that is already in it. The satisfaction of doing good work has real sweetening power. As G. Curtis Jones remarks in his book, *March of the Year*, "Current emphasis seems to be on getting ahead, rather than getting behind things that count."

One of the least creditable episodes in the life of Peter was when turning to the Lord he said, "Lo, we have left all, and have followed thee" (Mark 10:28; Luke 18:28), implying, of course, "What's in it for us?" Is this venture going to result in profit or loss? He must have been thinking of his fishing boats pulled up on the beach, and of his fishing trade that had passed into other hands. How sad that he could not see that fishing for men was reward enough in itself.

As one traces the concept of rewards through the Bible, he cannot help noticing how the emphasis has shifted. In the Old Testament, rewards were largely material. There are noticeable exceptions, to be sure, but it seems evident that the children of Israel endured the long marches of the wilderness, with their hardships and privations, not so much from the lure of idealism or obedience to God as from the fact that they were to be rewarded in a very concrete way. They were Israel, the chosen people of God, in whose lives God was committed to fulfill His promises, but many of them were not the true children of God, spiritually speaking, as Paul clearly states in Romans 9:6–8. They had been slaves in Egypt; they were to be property-holders in Palestine. "If ye be willing and obedient, ye shall eat of the good of the land" (Is. 1:1). Yonder is the Promised Land, "flowing with milk and honey" (Ex. 3:8). It is the land that the Lord thy God giveth thee. Go in and possess it (see Deut. 2:29).

When we come to the New Testament, the climate is changed. There is a promise, but not of a material possession. It is a condition, a state of being; it is the new birth, the kingdom of God. It is not something for us to possess, but for us to be possessed by. It is the kingdom that is within us (Luke 17:21).

In the Synoptic Gospels the concept of rewards is presented just as freely as the threat of punishments. Take Matthew 6:19–21 and Luke 12:33ff., for instance. Corresponding to the reward there is also a penalty for those who are disobedient to God (cf. Matt. 10:28; 11:20–24;13:40f.; 18:8f.; 18:23–35; 21:40f.; 23:37–39; Mark 9:43ff.; 12:9; Luke 12:5; 13:1–5, 34; 16:9; 20:15f.). In this connection it should be noted that reward and punishment are always future.

This close connection between reward and punishment helps to resolve the difficult question of whether God views His rewards or punishments as obligations or simply as consequences of our actions. If it were a necessity on the part of God, then it would be because of merit on our part. If God were obligated to pay us according to our work, then we would have the right to demand all that was coming to us. This is never the meaning of God's promises. He is faithful in fulfilling them, but His faithfulness is the result of His character, not of our merit. God never concludes bargains with any man; instead He fulfills the implications of His justice and mercy inherent in His character.

> Whence to me this tranquil spirit—
>   Me all sinful as I am?
> Is it thus descends the merit
>   Of the sin-atoning Lamb?
> Grace, all power to deliver,
> Gift of a Creative Giver,
> Like a full, refreshing river,
>         Ever flowing.
>
> Not my virtue or repenting
>   Earned the precious boon for me.
> Thine, my Savior, the relenting,
>   Thine the pangs which set me
> free—
> Gift of grace beyond all knowing,
> From the heart of Jesus flowing,
> Ever flowing, overflowing,
>         Flowing free.
>         —author unknown

## Reward and Punishment

Martin Luther, in his incomparable treatise on *The Bondage of the Will*, says:

> For those who do good and evil willingly, even though they cannot alter their will by their own strength, reward and punishment follow *naturally* and *necessarily;* as it is written: "thou shalt render unto every man according to his works" (cf. Ps. 62:12). *Natural* consequence is this: if you sink under water, you will be drowned; if you swim out of it, you will be saved. In a word: in the matter of merit and reward, we deal with either *worthiness* or *consequence.* If you have *worthiness* in view, there is no merit and no reward. If "free-will" cannot will good by itself alone, but wills good by grace alone (for we are speaking of "free-will" apart from grace, and inquiring into the proper power of each), who does not see that the good will, and merit, and reward, are of grace alone?

This is why one of the most important utterances of Paul in this whole discussion on rewards in 1 Corinthians 3 is the phrase, "according to the grace of God which is given unto me" (v. 10). If it were not for that grace, he would never have been able to will anything that would be acceptable to God. Therefore he refers to works by grace, those which are the consequence of grace. True, there is a will to do, but that will in the first place is the result of the grace of God.

> If, on the other hand [continues Luther] you have *consequences* in view, there is nothing, good or evil, that has not its reward. And hence comes the mistake, that, in the matter of merits and rewards, we ponder unprofitable thoughts and questions about *worthiness* (which is non-existent) when we ought to be discussing *consequence* alone. Hell and the judgment of God await the wicked as a necessary *consequence;* though they do not themselves desire or conceive of such a reward for their sins, and indeed think it abominable and, as Peter says, rail against it.

Second Peter 2:12 puts it very plainly: "But these [sensual and corrupt people], as natural brute beasts, made to be taken and destroyed, speak evil of the things that they understand not; and shall utterly perish in their own corruption."

> In the same way [says Luther] a kingdom awaits the godly, though they themselves neither seek it nor think of it; for it was prepared for them by their Father, not only before they themselves existed, but before the foundation of the world (cf. Matt. 25:34). Indeed, should they do good works in order to obtain the kingdom, they never would obtain it, but would belong rather to the number of the ungodly, who with an evil, mercenary eye seek the things of self even in God. The sons of God, however, do good with a will free from self-concern, seeking no reward, but the glory and will of God only, and ready to do good even if (though this is impossible) there was neither a kingdom nor a hell.
>
> These things are, I think, sufficiently established by that single saying of Christ which I have just cited from Matthew 25: "Come, ye blessed of My Father, receive the kingdom prepared for you from the foundation of the world" (v. 34). How do they *merit* what is already theirs, and was prepared for them before they were in existence? We

> could more accurately say that it is rather the kingdom of God that merits its possessors; so putting the merit where our opponents put the reward, and the reward where they put the merit. The kingdom is not in process of preparation, but was prepared before, and the sons of the kingdom do not prepare the kingdom, but are in process of being prepared themselves; that is, the kingdom merits the sons, not the sons the kingdom. So also hell rather merits and makes ready its sons; for Christ says: "Depart, ye cursed, into eternal fire, prepared for the devil and his angels" (v. 41).

When one chooses to obey God, he also chooses at the same time to abide by the consequences of that obedience. Those consequences can be said to be the reward of obedience. But you do not obey for the purpose of reaping the consequences. The person who chooses to do evil does not do it for the purpose of reaping the judgment of evil. That is built in as a consequence of evil. And God's spiritual laws contain the built-in consequences of every action.

> What then [continues Luther] is the meaning of all those Scriptures which promise the kingdom and threaten hell? Why is the word "reward" repeated so often in the Scriptures? "There is a reward for thy work" (2 Chron. 15:7). "I am thy exceeding great reward" (Gen. 15:1). Again: "Who rendereth to every man according to his work" (cf. Job 34:11). And Paul says in Romans 2: "To those who by patient continuance in well-doing seek eternal life" (v. 7); and there are many similar statements.
>
> The answer is that what is established by all these passages is simply a *consequence of reward*, not in any way a *worthiness of merit;* inasmuch as those who do good do not do so in a servile, mercenary spirit, with a view to gaining eternal life; so that their "seeking" is an earnest striving and diligent endeavor after that which regularly follows upon a good life. The reason why the future consequences of a good and a bad life are declared in the Scriptures is that men might be instructed, disturbed, awakened, and terrified.

That certainly creates a sense of personal responsibility (see Luther 1957, 181–93).

## What Kind of Reward Has God Promised to Believers?

John Calvin in his *Institutes of the Christian Religion* (Vol. 2, 123, 124) has a penetrating discussion on the subject of the rewards that the Lord promises for our works. He fully agrees with Luther that there is nothing meritorious in them but they are the natural consequence of God's grace. Commenting on 2 Timothy 4:8 he writes:

> How could he [the righteous judge] deem them [our works] worthy of reward, did he not with boundless goodness destroy what is unworthy in them? . . . Scripture humbles us more, and at the same time elevates us. For besides forbidding us to glory in works because they are the gratuitous gifts of God, it tells us they are always defiled by some degrees of impurity, so they cannot satisfy God when they are tested by the standard of his justice.

This is precisely what Paul refers to when he says that what we build on the foundation of Christ will be tried by fire. What is not fit and proper must be destroyed, if all that is of God in the superstructure of our lives is to abide forever.

I have found no more thorough discussion of the Greek word *misthós*, "reward," than in Gerhard Kittel's *Theological Dictionary of the New Testament*, volume 4, pages 695–728. The conclusion of that study is worth quoting:

> Jesus and early Christianity obviously spoke quite freely of reward. But for all the formal dependence, the Jewish idea of reward is completely transcended. The Christian cannot count on a reward either from men or God. Just recompense would mean for men absolute and definitive destruction, for God alone is good, Mark 10:18, 26f.; Romans 3:22–24, and consequently He alone is life and the living one. If the NT still speaks of reward, this is simply a temporally conditioned term for the incomparably rich gift of God's love to man in spite of all his weakness and sin.
>
> One may thus speak of reward in the NT sense only 1) as a reference to the fact that man is set before God, and that the most excellent fruit of faith which God demands and recognizes is not enthusiasm or ecstasy, but moral volition and action;

2) with an awareness that God's gift, that is, the kingdom, is so uniquely and incomparably great that it can only be given by God and no man can merit it, so that all reward is simply God's generous love;

3) in the faith that this final reward is God's gift because there is at the beginning endowment with God's Spirit and adoption into the living power of the kingdom of God, so man is conceivable as a child of God only in terms of his endowment by God;

4) with the clear perspective that the incomparable greatness of this gift frees man completely from calculating on rewards from men;

5) in the experience that the power of faith, the omnipotence of God, the possession of the Spirit, is a simple and natural incentive to moral action, so that there neither can nor should be any thought or talk of reward;

6) in the attitude of the child of God, who goes forward to the final decision of God, not with fear and uncertainty, but with uniquely great confidence and cheerful and childlike trust in the love of God which will perfect the calling of God's children in the glory of His kingdom. Thus what is said about reward summons to moral seriousness before the holy God but it is also an expression of blessing already experienced and of the most joyous certainty of the love of God which overcomes all things, including all man's weakness and guilt.

What will the reward be? Will it be something of a material nature? Let us recall the words of the Lord in Luke 6:35, "And your reward shall be great, and ye shall be the children of the Highest." It is not that we are to *receive* something, but that we are going to *be* something. Being is far better than having. "Ye shall be the children of the Highest."

Our Lord and Paul sometimes used material symbols to indicate spiritual values. "Crowns of glory" need not be thought of as literal; and even if they are, they should not be the important thing in our thinking. Our relationship to God is the most basic concept of Christianity. Being children of God is the state into which we enter when we believe. And does not a child partake of all that is available in the family? As St. Augustine said, "This is our highest reward that we should fully enjoy God, and that all who enjoy Him should enjoy one another in Him."

Yet even in family life, not all children enjoy its privileges equally. Their enjoyment depends on their obedience to and harmony with their parents. And that is how it is with us and our heavenly Father. In the first Psalm we are told: "Blessed is the man that walketh not in the counsel of the ungodly, nor standeth in the way of sinners, nor sitteth in the seat of the scornful. But his delight is in the law of the Lord. . . ." (vv. 1, 2).

And why is he blessed? Because "he shall be like a tree [something living, not just a post] planted by the rivers of water" (v. 3). "Follow me," said the Lord to Peter. "What do I get?" he asked. Nothing. "Follow me, and I will *make you to become. . . .*" The Lord makes us something, as we see in John 1:12: "But as many as received him, to them gave he power to *become* the sons of God" (see Phillips 1932, 15–24).

## Will There Be Degrees of Reward in Heaven?

Our Lord gave us two parables to illustrate the rewards that await believers when they stand before Him for judgment of their works. These are the parables of the talents and the pounds, in Matthew 25:14–30 and Luke 19:11–27.

One noticeable difference between the two is that in the case of the talents, the different servants had varying amounts with which to trade, and the profits were in direct proportion to these amounts; while in the case of the pounds all started alike but the results were different. But the nature of the reward was the same in both: "Thou hast been faithful over a few things, I will *make* thee ruler over many things" (Matt. 25:21, 23; cf. Luke 19:17, 19). "Who then is that faithful and wise steward, whom his lord shall *make* ruler over his household? . . . Of a truth I say unto you, that he will *make* him ruler over all that he hath" (Luke 12:42, 44). "If we suffer, we shall also reign with him" (2 Tim. 2:12). "And he that overcometh, and keepeth my works unto the end, to him will I give power over the nations: and he shall rule them. . . ." (Rev. 2:26, 27).

See also the special promise to the apostles, "Verily I say unto you, that ye which have followed me, in the regeneration when the Son of man shall sit in the throne of his glory, ye also shall sit upon twelve thrones, judging the twelve tribes of Israel" (Matt. 19:28). We shall be elevated to judgeship. We shall become something we are not now. The faithful servants of Christ will have dominion over nations or cities in the renewed earth. During the time of "building" now, the Lord is training rulers for His coming kingdom. None of us are yet in the fullness of our work for Him; we are only probationers in training.

There is no doubt that there will be degrees of reward, according to our proved capacity, as shown in the parable of the talents. Each man received a different sum, but the Lord expected the yield to be proportionate to the amount He had entrusted to each. Some will accordingly have authority over ten cities, some over five; all, we may be sure, up to the limit of their power to rule. In Matthew 25 the reward is twofold, an increased sphere of service, and fellowship in the joy of the Lord.

Daniel also alludes to degrees of reward: "And they that be wise shall shine as the brightness of the firmament; and they that turn many to righteousness as the stars forever and ever" (Dan. 12:3). This is a thought that Paul amplifies further: "There is one glory of the sun, and another glory of the moon, and another glory of the stars: for one star differeth from another star in glory. So also is the resurrection of the dead" (1 Cor. 15:41, 42).

And John writes to the elect lady and her children, "Look to yourselves, that we lose not those things which we have wrought, but that we receive a full reward" (2 John 8). We also find Peter writing of a long list of Christian graces, that by means of them we may secure an abundant entrance into the everlasting kingdom of our Lord and Savior Jesus Christ (2 Pet. 1:5–11).

Our title to heaven is secured by our justification, but our meetness for heaven arises from our sanctification. A king's son is heir-apparent to his father's throne by right of birth, just as a believer is assured of heaven by right of his new birth. Now suppose that the crown prince is educated with all the advantages, and possesses all the attainments, that are necessary to make him a complete monarch. His accomplishments, however great, do not entitle him to the kingdom; they only qualify him for it.

In the same manner, the holiness and obedience of the believers are no part of that right on which their claim to glory is found, or for which it is given. They are simply a part of that spiritual education by which they are fitted and made meet to inherit "the kingdom prepared for [them] from the foundation of the world" (Matt. 25:34).

Francis Xavier has voiced in a beautiful poem what every consecrated Christian considers his true reward to be.

Jesus, I love Thee, not because
  I hope for heaven thereby,
Nor yet because, if I love not,
  I must forever die.

I love Thee, Savior dear, and still
  I ever will love Thee,
Solely because my God Thou art,
  Who first hast lov-ed me.

Not with the hope of gaining aught,
  Nor seeking a reward;
But freely, fully, as Thyself
  Hast lov-ed me, O Lord!

Even so I love Thee, and will love,
  And in Thy praise will sing,
Solely because Thou art my God
  And my eternal King.

**LESSONS:**

1. The person who works for a reward is not as highly motivated as the one who works as a labor of love. However, such an individual can receive a source of gratification for recognition of work well done. The purpose of God's judgment of the works of Christians is to test their works for approval not disapproval.
2. We should examine our "works" against the Scriptures to see if they will stand in the day of judgment. "Work" means actual accomplishments, not efforts or wishful thinking. In the Scriptures we read that rewards will be given for steady, unswerving Christian faith and obedience.
3. The work for which God promises to reward believers is not necessarily full-time service, but rather the faithful execution of whatever task confronts them day by day. God rewards something no matter how great or small, as long as it is done for Him.
4. In Scripture rewards were promised for helping the poor and for spiritual service through witness and example, and for love and practical kindness shown to enemies. A special reward is promised to Christians who endure trials and conflicts and to those who love the Lord's appearing.
5. Serving God with the right motive can be a great source of satisfaction. The dedicated Christian does not serve God to get things from Him so much as to enjoy God Himself.
6. There is little doubt that there will be degrees of reward in heaven according to our proved capacity. The Lord entrusts different sums to each and expects proportionate yields.

# 1 Cor. 3:15 | *Will Your Work for God Survive the Test of Fire?*

> *If any man's work shall be burned, he shall suffer loss: but he himself shall be saved; yet so as by fire.*

Is your house fireproof? Maybe you have heard there is no such thing as a completely fireproof building. But just suppose there were, and you lived in it. If someone were to set a torch to it, you would see no need to jump out the window. But if you lived in a wooden house, and someone set fire to it, you would head for the nearest exit.

Well, something like that is going to happen to every Christian believer some day. Our spiritual house, our work of faith built on the foundation of Christ, will be put to the test of fire. In 1 Corinthians 3:15 Paul states, "If any man's work shall be burned, he shall suffer loss: but he himself shall be saved; yet so as by fire." This symbolism is in line with the fire mentioned in verse 13 that Paul said would test our work. If our spiritual house is made up predominantly of gold, silver, and precious stones (which Paul represents here as fireproof materials), it will stand. If our house of works consists mostly of wood, hay, and stubble (which are naturally combustible), it will burn down.

The whole idea is that God will one day judge the permanent worth of our Christian character and work. On that day, when Christ appears, we shall be entering our permanent state for eternity. Nothing temporal will enter that state with us, but will be destroyed.

Apparently this burning of useless works will take place at a specific time, once for all. This is indicated by the future tense of the verb *katakaíō* (*katakaḗsetai*). It is made up of the preposition *katá*, "down," and the verb *kaíō*, "burn." This means that, just as fire demonstrates the true permanence of any substance, God's fire of judgment will demonstrate the permanence of what is worthy in our character and works on that day when the Lord shall appear for His saints.

This, of course, will bring loss to many. Think of yourself as living in the house you have built on the foundation of Jesus Christ. Suddenly someone applies a torch to it. The verb *katakaḗsetai* is in the passive voice, indicating that the fire will be caused by God Himself. If your house is "fireproof," you need not run out. But if you see the walls burning, you will leave in a hurry. The Lord says in this latter case that you will have time to escape. You will suffer the loss of your house, but you yourself will be "saved." The word is *sothḗsetai*, the future indicative passive form of the verb *sṓzo*, which is used of material and temporal deliverance from danger, and of the spiritual and eternal salvation granted immediately by God to those who believe on the Lord Jesus Christ (see Acts 2:47; Eph. 2:5, 8). The word is also used for other types of deliverance, but here it undoubtedly refers to the salvation of man's soul.

Paul includes himself in this test by fire, since he refers to a building that he, too, is erecting during his lifetime. In verse 9 he stated, "We are God's co-workers," which of course included himself. In 1 Corinthians 9:27 he indicated that he would have to meet God's test on that day: "But I keep under my body, and bring it into subjection: lest that by any means, when I have preached to others, I myself should be a castaway."

As we have indicated in a previous study, the word "castaway" (*adókimos*) means "not approved;" applying the symbol of fire as the test—"not fireproof." It is the same word from which we get *dokimásei* in verse 13, translated "try," in the phrase, "each man's work shall be *tried* by fire of what sort it is." It is inconceivable that Paul would mean by the term "castaway" "not saved at last." How could that be the case with the apostle who wrote, "I know whom I have believed, and am persuaded that he is able to keep that which I have committed unto him against that day" (2 Tim. 1:12)? One thing Paul was sure about: on "that day" he would be among the saved, not because of any worthy house he might have built on the foundation of Christ, but because of his position on that foundation, of being "in Christ," as he emphasized over and over in the opening verses of 1 Corinthians. And this is true of every believer in Christ.

In the parable of the talents in Matthew 25, we read in verse 14 that the people the master was dealing with were "his peculiar [*toús ídious*] servants." They were not strangers. They are representative of believers, true and merely professed, as in the instance of the servant entrusted with the one talent, and the servant of Luke 19:20 who kept his pound hidden in a napkin. And in Luke 19:13 we read that these were "his very own (*heautón*) servants." When Paul says, "We must *all* appear before the judgment seat of Christ" (2 Cor. 5:10), some people might take this to mean all of mankind. But the context will show that he is speaking only of the saints, the saved ones—indeed, only of serving, ministering saints directly, and of all Christians by extension.

Thus here, as in 1 Corinthians 3:15, it is entirely a question of work done, not of life; and the word "we" evidently refers to those who are expected to be found pleasing to the Lord. But in a real sense the Lord expects no service, and accepts none, from any who have not first accepted Christ as Savior. The works of such people are "dead works," because they are performed by the spiritually dead, and must therefore be damning (Rev. 20:13).

**Are You Saved "Once for All"?**

As one of God's children neared the close of his life, he was in great distress of mind. His pastor tried to comfort and reassure him. The man listened with a distracted air. Then he said, "I am saved. I have no fear of dying. But what can I say at the judgment seat of Christ about the wasted years of my life? Will He understand?"

He did not fear the judgment of condemnation that awaits the unbeliever, which results in eternal separation from God. What troubled him was the judgment that awaits the believer for the works done in the body, which results in his unworthy works being "burned" in the presence of the Lord, though he himself is saved as one who escapes from a burning building.

Second Corinthians 5:10 clearly states: "We must all appear before the judgment seat [*bḗma*] of Christ; that every one may receive the things done in his body, according to that he hath done, whether it be good or bad." The Greek text says *diá toú sṓmatos*, "through the body or by means of the body." All that we did during our earthly lifetime, when our spiritual personality indwelt our body, will be reviewed before Christ. If our works for Him have been done worthily, this will be an occasion to look forward to, as well as an incentive to holy living.

Second Corinthians 5:10 and 1 Corinthians 3:15 indicate that this judgment will cause both joy and sorrow. The basic joy, of course, will be that by God's grace we are with Him because of our being "in Christ." But, as we see how Christ evaluates our works, we may experience both the joy of commendation and the sorrow of loss as we are made to realize what has been wood, hay, and stubble in our lives.

In heaven we will live under no illusions, and that is a good thing. We are to have a new beginning in our new resurrected bodies, and therefore all our past has to be reckoned with. As believers, all of us will experience some degree of sorrow and regret at seeing our unworthy works destroyed before our eyes. But Revelation 7:17 and 21:4 assure us that our sorrow will be quickly dissipated.

> And God shall wipe away all tears from their eyes; and there shall be no more death, neither sorrow, nor crying, neither shall there be any more pain: for the former things are passed away. . . . For the Lamb which is in the midst of the throne shall feed them, and shall lead them unto living fountains of waters: and God shall wipe away all tears from their eyes.

Both of these verses refer to a time after the judgment of believers. Not only do the tears and pain referred to in these verses represent the sufferings experienced in our earthly life, but also most probably the anguish caused by realizing how much of what we did in the body turned out to be worthless in the end. Oh, for God's Spirit to help us realize this now, that we may walk worthy of our calling, and thus reduce our loss, pain, and tears!

God's Word speaks of two major judgments. One is the judgment of men's salvation. The word generally used for this is *krísis* or *katákrisis*, "condemnation." It actually means separation. This is the separation of those who are outside of Christ from those who are in Christ. But believers do not have to wait until death, or until this particular judgment, to find out whether they are in Christ or not. They can know this at the very moment they receive Him as Savior. John 3:18 says, "He that believeth on him [Christ] is not condemned [*krínetai*, from *krínō* and *krísis*, 'judged']: but he that believeth not is condemned [*kékritai*, from the same root verb *krínō*] already because he hath not believed in the name of the only begotten Son of God."

And in 1 John 3:14 we read, "We know that we have passed from death unto life." John 5:24 dispels any doubt about the believer's salvation on that day: "Verily, verily, I say unto you He that heareth my word, and believeth on him that sent me, hath everlasting life, and shall not come into condemnation, but is passed from death unto life." The word translated "condemnation" here is *krísin*, "judgment," not *katákrisin*, "condemnation." In other words, believers will not be arraigned before God's criminal court to be condemned, because they have placed their faith in Christ. When men and women have passed from death into life, they will not be tried as to whether they are "alive" or not, but for what they did with their lives. Or, as Paul says in Colossians 1:13, the Father "hath delivered us from the power of darkness, and hath translated us into the kingdom of his dear Son." The decision about believers being "alive" in Christ has already been made.

Actually, believing sinners have already been judged, condemned, sentenced, and executed in the Person of their Surety, Jesus Christ; and since dying once exhausts the penalty, believers take their stand in a new condition of life. To translate this into personal terms, Christ and you cannot both die for the sin of one person, you.

The same immunity from ever coming into the judgment court is pledged again to believers in Hebrews 9:27, 28. "As it is appointed to men to die, and after that judgment, once, so the Christ was offered [died], to bear the sins of man [was judged], once: and by them that are looking for him, shall he be seen a second time, without [any recognition of sin] (literal translation).

## The Joy and Sorrow of the Christian's Final Accounting

When you believe in the Lord Jesus Christ as the Son of God, and receive Him as your Savior, the sin that separated you from God has been judged once and for all. At His Second Coming, the Lord will not bring you into court to be tried on the question of whether you have eternal life, or on the question of guilt.

But this does not mean that you will not have to face an accounting for your life in Christ. It will make a difference whether you have walked after the flesh or after the Spirit. Satan may try so hard to impress you with your safety from judgment that you will live carelessly, since you know you are not going to come into condemnation.

Paul tells us in Ephesians 1:8 that God abounds in wisdom and prudence. A wise God would not be so careless as to expose the riches of His grace to men's abuse without any countercheck. First Corinthians 3:15 provides this countercheck. True, Christ says of the believer that he "shall not come into judgment" (John 5:24). But Paul says in 2 Corinthians 5:10, "We must all appear before the judgment seat of Christ." And in 1 Corinthians 3:15 he tells us that it is possible for our work to be burned down and for us to suffer loss. Is there any contradiction between Christ and Paul? It may seem so at first sight, but not in reality.

We need to make a distinction here. In John 5 the Lord was alluding to a criminal court, where issues of life and death are tried. Everyone arraigned before that bar is tried for his life. Into such a court no believer can ever come, for the issue has been settled already. But Paul speaks of another and very different court, in which other issues will be tried. Life or death will not be mentioned at all. What will be determined is rewards for work done. It will not be a criminal but a civil court, a family investigation.

But, someone may wonder, will everything be made manifest at the judgment seat of Christ? Has not God said that He will remember our sins no more? (Is. 43:25). And we answer, Would you not like to view what you have done on earth in the light of His grace? Would you not like to know how much God appreciates the work of your lifetime in Christ? When a child has completed an examination, is he not anxious to know the teacher's opinion of what he has written, what grade he has received? Who would want to work and never know whether his efforts were appreciated or not? In this review of all that we have done in the flesh, it will be necessary to expose our sins, but this will be done in the light of the love that has forgiven them all.

Suppose that a young man has fallen into evil ways and involved himself heavily in debt. The father is willing to pay the son's debts, and does so at great sacrifice to himself. "Here you are, son. You are now free from debt. But what do you propose to do from now on?"

"I'll go and make something of myself in a far away country." And he does just that. Thirty years pass. "I'd love to see my Dad," he muses. His father welcomes him. They talk about old times. The father says, "You remember when I paid all your debts just before you went away?"

"Why, sure, Dad. How could I ever forget the kind way you handled that sad matter?"

"Well, did you ever know just *how much* I paid to clear you of your debts?"

"I really didn't have the heart to reckon them all up. I know it was a lot; I shouldn't be surprised if it was two or three thousand dollars."

"Would you like to see the bundle of receipts?"

"Why, yes, I would. I'd like to know how much you had to pay to save my neck."

So the father fetches the packet from the drawer in his desk. The papers are faded and brown with age, but there they are, the bills receipted in full. The son spreads them out on the table and looks at them with mingled feelings. He adds up the amounts and looks at his father in amazement.

"Dad," he says, "do you mean you had to pay thirty thousand dollars to clear me?"

"Yes, that was the sum."

"Well, Dad, I knew that you had paid it all, that no creditor had a claim on me for a single cent. But I never knew till this moment *how much* I am indebted to your love."

This is a hypothetical illustration, but it does serve to show how we shall feel at the judgment seat when all the receipted bills, all the forgiven sins are shown us. As Robert Murray McCheyne has put it in his well-known hymn, "Then, Lord, shall I fully know, Not till then, how much I owe."

I for one am eagerly looking forward to the revelation of how much the grace of God enabled me to do for Him during my lifetime, and to find out what works were or were not of permanent value. I am sure some of the things I did were mere rubbish—works that I would rather see burned up than to have to live with them through all eternity. I will feel deep sorrow over those, but great joy over the fact that I am in Christ, and that for some things in my life, at least, I will hear, "Well done, good and faithful servant."

## The Future Judgment of Believers

Suppose a wealthy merchant were to charter a ship to go to some distant country and bring back a valuable cargo. To encourage speed and faithfulness, the merchant offers a bonus to officers and crew if they bring the ship home by a certain date with the cargo intact.

The ship arrives at the foreign port and the cargo is placed on board. But unfortunately a quantity of whiskey is also taken on board, and on the way back the officers and men indulge in it too freely. They drive the ship upon the rocks, with the result that the cargo is lost. They send out an SOS, and men with life-saving equipment put out from a nearby port and save them. They are thus saved from death, but they have lost the bonus they might have earned. Unrewarded, and with the loss of all their possessions, they return to their home port at the expense of others.

This is similar to what awaits the unfaithful Christian when this life is over, when at the Second Coming of Christ he stands before Him for a final accounting of his earthly works—"saved, yet so as by fire," with the loss of all that might otherwise have been his (see Barker n.d., 35, 36).

We need not suppose any long period will be occupied with this judgment of believers. The Lord will already have formed His own infallible judgment of every case, from which there will be no appeal. Millions upon millions of experiences, no two exactly alike, will be judged. Yet, since the individuals will all be in perfected bodies, the results may possibly be communicated to, and apprehended by, each one, and all collectively, as well as to the hosts of surrounding and witnessing angels—this with a rapidity and a clearness of which a flash of lightning is but a feeble image. This judgment may be similar to the rapidity with which the resurrection of the dead believers and the transformation of the living ones will take place at the coming of the Lord: "In a moment, in the twinkling of an eye" (1 Cor. 15:52; see Zodhiates, *Conquering*, 1970, 730–33).

But Paul says the believer does not have to worry that he himself will be consumed in the fire of God's judgment. He will "suffer loss," but he himself will not be lost—just his work. "He will be saved, but only as if escaping through fire." Paul uses the term "fire" here as a symbol of that which will test the value of the believer's work. It cannot harm the believer himself, but neither can it improve his position. The New Testament never speaks of fire as purifying people or their sins. This is an Old Testament concept. In Isaiah 6:5–7, for instance, we read that a live coal off the altar touched the prophet's mouth and purged his sin. But in general Scripture speaks of blood as the cleansing agent. It presents Christ Himself as purging our sins (Heb. 1:3; see also

Matt. 26:28; John 6:56; 19:34; Acts 20:28; Rom. 5:9; Heb. 9:14; 1 Pet. 1:18, 19; 1 John 1:7; Rev. 1:5). This is not future, after death, but past and present for everyone who believes, and it is effective at the very moment anyone exercises faith.

Hebrews 9:14 says, "How much more shall the blood of Christ, who through the eternal Spirit offered himself without spot to God, purge your conscience from dead works to serve the living God?" That is here and now, not future. "And the blood of Jesus Christ his Son cleanseth us from all sin" (1 John 1:7). That is now—and it is by Christ's blood, not fire. Hebrews 9:22 says, "And almost all things are by the law purged with blood; and without shedding of blood is no remission."

The blood of Christ is for the sinner's redemption, past and present and as long as his earthly life shall last, as long as sin is a possibility, but not the future life. Fire is future, to test the believer's work of faith, not to test him as a person (i.e., for his salvation). Fire will be the means of evaluating him, not correcting him because there will be no opportunity for him to relive his life in the body he now inhabits.

What that fire actually will be we do not know. It is not mentioned elsewhere. The threat in Malachi 4:1, which bears a certain verbal resemblance to 1 Corinthians 3:15, does not apply to believers but to the wicked. It is not corrective, purgative, or restorative. It destroys the wicked. As for believers, Scripture never says God's judgment of believers will rectify their past. It is simply for the purpose of evaluating and rewarding their work, not going back to do it over.

The future judgment of believers must not be confused with God's present judgments on them. The "fiery trials" God permits in our lives now are corrective (1 Pet. 4:12). His fire now may even be punitive, as in the case of Ananias and Sapphira, whom He struck dead for lying to the Holy Spirit (Acts 5:1, 11). God may even bring death to those believers who partake of the

Lord's Supper unworthily (1 Cor. 11:28–32). First John 5:16 also confirms that there is a "sin unto death." Believers may therefore suffer in the body, or even incur death for their sins. (Again, this does not invalidate their eternal salvation.) But the fiery investigation and evaluation of believer's works is future; it will take place after this present life. "Therefore be ye also ready: for in such an hour as ye think not the Son of man cometh" (Matt. 24:44).

### Some Common Pitfalls to Avoid

The apostle Paul tells us that the trial by fire that is to judge the believer's works will take place in the future, on what he calls "the day" (1 Cor. 3:13). He distinctly warns us against making any decisive judgment now, in "man's day." Look at 1 Corinthians 4:4, 5: "But he that judgeth me is the Lord. Therefore judge nothing before the time, until the Lord come, who both will bring to light the hidden things of darkness and will make manifest the counsels of the hearts: and then shall every man have [his] praise of God."

That does not mean everything every believer does will "have praise of God." Not *all* ministry of the Word in the church of God will stand His scrutiny in that day. Not *all* preaching of the gospel to the world; not *all activity*, or enthusiasm, or organization; not *all* work done in the name of Jesus, some of which is even done by those who profess but do not possess Christ (Matt. 7:22, 23); no, not even *all* done by His own saints will earn His approval.

We sometimes hear a minister praised because "He faithfully preaches the gospel"—as if that covered everything. Yet he may be overlaying it, in his practice and teaching, with many things the Lord looks on as mere rubbish and stubble. True, he may be very active, energetic, and devoted. Think, then, of his regret at seeing so much of his cherished work burnt up. What sorrow to realize that most of it was done in the energy of the flesh. Another man, no more earnest and active than he, but more sensitive to the Lord's revealed will and more humbly obedient, will thrill to find his work appraised as "gold, silver, and precious stones," and to hear with joy the Master's words, "Well done!" (see Gosse 1884, 109–20).

How can we avoid the pitfalls of misjudging our present work? The Word of God gives us some practical advice on this.

First, let us look at Matthew 6:1, where our Lord says, "Take heed that ye do not your alms before men, to be seen of them: otherwise ye have no reward of your Father which is in heaven." Charity, prayer, and fasting, mentioned in Matthew 6, are wonderful works. But if you do them so that men will praise you, you have had your reward already. This is the meaning of the verb *apéchō* (Matt. 6:2, 5, 16; Luke 6:24)—they "have" their reward here and now. If they are looking for earthly recognition and reward from men, that is all they will ever get. *Apéchō* means "to be paid in full." If you have been paid in full down here on earth, don't look for further rewards when you stand before the Lord on "that day."

The second admonition from the Lord concerns confessing Him before men: "Whosoever therefore shall be ashamed of me and of my words in this adulterous and sinful generation; of him also shall the Son of man be ashamed, when he cometh in the glory of his Father with the holy angels" (Mark 8:38). Any Christian service we have undertaken with an eye to earthly glory or the approbation of men will be consumed as wood, hay, and stubble when Christ comes again. These very same works, if they had been done for the love of God and the glory of His name, would have been counted as gold, silver, and precious stones in His sight. Any Christian work will lose its reward if we are ashamed to let it be known that we did it for Christ's sake, and that all credit belongs "to the praise of the glory of his grace" (Eph. 1:6). We need to guard against two things: doing good works to be seen of men, and failing to confess Christ before men.

The third practical lesson is this: Because God is the Judge, we must never usurp that office. It is very easy to get into the habit of critically appraising the lives of others. Scripture warns against this. "But why dost thou judge thy brother? . . . for we shall all stand before the judgment seat of Christ. . . . So then every one of us shall give account of himself to God. Let us not therefore judge one another any more: but judge this rather, that no man put a stumbling block or an occasion to fall in his brother's way" (Rom. 14:10–14). Judgment is not your work but God's. You may lose your own reward by prematurely judging your brother. Here is a bit of advice I like: "Before criticizing another's faults, take time to count ten of your own."

And finally because God is our Judge, we need never be afraid of man's judgment. Paul said. "With me it is a very small thing that I should be judged of you, or of man's judgment: yea. I judge not mine own self. For I know nothing by myself; yet am I not hereby justified: for he that judgeth me is the Lord" (1 Cor. 4:3, 4).

Do not get upset by criticism. If it is untrue, disregard it. If it is unfair, keep from being irritated. If it is out of ignorance, smile. If it is justified, learn from it. Keep humble and commit your cause to God. "Behold, I come quickly," says Christ, "and my reward is with me" (Rev. 22:12). And again. "Behold, I come quickly: hold that fast which thou hast, that no man take thy crown" (Rev. 3:11). How wonderful on "that day" to stand with those who "cast their crowns before the throne. saying. *Thou* art worthy, O Lord, to receive glory and honor and power" (Rev. 4:10, 11; Eph. 1:6, 12, 14; see Marston 1913, 32–48).

**LESSONS:**

1. .On the day Christ appears we will enter our eternal state, and God will judge the permanent worth of our Christian character and work.
2. Believers cannot be arraigned before God's criminal court because they have placed their faith in Christ. This does not mean that they will not have to give an account of their life in Christ.
3. Avoid the pitfalls of misjudging present work. If you do acts of charity, prayer and fasting to the praise of men, you have your reward already. Any service we undertake with an eye to earthly glory will be consumed as wood, hay, and stubble.
4. It is easy to get in the habit of criticizing and appraising other's lives. Scripture warns against it. You may lose your own reward by prematurely judging your brother. And when you are criticized do not get upset, but be humble and commit your cause to God.

# 1 Cor. 3:16 | *Your Body, God's Temple*

*Know ye not that ye are the temple of God, and that the Spirit of God dwelleth in you?*

Imagine that you had built what you thought was a beautiful fireproof home for yourself. Then one night you had to rush out into the cold air and stand helplessly by while it went up in flames. You might well be forgiven if you shed tears. All that you had worked for destroyed in less than an hour! Yet that will be nothing compared to the sadness with which some Christians will see their works burnt up in the presence of Christ when He comes again. These are the unworthy works done in the body after one has received Christ as Savior.

That is why Paul asks a very solemn question in 1 Corinthians 3:16: "Know ye not that ye are the temple of God, and that the Spirit of God dwelleth in you?"

In the Greek text, what is translated "Know ye not" is *oídate*, which refers to intuitive knowledge. This is the knowledge that should come to a man instinctively when he becomes a child of God. It is like the instinctive knowledge of how to eat that comes to a child just born. Nobody teaches him this; it is part of his nature. In the same way, when you become a child of God through the new birth, you should know certain things instinctively. One of them is that you now possess the Holy Spirit, that God has come to dwell in you.

Ideally, nobody should have to teach you this, but, if you are not fully conversant with the teaching of Scripture, you may not realize what has taken place. It should be part and parcel of your nature as a child of God. Thus the question that Paul asks, *ouk oídate*, "don't you know?" in reality means, "Since you are a born-again child of God, you should have the instinctive, intuitive knowledge that your body is a temple of God, and that the Spirit of God dwells in you."

That was actually the purpose of the incarnation, of God becoming man in the Person of His Son. Look at John 1:1, 14. The first part of these two verses says, "In the beginning was the Word . . . and the Word became flesh." The second part says, "And the Word was with God . . . and dwelt in us." Observe that I translated that last phrase "in us," not "among us." The expressions in 1 Corinthians 3:16 and John 1:14 are equivalent, except that John 1:14 says "in us" (*én hēmín*) and 1 Corinthians 3:16 "in you" (*en humín*).

While it is true that Christ came to earth to dwell *among us*, that was only temporary. His permanent residence was and is *in us*, in our hearts, possessing our entire personalities. The first thing a man ought to realize who becomes a child of God through faith in Christ is that he is indwelt by God.

Some Scriptures indicate that we are indwelt by both Christ and the Holy Spirit. When the Lord Jesus was telling His disciples that He would send the Holy Spirit upon them after His physical departure from this earth, He said, "At that day ye shall know that I am in my Father, and ye in me, and I in you" (John 14:20). The Holy Spirit was going to make Christ's presence in the hearts of believers more evident than ever. Also, in His high priestly prayer, the Lord said, "I in them, and thou in me, that they may be made perfect in one; and that the world may know that thou hast sent me, and hast loved them, as thou hast loved me" (John 17:23).

Paul also states this clearly in his letter to the Galatians: "I am crucified with Christ: nevertheless I live; yet not I, but Christ liveth in me: and the life which I now live in the flesh I live by the faith of the Son of God, who loved me, and gave himself for me" (Gal. 2:20). And he prayed for the Ephesians, "that Christ may dwell in your hearts by faith; that ye, being rooted and grounded in love . . . might be filled with all the fulness of God" (Eph. 3:17, 19). Again in Romans 8:10 Paul says, "If Christ be in you, the body is dead because of sin, but the Spirit is life because of righteousness" (see also Col. 1:2; 1 John 3:24; Rev. 3:20).

In the same way, Scripture declares that the Holy Spirit also dwells within us. Ezekiel 36:27 says, "And I will put my spirit within you, and cause you to walk in my statutes, and ye shall keep my judgments, and do them." Here are some further Scriptures that make this teaching plain:

> Even the Spirit of truth; whom the world cannot receive because it seeth him not, neither knoweth him: but ye know him; for he dwelleth with you, and shall be in you [John 14:17].
>
> But ye are not in the flesh, but in the Spirit, if so be that the Spirit of God dwell in you. Now if any man have not the Spirit of Christ, he is none of his [Rom. 8:9].
>
> What? know ye not that your body is the temple of the Holy Ghost which is in you, which ye have of God, and ye are not your own? [1 Cor. 6:19].
>
> That good thing which was committed unto thee keep by the Holy Ghost which dwelleth in us [2 Tim. 1:14].

I am in Christ; Christ is in me—
My body His temple, sin's captive set free;
My heart His altar, divine love the flame,
Cleansing for service in His matchless name.
My life and His life co-mingled shall be,

With God's very Spirit enthroned in me.
—Frances Rhoads La Chance

**Indwelt by the Trinity**

Most Christians have realized instinctively that the Holy Spirit comes to indwell the believer who receives Christ by faith. But 1 Corinthians 3:16 also indicates that all three Persons of the Trinity dwell in the believer.

Look at the verse carefully: "Know ye not that ye are temple of God, and the Spirit of the God dwells in you?" That is a literal translation from the Greek. No definite article appears before *naós*, "temple," and no definite article before the first occurrence of the word *Theoú*, "of God." The absence of the article before *naós* indicates the quality of the man described, that is, he is "temple" to God; he is the place in which God makes His dwelling. The expression is similar to the third part of John 1:1, "And God was the Word." There is no definite article before "God" here either, in the Greek. This stresses the essence, the quality of the Word. He is God, not "a" God, not one of many, but one who possesses the quality, the essence of deity.

Thus, in 1 Corinthians 3:16, Paul declares that man possesses what it takes to be indwelt by God. But when no definite article appears before the word "God," *Theoú*, the implication is that the entire Godhead—God in His essence as Spirit, in His general character as eternity and infinity—indwells the human heart. Reference is here made to God the Father, God the Son, and God the Holy Spirit. This is identical with what we find in John 1:18, which says, "God [*Theón* without the article] no one has seen at any time." This refers to God's essence of omnipotence, omniscience, timelessness, holiness, and so forth, not to any one of the three persons (see Zodhiates *Was Christ* 1970, discussion of these vv. in John 1).

Thus 1 Corinthians 3:16 affirms that the entire Godhead, God, indwells the believer as He indwelt the temple. This reminds us of Christ's words in John 14:23, "If anyone loves me, he will keep my word, and my Father will love him, and unto him *we* [Father and Son] shall come and in him *we* shall make our abode" (a.t.).

But in the second part of 1 Corinthians 3:16 Paul proceeds to indicate that the Spirit of God indwells the believer in a particular way. "And the Spirit of God dwells in you." In the Greek text, the definite article appears before both words, "Spirit" and "God." This is the Person of the Holy Spirit, who in a very special way indwells and empowers the believer in his daily walk.

In 1 Corinthians 6:19 Paul asks, "Or don't you know that your [physical] body is temple of Holy Spirit in you, which you have from God [not *the* God], and that you are not of yourself?" (lit. translation). Again we see emphasis placed on the fact that the Holy Spirit in a very special way indwells the believer's body. Why? Because the body tends to obey the soul or *psuchḗ*—man's instinctive tendencies—rather than to obey man's spirit that has been regenerated by the Spirit of God. Man's physical nature needs spiritual guidance. The absence of such guidance would be catastrophic, reducing him to the level of the animal.

Paul, in deploring the carnality of the Corinthian Christians, reminds them that as a body of believers, and as individual believers, they are indwelt by the Spirit of God and should act accordingly. In 1 Corinthians 6:15 he asks again, "Know ye not [*ouk oídate*, the same Greek word referring to intuitive knowledge that occurs in 1 Cor. 3:16] that your bodies are the members of Christ?" In effect he is saying, "You as body personalities are members of the Body of Christ." They are the temple of God in which His Spirit dwells. Thus we conclude that the Holy Spirit dwells in every believer, and every believer is a member of the Body of Christ.

This is not merely a recognition that God pervades all of nature. We know that He is everywhere. David knew it when he asked, "Whither shall I go from thy spirit? or whither shall I flee from thy presence? If I ascend up into heaven, thou art there: if I make my bed in hell, behold, thou art there. If I take the wings of the morning, and dwell in the uttermost parts of the sea; even there shall thy hand lead me, and thy right hand shall hold me" (Ps. 139:7–10).

Although God is everywhere, He Himself in His uncreated essence is distinct from His creation. Man can never flee to a place where God is not. Thus in one sense the universe is the temple of God, and the Spirit of God dwells in it. How blind are those who challenge Him to make Himself visible to their physical perceptions! God does not yield to man's demand for a sign.

But Paul did not mean that the Corinthians were God's temple only in the sense of being part of His universe. Obviously man is differently related to God's omnipresence from anything else in nature. Man alone can feel it, acknowledge it, and respond to it. God is just as present with an animal or a plant as with man, but neither animal nor plant is conscious of it, and they can only offer unconscious obedience to God's law. Man in Christ, however, can know and adore God through the homage of his intelligence and moral freedom. However, apart from Christ this is impossible because of man's fallen condition. Thus the human soul is potentially a temple of God in a sense distinct from the rest of creation. The Christian is God's living temple.

### Indwelt by the Spirit

Divorces are granted on many grounds today, but one word that covers most of them is incompatibility: two people find it difficult, if not impossible, to live together because they are in perpetual disagreement. Though the Bible does not sanction incompatibility as a ground for divorce, it does recognize that two people cannot "walk together except they be agreed" (Amos 3:3).

This will help us to understand what happened when man sinned. God and Adam could "walk together" as long as they were going in the same direction, so to speak. But when Adam and Eve sinned, they began walking in the opposite direction from God. And in a way God departed from the soul of man, for holiness and sinfulness cannot dwell together in fellowship.

Yet in one sense God is present with all beings whom He sustains in life. But though He sustains them, He's not with everyone to approve and bless. How can He possibly bless the unrepentant sinner, when the powers God has given to him are perverted and used to produce what God hates? In a way, man in his natural sinful state is less a temple of God than the trees and beasts. At least they have done nothing to insult or grieve God, nothing to limit His authority or defy His will. The soul of fallen man, on the other hand, is in a state of normal contradiction, not just to rules laid down by God but to the very essence of His being. The sinful soul is hostile to those inherent moral and spiritual truths that are rooted in God's eternal self-consciousness, which in the very nature of God are not subject to change.

But to those of Adam's children who have been made alive in Jesus Christ, God manifests His presence by His Spirit. And this manifestation makes them His temples in an altogether more intense sense than is possible for unregenerate man.

This indwelling of the Spirit of God in the individual believer—in you and me—is not a transient visit but a permanent presence. The Greek verb is *oikeí*, from *oikéō*, which refers to dwelling in a house permanently. In fact, the word for "house," even in Modern Greek, is *oikía.*

The verb used in John 1:14 to refer to Christ as the eternal *Lógos*, the Word coming to earth, is *eskēnōsen*, which means "tabernacled, or tented, or camped among us or in us." His physical presence during His lifetime on earth, to which this statement refers, was a temporary one. But now the dwelling of the Holy Spirit in the heart of the believer is permanent. Our heart, our soul, our body, is His permanent dwelling. He does not come in for a while and then go out, never to return. Salvation is not a hide-and-seek affair. It is an eternal permanent act of God, when through His Spirit He comes in and makes us His temple, His dwelling place.

The Spirit of God "dwells," *oikeí*, in you, Paul declares. The verb is in the present tense, indicative mood, which denotes a continuous action or state. This state had a beginning, a time when the Spirit entered an individual heart and started making it His home. Jesus proclaimed that out of the heart of the believer "shall flow rivers of living water. (But this spake he of the Spirit, which they that believe on him should receive. . . .)"(John 7:38, 39).

Second Corinthians 6:16 uses the same word as 1 Corinthians 3:16, *oikéo*, but in the future tense, which involves the initial coming of God into human lives. "I will dwell [*enoikḗsō: en*, 'in'; *oikḗsō*, 'shall dwell'] in them, and walk in them; and I will be their God, and they shall be my people." We see, therefore, that Christ brings God into human lives in a very special and permanent way.

This presence carries with it the gift of a new principle of behavior, the character of God's sinless Son. The Spirit is said to be the Spirit of God, but He is also the Spirit of Christ because He makes us members of Christ's body (1 Cor. 12:12, 13). According to the New Testament, the Holy Spirit's work is not distinct from Christ's work, as if Christ's work for man on earth ended completely at His Ascension, and that of the Spirit began on the Day of Pentecost. Not at all. The action of the Spirit in the church is the continuation or prolongation of Christ's work in Christian history. It is the extension, and in a sense the perpetuation, of the incarnation in its power of making humanity partakers of the divine Nature. Therefore, "If any man have not the Spirit of Christ, he is none of his" (Rom. 8:9).

Along with this Spirit comes the gift of a new spiritual state of being, a new personal character, a new capacity and direction to the affections and will, and a clear perception of truth by the believer's renewed intelligence. "If any man be in Christ, he is a new creation" (2 Cor. 5:17). "The law of the Spirit of life in Christ Jesus hath made me free from the law of sin and death" (Rom. 8:2). "The fruit of the Spirit is love, joy, peace, longsuffering, gentleness, goodness, faith, meekness, temperance" (Gal. 5:22, 23). All this is simply the accompaniment of the gift of gifts itself, the indwelling of the Spirit of God bestowed on each Christian soul. And this gift dates from the first Christian Pentecost.

## Do Men See God in You?

In Shakespeare's play, *King Lear*, the king asks: "Is man no more than this? Consider him well . . . a poor, bare, forked animal."

The Bible answers that man is not merely a perishing animal gifted with life, a *psuchḗ;* he is an immortal spirit, a *pneúma.* Our Lord and His apostles distinguish carefully between the life of the animal human organism, which becomes extinct at death, and the immaterial, indivisible essence of man, which is indestructible, and which is the seat of the divine Presence.

Thus we see our Lord excusing the disciples for sleeping, instead of watching in prayer with Him in the Garden of Gethsemane, by drawing this distinction: "The spirit indeed is willing, but the flesh is weak" (Matt. 26:41). And at the moment of His death He commends His own spirit into the hands of the Father (Luke 23:46). Here it is obvious that His spirit cannot be the divine and Almighty Being. The word must describe a created being who, in some sense, needed protection and help. It stands for that aspect of Christ's human nature that did not become inanimate at death.

In line with this, Peter speaks of our Lord as having been put to death in the flesh, but quickened in the Spirit, in which also He went and preached to the spirits in prison (1 Pet. 3:19). Here, too, Scripture clearly recognizes that which remains of man after death as a conscious intelligence capable of understanding the good news of God. John alludes to living men as he might speak of disembodied spirits, simply as centers of thought and knowledge: "Every spirit that confesseth that Jesus Christ is come in the flesh is of God" (1 John 4:2). And Paul recognizes that man has a spirit, soul, and body (1 Thess. 5:23).

In other instances Paul contrasts the flesh and the spirit. In Galatians and elsewhere he shows that he usually associates the soul or *psuchḗ* with the animated body and contrasts it with the living spirit, which is above and distinct from it.

A life according to the flesh is a life in which natural or soulish—or call it animal—vitality and instincts control thought and action. A life according to the spirit is a life ruled by the immortal principle within man, which is renewed and reinforced by the eternal Spirit of God. In like manner, the spiritual man (*pneumatikós*) is contrasted both with the man of animal life and the man of the flesh—*psuchikós*, "soulish," or *sarkikós*, "carnal"—as being two aspects of the same thing (1 Cor. 2:14—3:4).

Man, as an immortal spirit, then, is at least potentially the temple of God, and if he is a believer, he is actually so. But we have no explanation of how the Spirit of God enters and tenants a human being. However we know it takes place when a man believes and receives Christ. The presence of the Spirit then, having its seat in the immortal spirit of man, is inseparable from the presence of the incarnate Christ, who renews and transforms man's inner life by incorporation with Himself (see Eph. 2:20–22; Liddon 1891, 329–40).

Why did Paul choose the symbolism of the temple of God, when referring to the human spirit in which the Spirit of God dwells? We can understand this better by examining the meaning and purpose of a temple. The Greek word translated "temple" is *naós* (1 Cor. 3:16, 6:19). This is the same word used for Solomon's Temple and other structures used for the worship of God. The temple localized the deity in the minds of people. That was so particularly with the heathen gods, to whom various temples were dedicated, in each of which the god was supposed to be personally present. In the case of the temple of Jehovah, the meaning is that the manifestation of His presence was localized in the temple that had been built by His direction. He took the name of "Jehovah-Shammah" (Ezek. 48:35), "and the Lord was there!" Of course, God in His intrinsic being can never be localized. However, the revelation of Jehovah was, by His will, manifested in a particular sense in and at the temple at Jerusalem (Acts 17:24; Is. 66:1, 2; 1 Kgs. 8:27).

Why did Paul say that we who believe in Christ are the temple of God? First of all because it is in the believers that God is localized as to His personal revelation. If people cannot see or find God manifesting Himself anywhere else, they ought to be able to see Him revealed in us. But do they? Remember that the reason Paul had to remind the Corinthian Christians that they were the temple of the Holy Spirit was that they were behaving like carnal babies. How could people see Christ in them if they were acting in such an unseemly manner? A temple of God should be a magnificent structure, able to withstand the test of time and fire. It should be constructed of the gold, silver, and gems of worthy works built on the foundation of faith in Christ.

The second purpose served by a temple was as a place for the worship of God. "I will worship toward thy holy temple," declared David in Psalm 138:2. Today we see Muslims worshipping with their faces turned toward their chief temple in Mecca. In the Old Testament we read of Daniel opening his windows and praying toward Jerusalem. And Deuteronomy 12:11 says, "There shall be a place which the Lord your God shall choose to cause his name to dwell there; thither shall ye bring all that I command you."

### Your Heart, God's Altar

Seneca, the Roman historian and philosopher, said, "No one is free who is a slave to the body."

In 1 Corinthians 6:19 Paul specifically refers to the *body* of the believer as the temple of the Holy Spirit. "What? know ye not that your body is the temple of the Holy Ghost, which is in you, which ye have of God, and ye are not your own?" Yet in 1 Corinthians 3:16 he says, "Know ye not that *ye* are the temple of God, and that the Spirit of God dwelleth in you?"

Is there a contradiction here between the body as the temple, and the whole person as the temple? No, both are correct. Our spirit pervades our body, and it is through the works of the body that the spirit, the real person, is shown. This is why the stress is on the body because that is what people can readily discern, while the spirit is immaterial. Paul knew that the body is the last area of man to be brought entirely under the Spirit's influence and power, just as the twigs and leaves are the last parts of a plant to be energized by the sap. Thus the bodily temple presents to us the complete picture of the fully consecrated man (see Cumming n.d., 306–11).

Temples were made of marble and stone and ornamented with precious gems and metals. They were built to be admired. Now, Paul intimates to the Corinthian Christians, you humans have taken the place of marble and stone. This is really a tribute to the dignity of man, created as he was in God's image. He is more than marble and stone, statuary and material splendor.

Everything was done to make the material temples beautiful and to preserve them from decay. Yet the great mass of men were degraded, corrupt, without faith and without aspirations. When Christ came on the scene, He dethroned material splendor and exalted the essential dignity of man. When He took upon Himself a human body, He made humanity the temple of God. The incarnation was the real starting point of human progress and elevation. In the glory of His person we discover our own worth. "Know ye not that ye are the temple of God"—better than the grandest buildings made with hands, richer than all palaces and treasure-laden shrines? You can think God's thoughts, share God's purposes. You can be thrilled with the very emotions of God. Your lives can shine with the very beauty of God. You are His dearest possession, bought not with silver and gold but with His own blood. Redeemed men rather than stone structures now make up the city of God.

A temple was something detached, cut off, separated, taken out of the common, secular, corrupt world, and marked out for other and higher uses. It was not to be employed for any service that was low, vulgar, profane, but only for what was pure and divine. It was to be kept holy, undefiled, and perfumed with the incense of sweet thoughts and prayers. Is your body, are you, thus consecrated, set apart, as the temple of God was? Think what our lives would be like if we could do all things with the consciousness that God is within us, over us, and all about us (see Greenhough 1896, 192–200).

The temple was the place where men offered their sacrifices to God. The central point of worship in the temple was the altar on which the sacrifices were made. Yet how casually we eliminate the altar in the temple of God, which is our body and our total being. "I beseech you therefore, brethren," says Paul, "by the mercies of God, that ye present your bodies a living sacrifice, holy, acceptable unto God, which is your reasonable service" (Rom. 12:1).

The key to the secret of a God-pleasing life is to yield up one's own will, to sacrifice oneself. There never was anything done in this world worth doing, and there never will be till the end of time, of which sacrifice is not the center and inspiration. As Christ is the one true temple, and we become temples of God by partaking of Him, so He is the one Sacrifice for sins forever, and we become sacrifices only through Him. If we are a temple, then we are an altar, and if an altar then a sacrifice. "Ye . . . are built up a spiritual house, a holy priesthood, to offer up spiritual sacrifices, acceptable to God by Jesus Christ" (1 Pet. 2:5). We become sacrifice, priest, temple, all in one; and all for the sake and by the might of that dear Lord who has given Himself a bleeding sacrifice for the sins of the whole world, that we may offer a sacrifice of thanks and praise and self-surrender to Him and to His Father God.

There is an altar and a throne
Within my ransomed heart.
If Christ as Lord shall reign therein,
Then self must have no part.

The choice is mine—oh, may I lay
Self on the altar, Lord, today!

I choose the altar—He alone
Shall evermore possess the throne!

—Avis B. Christiansen

## Is Sinless Perfection Possible?

The temple of God was a holy place, not to be desecrated in any way. You remember that Christ chased the moneychangers and merchants out of the temple in great moral indignation. When Paul said to the Corinthian Christians, "If any man defile the temple of God, him shall God destroy; for the temple of God is holy," he added the words, "which temple ye are." This is the only characteristic of the temple Paul brings out here, that of consecration and holiness.

We associate purity with the word holy or holiness, and rightly so. But the original meaning of *hágios*, the Greek word for "holy," is "separated"—not primarily in a negative sense, from certain things and sins, but in a positive sense, separated unto God. It is well known that Corinth was a flagrantly immoral city. This made a separated life especially difficult for the Corinthian Christians. The world around affected them with a strong downward pull. We encounter the same difficulty today.

After a temple was built, it was consecrated, set apart for God's use and service. If we look at the accounts of such consecrations in Scripture, we see that the temple first had to be purified from pollution by blood and fire, through an atoning sacrifice. Then there was the idea of full surrender of the building and its contents to the service of the one God, followed by an anointing with oil to signify the touch of God's Holy Spirit.

Paul presents three classes of people in 1 Corinthians 3:14–17. First, in verse 14, he speaks of the Christian who has built well on the foundation of Jesus Christ and who will be rewarded for his good works. Second, he mentions the Christian whose work will not prove acceptable but who will himself be saved though "as by fire." These two classes of Christians correspond to those Paul previously described in verses 1–3 as "spiritual" and "carnal."

But there is a third kind of person mentioned in verse 17 who, I believe, corresponds to what Paul previously described as the natural man. He speaks of him in verse 17 as one who corrupts the temple of God. This does not refer to the man's own body but to the all-inclusive temple of God made up of all the believers. And the reason I say this is that, after much study, I have come to the conclusion that Paul refers here to an unbeliever rather than to a carnal believer.

If we took this third kind of person to be a believer of a baser sort than the one whose work was burned up in verse 15, we would face some problems. This would mean that a man could be a believer and still deliberately try to desecrate the temple of God, the church of Jesus Christ as a whole, and the individual believers making up that whole.

The Greek verb used here for "defile" is *phtheírei* (which comes from *phtheírō*). It is in the present tense, indicative mood, active voice, which means that this individual is constantly and purposely working at the destruction of the Christian church, and those living stones, the believers, who make it up. This verb cannot refer to an occasional sin of attacking the church and the believers, but to the destructiveness of someone as an inherent part of his personality. The person who sins naturally, without any feeling of compunction, as part and parcel of his lifestyle, cannot be a regenerated Christian in whom the Spirit of God dwells.

The difference between an unregenerated sinner and a regenerated sinner is that the former sins as a rule of his life, whether he realizes it or not, and feels no need for repentance, while the latter sins as an exception, realizes it, and goes to Christ to confess it and seek forgiveness. The first man runs after sin, while the second, though chased by it, seeks to run away from it.

The Greek verb *hamartánō*, "to sin," in 1 John makes clear the distinction between living in sin and merely falling into sin. Take 1 John 1:10, for instance: "If we say that we did not sin [even once in our lives], we make him [Christ] a liar, and his word is not in us." There is no one who has never sinned, but there are many who, having been saved by the grace of God, do not sin as a matter of course.

Now look at 1 John 2:1: "My children, I write these things to you so that ye may not sin [not even once: *hamartḗte*, 2 aor. subj.]." John knew this to be impossible, of course, even for the Christian, for as James says: "To him that knoweth to do good, and doeth it not, to him it is sin" (James 4:17).

John earnestly desired that those to whom he was writing might not sin even once. But sinless perfection is impossible as long as we are in this body of humiliation and surrounded by so much evil. That is why John proceeds to say, "and if any man sins"—not regularly or as a matter of course, but sins once, as indicated by the verb *hamartánō*, being in the second aorist subjunctive, *hamartḗ*, as in 1 John 2:1. If you sin as an exception in your Christian life, you do not lose your salvation. Such sins are part of the work that is going to be burned up by the fire of God's judgment, but you are going to be saved, as is clearly stated in 1 Corinthians 3:15. We will go into this more deeply in our next study.

Lessons:

1. All that you have worked for can be destroyed in seconds. Even the believer will see his unworthy works burned up in Christ's presence.
2. God in His infinite Spirit indwells the human heart. Scripture affirms that the entire Godhead indwells the believer as He indwelt the temple of the Old Covenant. God's Spirit in the believer is not a transient visit but a permanent presence. This Spirit comes with the gift of a new personal character—a new creation.

3. When Christ took upon Himself a human body, He made humanity the temple of God.
4. We associate purity with the word *holy.* Because Corinth was a flagrantly immoral city, a separated life was especially difficult to establish. We face the same difficulty today.

# 1 Cor. 3:17 — The Man God Will Destroy

*If any man defile the temple of God, him shall God destroy; for the temple of God is holy, which temple ye are.*

No one can be quite so miserable as the man who loves God and knows he has offended Him. It may have been in some forgetful moment when he succumbed to a secret temptation before he could quite stop himself—some book he became intrigued with, some TV program he watched that was unchaste and unholy. It may have been in keeping silent when he should have spoken out in defense of the right, or in speaking out in anger when he should have been silent. Whatever the sin, whether of commission or omission, it hinders his fellowship with the Lord, and he is miserable.

The apostle John tells such a man what he can and will do if he is truly a child of God. He will go to Jesus Christ for forgiveness. In 1 John 2:1 he says, "We have a comforter or a pleader [*paraklḗton*] unto the Father, Jesus Christ the just one." In other words, since Christ is just, He will not destroy a person for a single sin, as He would destroy those who sin habitually because they have never been born-again, and are therefore not indwelt by the Holy Spirit.

Now look at 1 John 3:6: "Every one abiding in him [Jesus] does not sin [*hamartánei*, as a matter of course, constantly]."

Observe what follows: "Every one sinning [*hamartanṓn*, constantly, as part of his nature] hath not seen him [God], nor has he known him." Such a person, who sins because of his unregenerate nature, never saw, never knew God and does not see Him or know Him (*heṓraken*, "hath seen"; *égnōken*, "hath known"; both in the perfect tense).

And then in verse 8 John says: "He doing the sin [*poiṓn*, pres. part., doing as a matter of course, constantly] is from the devil, for the devil sins [*hamartánei*, constantly, this being his nature] from the beginning." In verse 9 John continues, "Every one who is born from God does not do sin." *Poieí* is the Greek verb here, in the present tense, indicative mood, which would mean doing as part and parcel of his nature.

In other words, he who has the divine nature within him does not sin as a rule of life. John tells us why: "Because his [Christ's] seed abides in him, and he cannot sin [*hamartánein*, pres. inf., indicating continuance of sinning]." The reason is given for the second time: "For he has been born of God."

The same truth is found again in 1 John 5:18: "We know that every one who has been born of [the] God does not sin [*hamartánei*, pres. indic., meaning continual sinning]."

The conclusion to which we come, and which is evident in the Word of God, is that he who continually sins cannot be a Christian, a born-again believer. Therefore the one who defiles or corrupts the temple of God constantly, as stated by Paul in 1 Corinthians 3:17, cannot be a Christian in any sense of the word, neither a spiritual nor a carnal child of God.

What is God going to do with him? He will destroy him. This is the identical word used in speaking of a man's actions in defiling God's temple. It is the verb *phtheírō*, but in a different tense. Man is said to *phtheírei*, "corrupt or erode," the temple of God. That is present indicative, denoting continuous action now. But when it speaks of God's action, it is in the future tense, *phthereí.* The King James Version translates the first occurrence "defile" and the second, "destroy," though actually in the Greek they are the same words but in different tenses. Man can defile or corrupt or destroy the temple of God, and God will destroy such a one.

Our body in its present state, for instance, is called "corruptible" (1 Cor. 15:54). It decays, it loses its strength, it deteriorates. In the case of the temple of God we could paraphrase it as "defile or desecrate." What is actually meant by God's action is not specified. "This one that corrupts or defiles or desecrates the temple of God, he will destroy." What kind of destruction is this?

Observe that it is the *person* whom God will destroy, not simply the work that he has done. In 1 Corinthians 3:15 it is clear that the work of the carnal Christian will be burned, while he himself will be saved. But in verse 17, the one who defiles the temple is himself destroyed. Therefore he cannot be the same person as the carnal Christian referred to in verse 15.

The only glimpse Scripture gives us of what is implied by the future destruction of this individual by God is in Galatians 6:8, where *phthorá*, the substantive form of *phtheírō*, is given as the opposite of salvation or eternal life. "For he that soweth to his flesh shall of the flesh reap corruption [*phthorá*], but he that soweth to the Spirit shall of the Spirit reap life everlasting." "Corruption," *phthorá*, versus eternal life. Therefore *phthorá* must be the opposite of eternal life. It must be identical with being lost.

Why is the same word used for the sinner's destruction of the temple and God's destruction of the sinner? Because Paul wants us to understand that God's punishment of the unbeliever is not any greater than what the unbeliever brings upon himself. Each one in reality brings upon himself no smaller destruction than

God will ultimately bring upon him. Punishment is built into the very sin itself.

### God's Indestructible Temple

What does Paul mean by the term "the temple of God" in 1 Corinthians 3:17? The New Testament uses two Greek words to refer to the temple in Jerusalem: *naós* and *hierón,* both translated "temple" in English. However, there is a distinction in meaning between them in Greek. *Hierón* is the whole structure, including the outer courts, the porches, porticoes, and other buildings subordinated to the temple itself. Matthew 24:1, which refers to "the buildings of the temple," is an instance of the use of the word *hierón.*

*Naós*, however, is the proper habitation of God (Acts 7:48; 17:24; 1 Cor. 6:19). It is the same as the *oíkos*, "house," of God (Matt. 12:4; Ex. 23:19). *Naós* is the heart and center of the whole, the Holy, and the Holy of Holies. This distinction existed even with reference to heathen temples. In Greek, *naós* denoted the "abode of the gods," hence "temple." It derives from *naíō*, meaning "to dwell, to inhabit."

The distinction is clear in the account of Zacharias entering the temple (*naós*, "*the* Holy of Holies"), in Luke 1:9. In verse 10 we read that the people were outside praying. They were in the *hierón*, not the *naós*, for only the priest was permitted in the latter.

When we read of the Lord Jesus teaching in the temple, He was in the *hierón*, the outer court (Matt. 26:55; Luke 21:37; John 8:20). Conversations and argument could be held there without any real interruption of the service of God. This temple was always the *hierón*, the porches and porticoes, excellently fitted for such discussions. Actually our Lord never entered the *naós*, the Holy of Holies, during His earthly ministry because being "made under the law" He could not have done so, the right of such entry being reserved for priests alone.

*Naós*, then, in 1 Corinthians 3:16, 17, means God's habitation, the inner sanctuary, so to speak. It is impossible here, however, that reference is made to the temple of Jerusalem, made by human hands. In John 2:21 we read that the Lord spoke of His body as the temple of God. This is equivalent to the statement in Colossians 2:9, "In him [Christ] dwelleth all the fulness of the Godhead bodily." In Christ's actual physical body dwelt the Triune God (*theótēs*, "Godhead," the only place this word occurs in the New Testament; different from *theiótēs* in Rom. 1:20 [see Zodhiates 1972, 108]). And the only reason God could dwell in that body was that it was sinless. But Paul is not referring to Christ's physical body in 1 Corinthians 3:17.

In 1 Corinthians 12:27 Paul says, "Ye are the body of Christ," referring, of course, to the believers, those individuals in whom the Holy Spirit came to dwell, making them the temple of God. As such they constitute the body of Christ, the greater temple. Christ, the great temple of God, is many members, many smaller temples, all baptized into one. "For as the body is one, and hath many members, and all the members of that one body, being many, are one body: so also is Christ" (1 Cor. 12:12).

Thus, in order to understand 1 Corinthians 3:17, we must view it as two distinct declarations: 1) "If anyone corrupts or erodes the temple of God, him will God destroy or erode." That is a hypothetical statement, starting as it does with the word "if." 2)"For the temple of God is holy, which [pl., possibly referring to holy temples] you are." I have been deeply disappointed as I studied every available commentary and sermon on this verse to find that no one ventures an exegesis of it. But I must make an attempt at it.

Let us take the first statement: "If anyone constantly corrupts the temple, God will destroy him—such a one." This person has to be an unbeliever. No believer can constantly seek to tear down Christ or His church, both being the temple of God, or even a believer in whose heart God dwells. Constantly to erode that which is holy—since *naós*, "temple," is practically synonymous with holiness, is to sin; and he who constantly sins cannot be of God. This is active opposition to God Himself, either dwelling in Christ, or in His church, or in the believer.

But is it possible to corrupt the temple of God? It is possible to try but not ultimately to succeed. This is implicit in the present indicative form of the verb *phtheírei.* An unbeliever can try to gnaw away at the temple of God, but he will never succeed in causing it to fall or disappear. No unbeliever's attempts can prevail against Christ, His church, or the individual believer. "And the gates of hell shall not prevail against it" (Matt. 16:18). "Nay, in all these things we are more than conquerors through him that loved us" (Rom. 8:37).

> Though many faults the church may have,
> And wounded though she be,
> Christ's love for her will hold her as
> His love at Calvary.
>
> A thousand foes shall whelm her not,
> And hell shall break her never!
> While Christ shall live the church shall live;
> And Christ shall live forever!
> —Lon Woodrum

## The Destruction of the Wicked

What did Paul mean when he referred to the temple of God in the phrase, "If any man defile the temple of God, him shall God destroy," in 1 Corinthians 3:17? It could not have meant the body or soul of the believer indwelt by the Holy Spirit, as Paul referred to it in the previous verse. No believer can constantly sin, erode, corrupt his own soul or body that is supposed to be holy. This would be antagonism of the natural against the spiritual, with the natural having the supremacy. In the Christian believer, the spiritual nature has dominance, in spite of the fact that the *sarkikós*, "carnal," sometimes rears its ugly head. But if it manages to keep it up there, it indicates that the person is none of Christ's. Romans 8:9,11 says: "But ye are not in the flesh, but in the Spirit, if so be that the Spirit of God dwell in you. Now if any man have not the Spirit of Christ, he is none of his. . . . But if the Spirit . . . dwell in you, he . . . shall also quicken your mortal bodies by his Spirit that dwelleth in you."

Anyone, therefore, who constantly seeks to destroy God's temple, Christ, His church universal or local, His believers, even anyone of them, will be destroyed by God. The verb *phthereí*, "shall destroy," is in the future tense. The unregenerate sinner mistakes God's longsuffering for a non-punitive attitude toward him, but He will mete out a fitting punishment in the end. The same word *phtheírō*, "destroy," used in the first declaration about the unbeliever's attack on the temple of God, is also used of God's retribution or punishment visited on the unbeliever. This is to show that the justice of God demands retribution or punishment commensurate with the sin committed. The unbeliever sought to destroy in his unbelief; therefore God will destroy him.

Observe that God's punishment is not spoken of as testing this man's work, as in verses 13–16 where Paul speaks about the believer's work of faith as a superstructure that is tested by fire, but as being visited on the person himself. The believer's work will be tested, tried, and what is of no permanent value will be burned, but the believer himself will be saved. In verse 17 it is a different story: "Him [this one, *toúton* in Gr.] God will destroy."

Just what this destruction (*phthorá*) is, we are not specifically told in this context. But it must refer to the punishment God will inflict on unbelievers, as proclaimed throughout the Scriptures in varying terminology. For instance, in Matthew 10:28 our Lord said, "Fear him [God] which is able to destroy both soul and body in hell." The word "destroy" here is *apóllumi*, the most commonly used term referring to the punishment of unbelievers. And in Matthew 25:41, 46 we read: "Then shall he say also unto them on the left hand, Depart from me, ye cursed, into everlasting fire, prepared for the devil and his angels. . . . And these shall go away into everlasting punishment: but the righteous into life eternal." The retribution referred to by the verb *phtheírō*, "destroy," in 1 Corinthians 3:17, must be of a similar nature.

In a peculiar way, though, the verb *phtheírō* and its derivatives refer to the body as a material entity. For instance, Paul tells us in 1 Corinthians 15:52 that when the believers hear the last trumpet they will be raised *áphthartoi*, "incorruptible." That is a form of the same word. And then in verse 53 he says, "For this corruptible [*phthárton*, the same word, referring to the human body] will be clothed with incorruptibility [*aphtharsían*]." In other words, man's body in its present state is corruptible, *phthárton*. It deteriorates. And that sphere is not complete as far as our spiritual redemption is concerned.

The redemption of our bodies, referred to in Romans 8:21–23; Ephesians 1:14 and 4:30, is their becoming incorruptible, not subject to deterioration. But apparently this incorruptibility will not characterize the resurrection bodies of unbelievers. In fact, 1 Corinthians 3:17 may refer to just that destruction or deterioration that God is going to cause to continue upon their resurrection bodies. Our Lord Himself said, "They that have done good, unto the resurrection of life; and they that have done evil, unto the resurrection of damnation" (John 5:29). This may very well be it.

Just as there will be "that day" when each believer's work will be manifested (1 Cor. 3:13), known as "the day of Christ," so there will be "that day," the "day of the Lord," when the unbelievers will be judged (see Zodhiates 1972, 126–28).

In connection with both the soul and body of unbelievers, their suffering and punishment is indicated in the awesome warning of Matthew 10:28: "And fear not them which kill the body, but are not able to kill the soul: but rather fear him which is able to destroy both soul and body in hell." Thus we see that the body of the unbeliever will be punished too, and this has to be his resurrection body. We conclude, therefore, that the phrase, "And God shall destroy [*phthereí*] this one," in 1 Corinthians 3:17, may refer to the particular punishment God will bring upon the bodies of unbelievers. While the resurrection bodies of believers will be *áphtharta*, "incorruptible," this will not be so with the bodies of unbelievers.

## How One Man's Sin Can Harm a Whole Church

Some people think that because they give mental assent to what the Bible and the church teach they are Christians. Yet, if Christ has never entered their hearts by faith, they have never experienced the new birth and are really not children of God at all. They are "head" believers, not "heart" believers, and are therefore not those whom Paul refers to in 1 Corinthians 3:16, when he says, "Know ye not that ye are the temple of God, and that the Spirit of God dwelleth in you?"

Now in verse 17 we see that God has promised to destroy anyone who corrupts or erodes this temple. Why? Because "the temple of God is holy." This is the same as saying that Christ, who is the temple of God, is holy, and so are the church and the individual believer who is indwelt by God's Spirit. A believer could never deliberately, as a rule of life, corrupt that which is holy. The temple of God is set apart for God. Therefore anyone who maliciously and deliberately defiles this temple cannot be a holy person in whom God's Spirit dwells. This is not to say that the occasional defilement of sin that occurs in all believers is unforgivable or merits destruction. Not at all. It is defilement or destruction of God's holy temple as a settled practice that is referred to here.

Paul concludes verse 17 by declaring, "who [*hoítines*—in the pl. form] you are." That is, "you collectively" are the temple of God. Each believer is God's temple, and all of them together are the temple of God.

The shift in persons in this verse has sometimes confused people. The verse begins, "If any man [anyone] destroys the temple of God." That is the third person singular, which here refers to any person at any time in history, although of course Paul is primarily addressing his remarks to the Christians in Corinth. These were in various stages of development: some spiritual, mature Christians; others carnal, infantile, atrophied Christians, and all stages in between. But of whatever kind, none of them could possibly be attempting to destroy the temple of God. They were the temple of God themselves; and anyone who attempts to destroy the temple of God cannot logically be the same as the one who is the temple of God.

The so-called destroyer of God's temple, then, is most certainly an unbeliever. That is why Paul does not say, "If you Corinthian Christians destroy your own body, which is the temple of God," but "If anyone destroys the temple of God." It is a mere hypothesis, of course, since it is impossible to destroy this temple because then Satan and his cohorts would be stronger than God. If this were possible, then Christ would be proved a liar when He said to Peter, "The gates of hell shall not prevail ['bear superior power,' *katischúsousin*] against it [i.e., the temple of God]" (Matt. 16:18).

Observe, now, how Paul shifts the subject in the last part of the verse: "which [pl., *hoítines*] *you* are [*humeís éste*]"—that *is*, holy temples or holy temple. Now he is directly addressing the Christians at Corinth. It is as if he were saying specifically to them, "You are God's holy temples. There will be those who will try to corrupt you, to cause you to lose your effectiveness as Christians, to separate you from Christ. But they will not be able to succeed because you are holy, separated unto God. Between you as Christians (and this also applies to the individual Christian) and the world stands Jesus Christ, who is your shield. If they can destroy Him, then they can destroy you, but be assured that since they can never destroy Christ they cannot touch you, much less destroy you."

It is true, of course, that we Christians touch the world at many points. How can we remain unspotted? Consider that little insect of which scientists tell us that, though you immerse it in water, the water never touches it. The reason for this is that the insect carries its own atmosphere with it, and because it is enveloped in a bubble of air it can bid the other element defiance, and though submerged in it remain untouched by it. This is how it is with the Christian. Christ is our holiness. When He indwells us and we dwell in Him, He is our immediate atmosphere. There is no way the enemy can get through Him to us.

However, no man can claim to be the exclusive temple of God. You are as much the temple of God as anyone else in whom Christ dwells. But at the same time you must remember that each individual believer is part of the whole. When you allow anything to defile God's temple, you not only hurt yourself but also all the other members of the body of Christ. None of us lives unto himself or dies unto himself. Each bears a responsibility toward the whole to maintain and promote holiness.

One member of a congregation who is living in open and unrebuked sin can cause God's blessing to be withdrawn from the whole congregation. Paul warned the Corinthians about this in 1 Corinthians 5:6, 7, when he reproved them for tolerating a licentious believer in their midst. There must be constant watchfulness in the church, and in our individual lives, lest we allow pollution to creep in and remain unchecked.

## What Will Your Resurrection Body Be Like?

Man is presently constituted of matter (his body) and of soul-spirit (which is immaterial). God is essentially spirit (John 4:24), that is, immaterial. At will for a season He has taken upon Himself a materially visible form, as in the Old Testament theophanies, and permanently in the incarnation in the person of Jesus Christ.

In their essential being, then, man and God are really distinct. Man is created matter plus finite created spirit, though the highest of God's creation on earth. God is pure spirit, the uncreated Creator. That is one reason at least why man can know God only in part (1 Cor. 13:9). Man holds only a spirit in a sense in common with God, though a created spirit, and if he is a natural man, his spirit is yet unredeemed and can have no real communion with God.

But even when by faith a man appropriates Christ and His work, and thus becomes a child of God, he is still not fully able to know God because he is encumbered by his body. As 1 John 3:2 says, "Now are we the sons [children] of God, and it doth not yet appear what we shall be." That last clause refers to our future make-up, the transformation of our bodies. "But we know that, when he [Christ] shall appear [be made visible to our physical eyes—*ephanerṓthē*], we shall be like him; for we shall see him as he is."

Two things will happen at the appearance of the Lord: 1) The dead in Christ are raised (*aphthartoí*) incorruptible (1 Cor. 15:52); they receive new bodies and are thus able to see the Lord as He really is, not merely as He appeared from time to time on earth. 2) The believers who are alive will be changed and raptured to meet the Lord.

But the unbelievers will also be raised from the dead. This is clearly taught in John 5:28, 29. "Marvel not at this: for the hour is coming, in the which *all* that are in the graves shall hear his voice, and shall come forth; they that have done good, unto the resurrection of life; and they that have done evil, unto the resurrection of damnation."

However, the resurrection of believers will take place at the appearance (*parousía*) of Christ (1 Cor. 15:23), in the manner of Christ's own resurrection (see Zodhiates *Conquering* 1970, 308–24). This is "the first resurrection" according to Revelation 20:6. Luke 14:14 refers to it as "the resurrection of the just." These believers will put on *aphtharsían*, "incorruptibility," and *athanasían*, "immortality" (1 Cor. 15:54). Both words refer to the essence of the resurrection body, not to the soul or spirit. The believer's resurrection body will not be like the present one, subject to deterioration, disease, and finally death (i.e., separation from the spirit-soul). Since the believer's future body will not deteriorate, it will never die. Our spirit will never be separated from our resurrection body. That is what Revelation 20:6 declares and 1 Corinthians 15:54 means (*Ibid.*, 746–57).

But this will not be true with the resurrected body of unbelievers that takes place at the end of Christ's millennial reign on earth, as brought out in Revelation 20:7, 11–14. Punishment is imposed upon unbelievers—punishment inflicted on their soul-spirits, unredeemed because of their rejection of Christ and God's witness to them, as well as on their resurrected bodies. Scripture nowhere says that the resurrected bodies of unbelievers will be incorruptible. Revelation 20:14 tells us that their punishment from God will be the lake of fire, a physical and material punishment. Their resurrected bodies, then, must be so constituted as to be able to suffer physical pain.

That is what I believe the apostle Paul meant in 1 Corinthians 3:17 when he said that "him will God destroy." Destruction will come upon the consistent unbeliever who during his lifetime tried to destroy the temple of God, that is, the church or the individual believer. Bear in mind, also, that destruction here does not mean annihilation. It means pain and physical suffering, in a susceptible body, in contrast to the incorruptibility of the resurrection body of the believer.

In considering the verb *phtheírō*, "corrupt or destroy," in order to see this special relation to the body, I would like to refer to Acts 2:31, where Peter, speaking of Christ as having died, said, "He seeing this before spake of the resurrection of Christ, that his soul was not left in hell [*hádēs*], neither his flesh did see corruption [*diaphthorá*, from *diá*, 'through,' and *phtheírō*]." He refers to the flesh of Christ not having experienced corruption in the grave.

And Paul says in Philippians 3:21, "Who shall change our vile body, that it may be fashioned like unto his glorious body." There you have it. One of the greatest rewards of the believer will be the refashioning of his present corruptible body. And one of the greatest punishments of the unbeliever for corrupting or eroding the temple of God, Christ, His church, and the believer, both in soul and body, will be the corruptibility, the susceptibility to pain, of his resurrected body (see Zodhiates, *What Happens After Death*; Trench 1953, 10–12; Kittel, *Theological Dictionary of the New Testament*, 880–91; Meyer 1877, 100, 101).

LESSONS:

1. A man who loves God and knows he has offended Him is miserable. Because sin hinders fellowship with the Lord, such a man will go to Jesus Christ for forgiveness
2. Anyone who sins continuously does not know God and is not born again. God will destroy him and his work. By contrast, the carnal Christian's works will be burned while he himself will be saved.

3. The body of Christ refers to believers in whom the Holy Spirit dwells and makes into the temple of God. An unbeliever who corrupts (erodes) the temple of God will be destroyed.
4. The unregenerate sinner mistakes God's longsuffering for a non-punitive attitude toward him, but God will mete out a fitting punishment in the end when He destroys him.
5. There are those who try to corrupt Christians so that they might lose their effectiveness, to separate them from Christ, but they cannot succeed.
6. The resurrection of believers takes place at the appearance of Christ when the rapture occurs. Believers will put on incorruptibility, a word which refers to the resurrection body, not to the soul or spirit. The unbeliever's body is resurrected at the end of Christ's millennial reign on earth and is constituted to be able to suffer physical pain.

# 1 Cor. 3:18 | *Wise Men and Fools*

*Let no man deceive himself. If any man among you seemeth to be wise in this world, let him become a fool, that he may be wise.*

If I were to ask you how tall you are, you would be able to tell me exactly because there is a generally accepted standard for measuring length. But if I were to ask you how good-looking you are, you would have to say, "That's a matter of opinion." Beauty is a matter of subjective evaluation. Each of us sets up his own standard as to what is beautiful and what is ugly. And it is the same with wisdom. If I were to ask you how wise you are, your answer would be simply a matter of personal opinion. Wisdom is a quality that cannot be evaluated with complete objectivity.

When the apostle Paul writes to the Christians at Corinth, "Let no man deceive himself," he is cautioning against making false judgments as to who is wise and who is not. The main reason it is so easy to be deceived in this matter is that man has freedom to choose for himself what his standard of measurement is with regard to wisdom, as well as what is ethical and moral and what is not. This is where situation ethics comes in—in man's seeming freedom to set up his own standard and then judge his beliefs and actions by that standard.

Paul does not believe in situation ethics. He categorically denies that man has the right or the wisdom to set up his own standards of wisdom and proper conduct. Let us test the logic of this. Take the physical world as an example. The laws of nature ordained in the beginning by God are inexorable. You cannot defy the law of gravity without incurring serious injury or even death. If you refuse to eat or drink, you will get the same result. No matter how sincere you may be in thinking you can disobey natural law, you will soon find there is little freedom as to what course you must follow in order to live.

Now the same God who made nature and its laws also made man a spiritual being and ordained the laws of the Spirit. These are just as absolute as physical laws. You cannot choose to obey the one and disregard the other without reaping the consequences. The reason man so readily obeys physical law and so thoughtlessly disobeys spiritual law is that the consequences of the first are immediate, while the consequences of the latter are often temporarily postponed.

If you disobey the law of gravity by throwing yourself from the roof, the result of your disobedience is that you fall and in all probability break your neck. If you refuse to eat you will die. But if you refuse Christ's offer of salvation and eternal life, you may not be conscious of any immediate harm that results to yourself as a spiritual being. You do not realize that you are dead in your trespasses and sins (Eph. 2:1).

You can put a dead body into a furnace and it will feel nothing; it has no consciousness of what is taking place. And that is exactly the condition of a spiritually dead person. The effects of his disobedience to God's spiritual laws are not immediately felt. His realization of them is postponed until that day when the Lord will destroy those who try to destroy the temple of God (1 Cor. 3:17)—that is, those who disobey God and His standards and refuse His invitation to salvation, as well as those who try to destroy individual believers and the church by persecution, deliberate deception, and so on.

Paul is here trying to combat the attitude of the natural man, the unbeliever who has rejected the gospel and feels he has done nothing wrong. "I don't need what the gospel offers" was the prevalent attitude of the worldly wise man then, even as it is now. And by taking that attitude he did not feel he was a fool but wise. Not only that, he felt that believers were fools for believing. Is that not the attitude of many so-called wise persons today?

"Let no man deceive himself. If any man among you seemeth to be wise in this world, let him become a fool, that he may be wise," warns Paul. I believe this applies first to the area of faith. It applies to the unbeliever who considers the cross of Christ foolishness. Do not deceive yourself by setting yourself up as the judge of what is wise and what is not. Man cannot be the judge of God. You may think you could have done better than He in establishing the laws of nature and providence, but the fact remains that you lack the power even to alter those laws. You remain their slave and find physical salvation only in blind obedience to them. Disobedience to the laws of nature brings misery.

What, then, makes you think it will be any different with the laws of the Spirit? You have to apply the same standard to the spiritual as to the physical. You cannot regulate the laws of nature because you were not their creator. You have to accept them without criticism. Prove yourself equally wise in accepting Christ and His cross, foreordained by God for your spiritual forgiveness, reclamation, and eternal salvation.

> I look at the sun, and I think of the power
>   And majesty of God;
>
> I look on the earth where the flowers bloom,
>   And I think of the path He trod.

I look at the trees, and think of the wood
Which made His cross of shame;

Then I look in my heart, and see my sin,
And believing, I've life through His name.
—author unknown

## The Day of No Return

To play the fool with regard to matters of spiritual life and death is bad enough, but to think you are being smart while doing it is the crowning folly. When Paul wrote in 1 Corinthians 3:18, "Let no man deceive himself," he was connecting that admonition with the discussion he had carried on in chapters one and two regarding the cross of Christ being the wisdom and power of God for salvation. Now in this verse he warns the natural man to beware of deceiving himself by thinking he is wise when he is really playing the fool.

It is interesting to note that verse 18 begins somewhat like verse 17, in the third person singular. "If anyone destroys the temple of God" and "Let no man deceive himself." Paul is not directly addressing the Corinthian Christians here because this admonition does not primarily affect those of the household of faith. He is speaking to any individual who is criticizing the gospel, trying to destroy it, and calling it "foolishness." He does not say, "If *people* destroy the temple of God," or "Let not *people* deceive themselves." The matter is personal.

Do not think that your personal responsibility can be overlooked or lost in the collective actions of others, whether bad or good. Each man must give an account of himself. You cannot blame the whole for your individual action. You cannot say, "These people deceived me." You are responsible for what you do. If you are an unbeliever who calls the cross of Christ foolishness, you are deceiving yourself. It is time you faced up to the personal consequences of your unbelief.

Just what is the meaning of "deceive yourself"? The Greek word *is exapatátō*, made up of *ék* or *éx*, which intensifies the meaning, and *apatáō*, which means "to beguile." It means to deceive or beguile thoroughly. It occurs in Romans 7:11, where Paul speaks of sin thoroughly beguiling him. Sin can deceive you completely and kill you without your realizing it.

The word also occurs in Romans 16:18, where Paul speaks of those who bring divisions into the Christian church, and who, after serving their own appetites, thoroughly deceive the hearts of the simple ones. How many such deceivers there are today, who fatten their own pocketbooks by slyly perverting the truth and holding out glittering promises contrary to the plain truth of revealed Scripture. "To the law and to the testimony," says Isaiah. "If they speak not according to this word, it is because there is no light in them" (Is. 8:20). You are responsible for examining whatever a speaker says in the light of God's Word—and if it cannot meet that test, you are to reject it.

Again the word occurs in 2 Corinthians 11:3, where Paul warns the Corinthians against being corrupted from the simplicity that is in Christ in the same way that Eve was thoroughly beguiled by the serpent into disobeying God, with the promise that nothing harmful would happen to her. And yet it did. That is the master plan of Satan. "Go on," he says, "do your own thing. You will find new freedom and enjoyment that way." If you believe that, you are only deceiving yourself. Deception is a matter of your own personal sinful will. Eve chose to obey Satan and to disobey God, and she had to bear the responsibility and consequence of acquiescing in the deception.

And finally the word occurs in 2 Thessalonians 2:3, where Paul speaks of the attempts of some to deceive Christians thoroughly about the Second Coming of the Lord. There is more deception about this than almost anything else as far as Christian teaching is concerned. Do not be deceived, says Paul, into thinking that the Lord will come to set up His millennial kingdom until the Antichrist comes, along with the prerequisite apostasy.

But Paul's admonition in 1 Corinthians 3:18 can also apply to the immediate context of verses 10–16, where he speaks of the building of a Christian edifice on the foundation which is Christ. As a Christian, you may think you are building with gold, silver, and precious stones, when actually you are working with wood, hay, and stubble. Just as a day is coming when the unbeliever will reap the results of his unbelief—God's destruction—so you, in the day of Christ, will receive the proper evaluation of your work of faith. The unbeliever *himself* is judged. But for the Christian it is his *work* that is judged. So be careful.

Remember, "All that glitters is not gold." Do not be deceived by specious promises or accept anything less than God's standard of what is right conduct for a Christian. Do not wait for the day of Christ's return to examine your work of faith. Do it now. It is so easy to be deceived in your estimate of what is important and God-pleasing in what you do with your life, your time and money. Stand back and take a good look at the structure you are building. Then make whatever changes God indicates, while you have time to make up at least some of what has been lost. Christ's day of judgment is the day of no return.

## Two Kinds of Wisdom

In first century Corinth, all you had to do to insult a Greek was to question his wisdom. He was not particularly vain of his personal appearance, of his clothes, or of his property, but he was puffed up with intellectual pride. He preferred an empty purse to a thinly furnished head. He would rather be known as a criminal than be regarded as a fool. And yet the apostle Paul did not hesitate to point out the foolishness of the worldly wisdom so dear to the hearts of the Corinthians. "If any man among you seemeth to be wise in this world," he said, "let him become a fool, that he may be wise" (1 Cor. 3:18).

The telling phrase in this verse is what is translated "in this world." In Greek the expression literally rendered is "in the *eon,* this one." The Greek word *aiṓn* should more correctly have been translated "age" instead of "world." *Kósmos* is the Greek word for world, and has to do with space. It is the material world we are aware of through our physical senses. But *aiṓn*, "eon or age," must be thought of in terms of time or the course of history. The Scriptures do not speak of the end of the world, as the translators have led us to believe. The Scriptures do not use the word *kósmos* ("world" as space), but instead they speak of the end of the *aiṓn*, *"age,"* of a particular time period.

Note that in the following passages the word *aiṓn* is incorrectly translated "world" instead of "age": Matthew 13:39, 40, 49; 24:3; 28:20; 1 Corinthians 10:11; Hebrews 9:26. The Scriptures predict that the present period of God's grace will end, and the age of judgment will be ushered in.

The apostle Paul calls the wisdom that is unacceptable to God "the wisdom of the world" in 1 Corinthians 1:20. "Where is the wise? where is the scribe? where is the disputer of this world [*aiṓnos*, the gen. of *aiṓn*, 'age']? hath not God made foolish the wisdom of this world [*kósmou*, the gen. of *kósmos*, 'world']?" The same expression is found in 1 Corinthians 3:19. The wisdom of man which is foolishness to God is of this *kósmos*, this material world.

This all-important word occurs in the writings of John more than a hundred times, meaning most often the material universe or the external framework of things in which man lives and moves, which exists for man and of which he constitutes the moral center (see John 1:9; 3:16; 4:42; 2 Cor. 5:19). "For God so loved the world [*kósmou*, acc. of *kósmos*]"—all sinful humanity living in the material world. Therefore "the wisdom of the world," *kósmos*, means the wisdom of the material world and a sinful humanity. It is the wisdom of sinful man that limits itself mainly to the consideration of the material and not so much to the spiritual. It is materialistic wisdom, and its spirituality if any is deficient and distorted.

God considers the person who thinks only of material things a fool, in spite of the fact that he may consider himself wise. Furthermore, God tells us that most of humanity is materialistic and needs to acquire a regenerated spiritual dimension, at which time their wisdom will be converted from the wisdom of the world to the wisdom of God. God is Spirit in His essence (John 4:24). Man cannot be considered wise by God until such time as he thinks on the higher level of the Holy Spirit. This is essentially the difference between men of the world and men of God. The first are materialists—natural men though they may profess to be spiritual as do some adherents of cults or false religions—and the second are spiritual.

Paul concedes that there are natural men who can think, but their thinking is one-sided—basically materialistic. To look at the universe in all its beauty and regularity and to recognize no unseen personality behind it is to be a fool. The visible things of the creation ought to lead men to realize the existence of the invisible (Rom. 1:20).

The poet Shelley, though able to produce the most beautiful verses about nature, amid the glorious scenery of the Alps and surrounded by the sublime manifestations of God's power, had the audacity to record his atheism by writing against his name in the record kept for travelers, "An atheist!" Another traveler who followed, shocked and indignant at this inscription, wrote beneath it, "If an atheist, a fool; or if not, then a liar!"

The difficulty with the person who denies the existence of anything beyond his physical senses is that he gives himself wholly to the material universe, placing all his thoughtful ingenuity in the crucible of matter. He is wise in the things of the world. He discovers the laws of nature. He depends fully upon their precision. Yet he thinks there is no inconsistency in saying there is no God.

What a calamity to see those considered truly wise by the world acclaimed by their fellows as great, and yet to be considered fools by God! Their minds are blinded in the direction of the spirit. All is basically matter, says many a wise man of this world.

## Portrait of a Foolish Wise Man

A Sunday School teacher said to her class of juniors,

> Some say that the moon, the stars, the sun, and the planet on which we live—the earth—just happened, and that there was no all-wise and all-powerful Creator who made them. I hold in my hand a small wristwatch. Suppose I should say, "This wristwatch just happened. Its screws, its springs, its wheels, its case, its hands, its face, and its crystal began to twirl and twist and finally came together just as you see it in my hand." Why, you would say, "Poor teacher! A cog has slipped in her mind." You would be right if I should make such a claim for my watch. Yet people who are otherwise sensible and intelligent say the universe just happened. They deny that a great and mighty God created all things and established order throughout the universe.

A man who thinks that way, and lives for this world alone, is not generally regarded as a fool, especially if he is moderately successful. The rich man in the parable of Luke 12:16–21, who was heaping up an immense store of goods, planning to build new barns in which to place them, and calculating on an easy, luxurious, and well-endowed old age, had not the slightest idea that there was any deficiency of sense in these proceedings. He was smart and thrifty, with an eye on the main chance. It never occurred to him that anyone would regard him as a fool. And the probability is that all his neighbors applauded his prudence, sagacity, and judgment. In fact, this applause and approval by the people of the world for the materialist is suggested by Paul in 1 Corinthians 3:18: "If anyone among you thinks himself to be wise in this age." Not only does this person consider himself wise, but others like him, seeing how materially successful he is, consider him wise, too. Who would have considered this rich, successful farmer a fool? Not the world.

But God did. He said, "Thou fool, this night thy soul shall be required of thee" (Luke 16:20). And that is just what he was—a fool. He was preparing for old age, but not for what would follow.

In 1 Corinthians 3:18 as well as 2:6, Paul calls the wisdom of the man of the world "the wisdom of this age"—not "of this world," as he refers to it in 1 Corinthians 1:20. As we saw, "the wisdom of this world" refers to the wisdom of materialism. But "the wisdom of this age" is the wisdom of the here and now. It is that human wisdom that shuts out eternity from man's consideration. This philosophy of "Who cares what happens later?" is a natural sequence of materialism. Matter is transitory, ephemeral, whereas the spirit is eternal.

The nature of worldly wisdom, then, is that it concerns itself with material things, with transitory concerns in the here and now. It is contemporary wisdom. The consistently worldly wise individual seeks the goods of this world, the possession of riches and influence, reputation and power, together with all the conveniences and pleasures possible. In pursuit of his purpose he is not always scrupulous in his choice of means. Whatever promises to make him successful in material acquisitions is wise as far as he is concerned.

What he appears to the world is important, not what he really is in the sight of God. He is therefore careful to conceal his true nature, even from himself at times. He may even be more devoted to the achievement of his materialistic ends or natural accomplishments than the Christian is to the achievement of his spiritual goals. Our Lord said it in plain words: "The sons of this age [*aiṓnos*, the gen. of *aiṓn*] are brainier [wiser, *phronimṓteroi*] than the sons of light in their own generation," (Luke 16:8).

The contemporary materialist in any historical age is a man of selfish disposition. Friends, country, duty, honor, are often secondary when his own interest is at stake. His mind is clever, but his heart is hard. He is a man who has few loving friends. You remember how few friends the prodigal son ended with? Similarly, as long as the materialist is successful and important, he is surrounded by opportunists who profess to be friends.

He thinks it wise not to trust others. He sees others as a projection of himself. He proceeds on the assumption that all men are carrying on self-interested designs of their own, and of course he is ever on his guard against them. He is wrapped up in himself. He is wise in that he is not an open enemy, but nevertheless he cannot but be suspicious and unforgiving.

He considers that man wise in our world today who has the ability to advance himself materially, even over the wreckage of others. He is the clever person who can flatter and deceive, who can smile in your face while he is contriving plans for your ruin. He does not basically care about what is right and honorable, only what is expedient and useful to serve his own ends.

Why does God detest such wisdom? Well, how would you like to have such a man as your brother, husband, son, employer? Could you honor such a man as a parent, or respect him as a judge, or wish to live under his political leadership? Of what real value, then, is that boasted wisdom of the world that can neither evoke love, nor produce trust, nor command inward respect?

### When It Is Wise To Be a Fool

Hardly a day passes that we do not hear of some political figure being found out in a shady deal, whether it be in taking bribes or cheating on his income tax. But the great number of those who are not found out would probably astound us. Lawyers grow fat on advising wealthy clients how to get around laws that were meant for the protection of the people. Nevertheless, a day is coming when God will say, "Thou fool, this night thy soul shall be required of thee" (Luke 12:20). All their vaunted wisdom will avail them nothing under the withering fire of divine judgment.

Makc no mistake, however; the wise man of this age may be a person of considerable abilities. He may display talents, genius, learning, and courage. But if he has no regenerate spiritual values and no belief in eternity he is devoid of true morality and righteousness in God's estimation. That is the principal evil of our day. We have too many wise men without God and eternal values. They are clever at doing their own thing but not in pleasing God. An evil man with a brilliant mind is far more dangerous than a stupid one. Our world is honeycombed with such clever wise men at every level of business and government; hence the unprecedented moral mess we find ourselves in.

Paul's advice to such a man who thinks himself wise is to become a fool. The verb translated "thinks" in Greek is *dokeí*, which refers to man's own mental estimate of himself and not to what he really is. That fully agrees with the command with which 1 Corinthians 3:18 begins, "Let no man deceive himself." And what is that deception? To think himself wise when he is not. And the remedy? To "become a fool." Not "think himself a fool," but to become one (*mōros génesthō*).

The word "fool" here means "something that the world will consider foolish." When you confess your sinfulness, the world will call you "soft in the head." Who acknowledges his guilt nowadays? Cover-up is the order of the hour and the height of worldly wisdom. The worldly wise individual feels that only a weak-minded person or a child would believe that by looking to the crucified Christ in faith he could receive eternal life and have his whole being transformed.

Interestingly, in Modern Greek the word for baby is *mōron* (from which we get the Eng. word "moron"). The reason for this is that a child is not yet intellectually developed. Yet did not our Lord tell us that unless we become like little children we cannot enter the kingdom of God? It is not enough to think of yourself as a little child; you must actually become one in recognizing your dependence upon the guidance and sustenance of God.

Man is a fool who thinks only of material things and of this present world, no matter how wise he considers himself to be. Stop thinking of yourself as wise in being what you are, is Paul's advice, and become exactly the opposite of what you are. Instead of seeking to be wise in the eyes of the world, become a fool according to the estimate of God. And when you say, "Lord, I am a fool in not thinking of Thee and eternity," He will make you truly wise. God will come to dwell within you, and you will live with eternity's values in view, and not just for the here and now. But no one can be filled by God unless he first empties himself. "Become a fool so that you may become wise"—wise unto God, that is.

The daughter of an arrogant and defiant unbeliever became critically ill. The girl's mother, a devout Christian, had often prayed for her daughter's conversion. As the girl grew progressively worse, she said to her father, "Daddy, Mother has often tried to get me to become a Christian, but your influence has kept me from trusting Christ to save me from sin. I know I am going to die, and I am not ready to die. Am I to follow your infidelity, or am I to take my mother's God and trust her Savior to save me?"

The father was deeply moved. He greatly loved his daughter. Weeping, he said, "Daughter, my infidelity holds out no hope for you in this dark hour. In God's name, turn from it. Take your mother's God and your mother's Christ and your mother's Bible."

"For the wisdom of this world [*kósmou*, the gen. of *kósmos*] is foolishness with God" (1 Cor. 3:19). That is the reason you should become a fool. When you become spiritually wise, you will be considered a fool by the worldly wise. But it is far worse to consider yourself wise and to be a fool in the estimate of God. It is better to have the world think you a fool than actually to be one as far as eternal values are concerned.

One of Aesop's fables tells of a lottery that Jupiter held for the gods. It happened that the best prize, "wisdom," fell to his daughter Minerva, upon which a general murmur arose that the wheel had been rigged. In order to punish and silence the protesters, Jupiter awarded them the prize of "folly" instead of "wisdom," and they went away perfectly well contented. And from that time, it is said, the greatest fools have looked upon themselves as the wisest men.

### When Is It an Honor To Be Called a Fool?

The apostle Paul was speaking from personal experience when he said, "We are fools for Christ's sake" (1 Cor. 4:10). The local rulers appointed by Rome—Festus, Felix, Agrippa and all that class—regarded the Christians as deranged. And it certainly did seem an absurdity for any man to choose such a life as that which Paul lived. He was well-born, well-educated, with marvelous energy and exceptional intelligence. There were few positions in the Jewish nation, and perhaps not many in the Roman Empire, to which he might not have aspired. He certainly had it in him to acquire great wealth and distinguished honors.

Instead he preferred a career of persecution, poverty, and continual hardship. He met with tears, stripes, and imprisonment at every step—with no money at the end, no reputation, only ignominy, a violent death, and an unknown grave. If such a man were found today, most people would call him just what the world called Paul—a fool. But in God's eyes he was supremely wise, and time has vindicated that judgment. This man has a name that will endure forever. He has won a crown of eternal honor, and, if we had to choose, every born-again believer would a hundred times rather be a St. Paul, with all his sufferings, than the prosperous man of the parable whom the Lord called a "fool."

Was not our Lord also accused of madness by those who persecuted and crucified Him? His life, with its hunger, loneliness, and weariness, its high ideals and daily rejections, and its apparent utter failure at the last, seemed to that dark, blinded world a senseless, aimless, insane sacrifice. Yet now we declare that in Him are hid all the treasures of wisdom and knowledge. And though the world called Him a fool, today millions adore Him as divine.

The world will call you a fool, too, if you actually follow the footsteps of the Lord Jesus. An honest life will not always be called wise; a life of purity will occasionally win cheap sneers. If you pursue great ideals; if you kneel in prayer; if you spend your energies in self-denying labors; if you give freely to help others; if you often lift your eyes from the dust toward the heavenly crown; if you seek God's "Well done!" rather than the praise of men, you are sure to be called by the baser sort, as all good men have been, a fool.

Take it with a smile. Pin the name upon your breast as a mark of honor. For it is an honor to have that name conferred by those who have no greatness of soul. You are following in the way of God's wisdom, and it is of infinitely more consequence, both now and hereafter, that you should not be deemed a fool by Him, whatever you seem to be in the eyes of men.

Has not the Lord demonstrated that His wisdom is sufficient? Did He not take the weak things of this world to confound the mighty? In the early history of Israel, when an unorganized, badly scattered people needed a wise ruler, God passed by those in places of eminence, and over the seats of learning, that in the open fields He might crown David, a shepherd lad.

Later on, when Jerusalem was a ruined city, overgrown with weeds and briers, God ignored commanding generals and ruling monarchs and instead honored Nehemiah, whose conquering courage rebuilt the city.

When, mad with power and wild excesses of sin, the mighty nation of Babylon needed restraint, God stepped over the royal houses as though they were playthings upon the nursery floor and lifted Daniel, an exile, to become the condemning conscience for those who had slain their consciences. He became a radiant hope for those who were enslaved and had lost all courage.

During His earthly ministry, whom did the Lord first choose to proclaim His gospel and confound the learned? Fishermen. Was He a fool? The events prove otherwise.

Not that Christianity places a premium on ignorance, but even common sense will tell you that the highly educated man is not necessarily the wisest. Often such men are theorists, who know all the answers from books but lack the ability to relate their knowledge to the practicalities of a given situation. Highly educated economists hold widely divergent views on how to control inflation during times when it is soaring out of control. Government officials seek to regulate crop production, only to find they have created shortages or surpluses.

And when men enlarge their horizons by acquiring all possible knowledge, they still find they cannot be saved by learning alone. Ultimate success depends upon being in right relationship with God and man. That is true wisdom, and the humblest individual may possess it (see Blair 1818, 340–58; Anderson 1922, 92–93; Greenhough n.d., 142–44).

**LESSONS:**

1. God who made nature and its laws also made man a spiritual being and ordained the laws of the spirit. Although these laws are as absolute as physical laws, the physical law is immediate while the consequences of the spiritual are often postponed. Man readily obeys physical law while thoughtlessly disobeying the spiritual.
2. Be not deceived. Deception is a matter of your own personal sinful will. Some people attempt to deceive Christians about the Second Coming of the Lord. However, the day is coming when the unbeliever will reap the results of unbelief.
3. The wisdom of man is of this world and is foolishness to God.
4. The rich man laid up an immense store of goods, planned new barns, and calculated a well-endowed retirement for himself. This man considered himself wise, as did those who knew him, but God accounted him a fool.
5. The man who thinks only of worldly things to the neglect of spiritual things is a fool. No one is filled with the Spirit of God who is not self-emptied. From the perspective of eternity, it is better to have the world think you are a fool than actually to be one.
6. Christianity does not place a premium on ignorance, but common sense says that a highly educated man is not necessarily the wisest. When men enlarge their horizons, they still find they cannot be saved by learning alone.

# 1 Cor. 3:19 | *How To Keep a Receptive Heart*

*For the wisdom of the wise is foolishness with God. For it is written, He taketh the wise in their craftiness.*

To become a fool as Paul advises in 1 Corinthians 3:18 is to become humbly receptive to outside truth. As long as human beings feel that they know enough through their own personal discoveries, they consider themselves wise. But Phillips Brooks warns against such complacency. In his illuminating sermon, "The Principle of the Crust," he says, "Life tends to encrust itself, to imprison itself within itself. Its crust needs to be constantly broken and returned into the general mass out of which it was formed, in order that the best influences may be received."

Observe the language of Paul: "If anyone thinks himself to be wise"—not to have wisdom, but "to be wise." This is not something that he has acquired from the outside world, but something that he has developed from within himself. It is not like money that is added to his possessions from an outside source. He can lose that just as easily as he can acquire it. But it is "being wise"—a state that develops from within.

As Brooks says: "No other possession so becomes a very part of the possessor. The thing you know is part of you. No man can take it from you. Its subtle essence is in your heart and character. A man loves what he is more than what he has." Therefore in Christianity, before you can become what God wants you to be, you have to humble yourself by putting aside what seems to be your wisdom. You have to lose before you can gain.

Our Lord said it clearly and succinctly: "Whosoever will save his life shall lose it" (Mark 8:35). "Sell all that thou hast" (Luke 18:22). "Except ye be converted, and become as little children" (Matt. 18:3). And Paul adds, "The man who considers himself wise must become a fool to gain true wisdom, the wisdom of God which comes from God."

Two kinds of obstacles may prevent a power from outside reaching you. One is external—something that stands between God and you. That could be the devil, or another person, or another philosophy—whatever obstacle originates outside yourself, something other than yourself.

But the second may be your very self as the surface of your heart and mind harden, like the top that hardens on a loaf of bread and becomes the crust. This crust, made of the very same substance as the bread itself, keeps outside elements from reaching the soft part of the bread within the loaf. The crust is self-produced protection from outside influences.

Again, your inner barrier may be compared to a river that freezes over. The ice on top is the river's own water, frozen. It shuts out the river's water from the sunshine and the rain.

A third illustration is that of the ground when it is trodden down hard. That is the very earth itself with a crust on top. It is hard and impenetrable. No seed can enter into the soft part of the ground to grow into a fruitful plant.

The crust is bread itself; the ice is the very water of the river; and the hard ground is the very soil of the earth. It is the very substance of the thing that it imprisons. It is not foreign material, but the thing itself, grown hard and rigid. It shuts the soft and tender and receptive portions of the thing away. The influences from outside are powerless to reach it. Not until the crust is broken, and the ice melts once more into the stream, and the hardened ground is crumbled into the general system of the soil again, can outside influences enter into their substance.

That is exactly what happens to man. The crust, the ice, the hardened soil must be broken up. His own wisdom has to go. What he is and has is the barrier to God reaching him with His wisdom. A child is fit for the kingdom of God because he has not yet formed a crust.

One of these crusts is *prejudice.* That is simply the premature hardening of opinion. A man may be thinking and studying, seeking after truth. He is open to all light and influence. He is ready to be taught on every side. The surface of his life is free. But suddenly or gradually the man stops. It is as if a cold wind touched the stream and froze it. The water turns itself into a wall of ice. Nothing can break through it. It is a crust. It is made of the thought it imprisons. This is the essence of all prejudice. And man is so blind that he calls it wisdom!

Another crust is *formalism.* Truth utters itself in outward symbols, such as in making the sign of the cross. When repeated three times, this is supposed to express belief in the Trinity, as well as life through the crucified Christ. Forms are not self-defeating if they express an inner faith. But when they cease to do this they become empty formalism, shutting outside truth from reaching character. Forms ought to be the medium through which truth comes to the inner nature. Be wary of formalism—not necessarily by discarding forms but by keeping them soft, refusing to let them grow hard. When they cease to express faith, break them up, return them to the ground again, and ask God to feed you directly with His truth. Reformation is nothing but breaking up of a formalism that has become a crust.

## The Knowledge That Can Keep You Ignorant

Jonathan Swift once observed, "A man should never be ashamed to own he has been in the wrong, which is but saying, in other words, that he is wiser today than he was yesterday."

In our last study we were speaking of crusts that form out of a man's own nature, that prevent truth from reaching him from the outside. One was the crust of prejudice, another the crust of formalism.

A third crust is *the conceit of knowing*. The most ignorant person may well be the one who thinks he knows just about everything. His knowledge becomes the crust that shuts out further possibilities of illumination. The eagerness to know more can only come to him through a recognition of the inadequacy of that which he knows of himself. The moment he recognizes he knows nothing in comparison to what is to be known, he stands a chance of absorbing the most. That is what Paul means by his admonition that we become fools—getting rid of the crust of life in order that life itself may be open to light from outside.

God sometimes uses a crisis to break the crust of our supposed wisdom and knowledge. We lose a loved one, lose all our money, become homeless, have our prejudices knocked down by some humiliating discovery. We are crushed. The crust is gone. The sunshine enters the substance of our being. When we find ourselves without answers, we recognize what fools we have been right along, and we allow God's wisdom to penetrate our crust. Thank God for such crisis experiences. They help to break the crust of our self-sufficient wisdom and turn us to Himself. Is not that what happened to Paul on the road to Damascus? Hot in pursuit of Christians whom he believed to be God-dishonoring heretics, he was struck down by the illuminating manifestation of the Son of God speaking from heaven. All his preconceived notions were knocked flat. All the conceit was taken out of him, and he humbly opened his heart to receive that "wisdom that is from above" (James 3:17).

In 1 Corinthians 3:19 Paul intimates that the wisdom of God should take the place of man's own futile wisdom. "Let him become a fool so that he may become wise." We tend to become what we yearn to become, but we are unable to achieve this without permitting Someone from outside ourselves to enter in, namely God in Christ. When we become "fools" in this sense, we do not become ignoramuses. What happens is simply that the crust of our conceit is broken so that we may receive a higher, heavenly wisdom.

The man who develops a crust is ignorant because he isolates himself from God's wisdom. The opposite of human wisdom is not human ignorance but divine wisdom. The Christian life is not one of ignorance but of that higher wisdom that cannot be obtained through a man's own efforts. This wisdom is a separate, a higher region of knowledge than that to which we generally give the name, but it is knowledge still. It is the apprehension of truths, of those vast truths that the senses cannot discover or the intellect evolve, but which through the open avenues of the spirit enter in and occupy the life.

This spiritual and eternal wisdom is the ultimate treasure of the human soul. When by God's grace we break up the crusted conceit of human wisdom, its fragments make part of the simplified and softened human nature into which God can pour the higher wisdom of His grace. Only the overwhelming love of God taking possession of our soul can accomplish this. This is the new birth. It is Christ being born in the human heart. It is His wisdom replacing ours. To know Him is the only satisfactory attainment of a human life. If we reach that, whatever else we miss, our lives are rich. Missing that, whatever else we gain, our lives are poor. Reaching that, whatever else we gain, our knowledge of God will dominate it all (see Brooks n.d., *The Mystery of Iniquity and Other Sermons*, 153–70).

Justin Martyr, one of the early church fathers, started out in his youth on a search for the highest wisdom. He tried a stoic, who told him that his search was vain. He turned to a second philosopher, whose greed for money quenched any hope of assistance from him. He appealed to a third, who required a preliminary knowledge of music, astronomy, and geometry.

Just think of a soul thirsting after God and pardon and peace, being told, You cannot have any of this until you have a college degree. How many would be shut out from God's presence! In his helplessness, Justin Martyr applied to a follower of Plato, under whose guidance he began to have some hope that he was on the right track.

But one day, when earnestly groping after the truth, he was met by a nameless old man who talked to him about Jesus Christ. Immediately he felt he was at the end of his quest. "Straightway," says Justin, "a flame was kindled in my soul," and if not in the actual words, yet in spirit he sang, "Thou, O Christ, art all I want;/More than all in Thee I find."

LESSONS:

1. In Christianity before you can become what God wants you to be, you have to humble yourself by putting aside the wisdom of the world. You must lose this to gain Christ, the Wisdom of God.
2. A man is wiser today than yesterday if he admits he is wrong. The wisdom of God should take the place of our own futile wisdom. Spiritual, eternal wisdom is the ultimate treasure of the human heart.

**1 Cor. 3:19–21a**

# *Caught in God's Net*

*For the wisdom of the wise is foolishness with God. For it is written, He taketh the wise in their own craftiness. And again, the Lord knoweth the thoughts of the wise, that they are vain. Therefore let no man glory in men.*

To support his argument that human wisdom is worthless without the wisdom of God, the apostle Paul refers to a saying from Job 5:13, "He taketh the wise in their own craftiness." Read that whole chapter of Job to see the shaky foundation on which man's safety and possessions rest. God can interfere suddenly and resolutely, causing man to recognize how little he can trust in his own wisdom and sufficiency.

The Greek word for "He taketh," in 1 Corinthians 3:19, "He taketh the wise in their own craftiness," is the present participle *ho drassómenos*, from *drássomai*. Nowhere else does this verb occur in the New Testament. Essentially it means "to grasp with the hand, to lay hold of, to trap." It implies that this activity of God is an essential part of His character. He does not just do this occasionally, but, whenever He sees the conceit of a man who thinks himself wise and secure in his own way, God acts to bring him to Himself. He takes hold of him in His hand. He catches him. Our crises are God-given to break up the crust of our vaunted human wisdom.

The verb *drássomai* implies speedy action, taking advantage of an opportunity. In fact, in Modern Greek it is used in the expression *drássomai tḗs eukairías*, "I take advantage of an opportunity." God takes advantage of the humanly wise when they are showing their craftiness, in order to rescue them from themselves. The word "craftiness" in Greek is *panourgía*, which comes from *pan*, "all," and the root *érgon*, "work" (see also Luke 20:23; 2 Cor. 4:2; 11:3; Eph. 4:14). All the work of earthly wisdom is cheating, is craftiness, simply because man in his sinful state seeks his own.

God has a way of catching him in this. One of the most dangerous characters in the world is a clever person who is not saved by the grace of God. He is crafty. But he cannot escape God's net. That is what the expression from Job 5:13, quoted by Paul in 1 Corinthians 3:19, means. "He taketh the wise in their craftiness."

But Paul quotes another saying from the Old Testament, as found in Psalm 94:11, when he says in 1 Corinthians 3:20, "The Lord knoweth the thoughts of the wise, that they are vain." In the quotation from Job 5:13 we are told that God hastens to catch the worldly wise in all that they do, in their works. In this quotation from Psalm 94:11 we are told that God really does not need to wait to see their works in order to know what they are up to. He knows their thoughts before they become works (*érga*, in *panourgía*).

The word "thoughts" in Greek is *dialogismoús* (pl. acc.of *dialogismós*), which is made up of *diá*, "through," and *logismoús*, "thoughts, reasonings, opinions, concepts." It is those things that pertain to *lógos*, "intelligence." God has a way of penetrating the mind of the worldly wise. He knows what their concepts are before they become evil works. It is as if Paul wants to show us that the thoughts of the worldly wise cannot help but result in craftiness. And God allows them to be demonstrated in evil works so that there can be no excuse. Who can prove a man guilty merely on the grounds of evil thinking? It is only in the execution of evil that a man can be proved guilty and receive punishment.

God knows the thoughts of the worldly wise to be vain, declares Paul. In Greek the word for "vain" is *mátaioi*, "aimless, empty of any beneficial result." The thoughts of the worldly wise can never be beneficial; they are hollow. Take God out of human wisdom and it is hollow, aimless, and cannot accomplish anything of genuine significance. Put God into the human mind and heart and the result will be good works and beneficial thoughts.

It is so easy to deceive yourself as to how wise you are. And it is equally easy to boast about the wisdom of other human beings of whom you hold a high opinion. Paul, as a master psychologist, warns us about both tendencies. In 1 Corinthians 3:18 he tells us not to deceive ourselves about being wise in the things of this world. That is, we are not to measure ourselves by standards that are earthly and temporary. Then in verse 21 he says, "Therefore let no one boast in men." The danger is that you will elevate another human being in your esteem to such a degree that you will miss the good in others. Watch your opinions about yourself and others. That is good down-to-earth advice from a man of God who was also a keen observer of human nature.

You remember that Paul closed chapter one of this epistle with the words, "Let him that boasts, boast in the Lord" (v. 31). Man has to boast about something or someone. Boasting or glorying or being proud of somebody or something is not necessarily evil. It all depends on the object of your pride. Whom and what you boast about is very revealing. If you boast about yourself, you are conceited. If you boast only about other men, you are misguided. If you boast in the Lord you are committed to Him. Of whom you speak, and what you say about them, show the character of which you are made.

**Lessons:**

1. The wisdom of the world is altogether worthless. God interferes in the life of the man who trusts his own wisdom. He destroys the wisdom of the wise.
2. A person not saved by the grace of God is crafty. However, he cannot escape God, for God knows the thoughts of men before they think them. It is so easy to deceive ourselves. Man has to boast about something or someone.

# 1 Cor. 3:21 — *Give Glory to God, Not Men*

*Therefore let no man glory in men. For all things are yours.*

Two things may be deduced from Paul's warnings about boasting. In fact they stand out like commands, since both verbs are in the third person singular present imperative: *exapatátō*, "let him not deceive himself" (1 Cor. 3:18), and *kauchásthō*, "let him boast."

First, your wisdom can deceive you when it comes to judging those things that transcend the world and time. Second, no man is worthy of your boasting when it comes to spiritual truth, since no man has it all concentrated in himself. "Therefore let no man boast in men," says Paul. Since he is addressing Christians, he refers to boasting by believers; and by the word "men" he means primarily those who teach spiritual truth. In the case of those in Corinth, these teachers were Paul, Apollos, and Cephas or Peter. No teacher, not even I, Paul says, has so much spiritual wisdom that he deserves to become the object of our boasting.

It is possible that we preachers, sometimes unconsciously—but too often I am afraid consciously—seek to draw admiration to ourselves, forgetting we are but men. Martin Luther said, "I am more afraid of my own heart than of the Pope and all his cardinals. I have within me the great pope—self." And R. A. Torrey stated, "I believe more promising Christian workers have failed through self-sufficiency and self-esteem than through any other cause."

One day as G. Campbell Morgan prayed, the Lord seemed to say to him, "Which do you want to be—a servant of Mine or a great preacher?" Morgan replied, "May I not be both, Lord?" A spiritual struggle ensued as he thought, God may want me to be an unknown minister in an obscure place. Then Morgan submissively prayed, "O Lord, my greatest wish is to be a servant of Thine!" The Lord responded by making him one of the greatest preachers of his time.

Let what an American novelist said become the guideline of every one of us who preaches God's truth: "The best sermon is not the one which causes the hearers to go away praising the speaker, but the one which makes them go away thoughtful and serious, and hastening to be alone."

The greatest danger for any preacher is to overhear someone telling others how great he is. Let us who preach God's Word be careful lest we encourage followers of truth to degenerate to the point of becoming followers of us. The burden rests as much upon us to discourage others from boasting about us as it does upon the boasters to abstain from idolizing us. He who secretly exults in such boasting sins more than the one who does the boasting.

Certainly it was not jealousy that prompted Paul to warn against boasting of human preachers. In naming those spiritual teachers who were being boasted about, he places himself first. It made no difference to him whether they were bragging about Paul, or Apollos, or Cephas; it was wrong. He might even have been more tolerant if their boasting had not included him.

Ask yourself, preacher, how you would feel if some of your people were praising other preachers and not you. Would you be hurt and offended, or would you rededicate yourself to the Lord? Paul was not angry because the Corinthians included two other human stars in their spiritual sky. He would have been far more upset, I believe, if they had considered him the only star in their spiritual horizon. He was determined to raise them above the stage of glorying in men. May his warning raise our own sights as preachers and followers to glory in the Lord and not in men.

When a person glories in any particular man, it is an indication that his concept of greatness or holiness is small and inadequate. There is an unconscious attempt to imitate greatness and holiness. But these are qualities that cannot really be imitated. They are developed from within through God's own work in us. And when a person glories in any particular thing of an earthly kind, it may be that he has not much else to glory in, or at least is not conscious of having much else. You do not find people of the highest position and attainments boasting much in things. Glorying or boasting is a sign of deficiency in one direction or another.

This was the general principle that Paul went upon in saying, "Let no man glory in men. For all things are yours." If the Corinthians had realized that all things were theirs in Christ, they would not have gloried in men or in anything else. If Christians today only knew that all things are theirs in Christ, they would cease to glory in their money, or their property, or their friends, or themselves.

Paul wants to give us a larger vision of our possessions as believers. Why glory in something that is less than what we possess? We possess Christ, and in and through Him we possess all things. When we see that we have all things and the Creator and Sustainer of all things, we cease boasting about anything or anyone in particular. We only boast in the Lord. As Paul states in 1 Corinthians 1:5, "That in all things [or in everything] ye were enriched in him." When you have so much in Christ, why boast about any gift or any man or anything? "All things are yours."

**Putting God First**

How can you tell whether you put the Lord first in your life, or whether another person preempts the glory that should rightfully be His? The sin of glorying and boasting in men is as prevalent among Christians today as it was among the Corinthian Christians of the first century. Therefore we need a few diagnostic guidelines to help us spot the symptoms of this sin of the spirit.

Remember God's command that we should have no other gods before Him. This includes the deification of human beings—a perilously easy thing to do. We become so wrapped up in a husband or wife, a father or mother, a son or daughter, or even a preacher, that the person may very well become a god to us. If anyone whom you see closely and toward whom you feel intimately blurs your view of God and His sovereignty, tread softly. You may be in danger of overstepping the line between a proper love and regard for a fellow human being and the adoration that should be given only to God.

It only takes a half dollar held close to your eye to blind you to the sight of the sun. Alexander the Great, full of pride over recent triumphs, once came upon that wise philosopher Diogenes who was basking in the glory of the noonday sun. The powerful ruler condescended to speak to the philosopher, asking if there was anything Alexander could do for Diogenes. "Yes," was the reply, "Alexander can step aside from between me and the sunshine." Diogenes was wise in this respect. Alexander was great in conquest, but he was a fool to think he was more important to Diogenes than the sun. Anyone who considers himself great enough to blot out God from your full sight, worship, and glory is a fool, and you should not boast in him but should tell him to get out of the way.

Beware of anyone who says he can do what only Christ can do for you. Anyone who tries to mediate between you and God for any personal gain ought to be regarded as one over whom you should not boast.

Watch out for that person who seeks your admiration for what he does for God. In fact, watch out for that same tendency in yourself. So often you may be tempted to take credit for what God does in and through you, instead of giving Him the glory. Are you the central star in your congregation, your Sunday School class, your missionary society, or any other area of Christian service? No work or accomplishment should cause you to preen yourself on your abilities; none are sufficient to cause you to merit glorification.

Take heed when you find yourself more anxious to please any servant of Christ than you are to please Christ Himself. In Galatians 1:10 Paul says, "Do I seek to please men? for if I yet pleased men, I should not be the servant of Christ."

Be on your guard when you find yourself placing absolute trust and confidence in another human being, resting and hoping in him, instead of depending on God alone for the supply of your deepest needs. It is so easy to trust in earthly visible power and greatness and not by faith to see the invisible God who is greater than all and above all (Heb. 11:27).

Beware of thinking that any human teacher or any denomination or church can do no wrong, and therefore merits your blind obedience and loyalty. In judgment, the excuse that you accepted what you were taught without question will never absolve you of personal responsibility. The disciples of Berea were commended because they searched the Scriptures to find out whether what they were taught agreed with God's Word or not (Acts 17:11). Any pastor or Bible teacher who claims to be right in all his interpretations, and who holds that no one who has a different view can be right, is someone to watch out for. If you follow him implicitly, he has become for you "a human over whom you boast," contrary to Paul's admonition.

Watch out for any man who harps on part of the truth and demands your allegiance to that aspect of truth to the neglect of the whole counsel of God's revelation. "He that glorieth, let him glory in the Lord" (1 Cor. 1:31). If he glories in being a Baptist, a Presbyterian, a Lutheran, a Catholic, an Orthodox, a charismatic, or whatever, you may well know that he is one of those in whom Paul does not want you to glory. The center of your glorying should be the Lord Himself. "God forbid," says Paul, "that I should glory, save in the cross of our Lord Jesus Christ" (Gal. 6:14).

As S. M. Zwemer said, speaking at Keswick:

> Most of us have never realized our possessions! Most of us live on the narrow coast, and we have never ventured inland. We are afraid; we are timid; we are sectional; we are parochial; we are sectarian souls; poverty-stricken, emaciated weaklings. The smaller the diameter of your brotherly love, the smaller the circumference of your spiritual power [*The Keswick Convention*, 1937, 217].

> The dearest idol earth has known,
> Whate'er that idol be,
> Lord, I would tear it from its throne
> And worship only Thee.
>
> —author unknown

LESSONS:

1. Wisdom can deceive us if we attempt to judge things that transcend our world. No man is worthy of boasting when it comes to spiritual truth.
2. Although there is an unconscious attempt to imitate greatness and holiness in all of us, these qualities cannot be imitated. Spiritual people do not boast in things so much as in Christ.

3. We should be on guard against the temptation to take credit for what God has done in and through us.
4. Remember the Berean Christians, who were commended for searching the Scriptures daily to be sure that what they were being taught agreed with God's Word.

# 1 Cor. 3:21, 22 | *Why Man Lost His Mastery Over the World*

*All things are yours; whether Paul, or Apollos, or Cephas, or the world. . . .*

When Paul said that all things belong to the Christian, and included the world itself, he was not being visionary. But how can a man without a foot of land say, "The world is mine"? Yet to say that the fields and hills are ours only when we have a legal deed made out in our name and locked in a safe-deposit box is to take an artificial view of proprietorship. That is truly ours which enlarges our mind, rejoices our heart, and purifies our life.

Are you a Christian in the true sense of having given your heart and soul to Christ? Then the world is yours because:

The world stands out on either side
No wider than the heart is wide;
Above the world is stretched the sky,
No higher than the soul is high.
The heart can push the sea and land
Farther away on either hand;

The soul can split the sky in two,
And let the face of God shine through.
But East and West will pinch the heart
That cannot keep them pushed apart;
And he whose soul is flat—the sky
Will cave in on him by and by.

The basic truth Paul taught when he declared that the world is ours is that the world is realized only in the redeemed man. Let us not think of nature as being over there and us over here. The world does not lie entirely outside of us. It is not a creation independent of our presence and powers.

Let us not forget that, except to God, the world was only a mass of dark force, a dance of atoms, a whirlpool of vibrations, until Adam came. Again except to God, the sun did not shine until there was a human eye; there was no music until there was a human ear; there was no fragrance until there was a human nostril; there was no sweetness until there was a human lip.

From the human viewpoint, the world realizes itself only on man's nerves, in man's brain, in man's soul. The glory of the universe is revealed only in the sense and in the thought of humanity. All the splendor of the world shone out for the first time in the brain of the first man; and when the last man closes his eyes the splendid world will lapse again into silence and darkness, to be replaced by a new heaven and a new earth.

The world is not only realized in man but is comprehended only by man. Who but man has a passion for mastering the secrets of nature and a capacity for understanding at least some of those secrets? The world is ours because we can comprehend its laws, perceive its unity, mark its developments, rejoice in all its wonderful movements and manifestations. A thing is preeminently made for the mind which comprehends it, appreciates it, and finds in it a source of gratification and development. Surely there is no truer criterion of proprietorship than this.

But nature, the world, is not only realized in man and comprehended by man; it is also claimed only by man. Man instinctively acts as if the whole world belonged to him, and in a thousand ways he proceeds to exercise lordship over it. Did not the Psalmist say, "Thou madest him to have dominion over the works of thy hands; thou hast put all things under his feet" (Ps. 8:6)?

It is this sense of lordship that has put man on the moon. The wealth of the world is ours in a sense in which the animals and the fowls of the air cannot participate. Our place in nature is that of the sun in the solar system, solitary and supreme. Apart from us, the world has no meaning; it does not realize itself; it is not understood; it is not utilized to any large and adequate end.

But Paul indicates that man in his sinful state is not the world's actual undisputed head and lord. In many respects the world has been wrested from his grasp. It is often his master. It tyrannizes over him. It crushes him. But in Christ the proprietorship and government of the world are being fully restored to us, and thus the ideal becomes the actual.

Man has idolized nature in his sinful state. That which he could not master he made his master. Thus we find in Egypt, Greece, and Rome that the powers of nature were regarded as divine, and the God who is above was denied. Today science has become God to many, who worship the laws but deny the Lawmaker. That is why men have lost their mastery over the world because they have lost the Lord of the world. Many men have worshipped nature, looking upon themselves as wholly inferior to the world, as the slaves of the sun, the sea, the sky, the stars.

The theology of the natural man is geology, astronomy, and other forms of science. To him God is nature, the material universe with its laws and forces and movements. But Christ came to deliver us from this tyranny of superstition by making manifest to us "the God that is above."

### Getting the Most Out of Life

Christians are sometimes accused of missing the enjoyment of the present because they are living only in the prospect of the life to come. This is not true. The Christian, says the apostle Paul, not only enjoys and possesses the best of this world but also possesses a rich and full life.

As Dr. Doddridge expressed it, in a poem based on his family motto of arms, "While we live, let us live"—

> "Live while you live," the Epicure would say,
> "And seize the pleasures of the present day."
> "Live while you live," the sacred preacher cries,
> "And give to God each moment as it flies."
> Lord, in my views, let both united be:
> I live in pleasure while I live to Thee.

"Life," as Paul refers to it here, means the consciousness and purpose of being, the direction of being. The man who places a spiritual value on life enjoys it most. The pleasures that others pity him for missing are usually those of a transitory nature. In this connection I like the story of the little girl vacationing with her mother in Maine. Someone offered her a beautiful Angora cat. Her mother, thinking it would be too much bother to care for the cat on the long trip home, offered to buy her daughter off with a bribe. "Honey," she said, "if you'll say no more about the cat, I'll give you a dollar to spend as you like." The little girl looked thoughtful for a moment, then said, "But, Mama, how much longer a cat will last than a dollar!" That is the attitude of the true Christian. In his choice of joys, and in the things he prays for, he selects those pleasures that endure. As between cats and coins, let us choose cats.

Now in saying that "life" is the possession of the Christian, Paul does not mean anyone can ultimately control the circumstances of his life. He knows, however, that the circumstances are controlled by God. And, since God is his Father, he is satisfied that they are for his ultimate and eternal good.

The difference between a Christian and a fatalist is that the Christian believes God is behind every circumstance, while the fatalist believes that circumstances are blind, often harsh, and purposeless. He acknowledges no moral cause behind them. The Christian sees God in the circumstances of his life. True, he cannot direct their course except by his obedience to the one he believes directs them. But the fatalist sees nothing but chaos. The Christian accepts life as a gift, not as a right. He is therefore thankful for whatever shape it comes in, and whatever color God paints it with. He discerns that in God's providence all things have a purpose. And, since he knows that the omnipotent God is his Father, he knows that that purpose would not be evil.

As Christians, we are not slaves of circumstance. We do not say with the poet, "Neath the fell blows of circumstance my head is bloodied but unbowed." We do not brag about our stoicism, our ability to meet courageously whatever fate sends. We believe circumstances are made to serve God's purpose for each of our own individual lives, as well as to fit into God's overall plans for the working out of His larger purposes.

Christ liberates us from the bondage of the outside world. Man apart from Christ fights circumstances. But the Christian lives in the spirit of that centuries-old prayer, "Heavenly Father, give us serenity to accept what cannot be changed, courage to change what should be changed, and wisdom to know one from the other." He helps and remedies what can be helped and remedied. But he interprets what cannot be helped or avoided as God's speech in action.

This explains why the natural man may be inflated by success and crushed by failure, why he may be made proud and selfish by abundance. Leisure may make him slothful, pessimism make him fretful and complaining. Health may make him shallow, and sickness bitter. But in the knowledge and strength of Christ we are freed from the bondage of circumstance; life becomes ours, and we use the manifold events and circumstances of the outer world toward the attainment of that ideal moral and spiritual perfection that is the mark of the prize of our high calling of God in Christ Jesus. Amid the multiplied and complicated changes of the outer life we select and reject, accept and resist, suppress and encourage, fight or fly, act or wait, so that each day, each hour, works in us a deeper, truer, nobler spirit.

The grand service of Jesus Christ to us in this matter is, He instructs us how to use the outer life for the inner life, and He so strengthens us that we constantly subordinate the outer life to the training and perfection of that inner life.

"Life is yours," says Paul. You are not the poor slaves of the outside forces. You are free to use the world and to be served by it in the very largest and best sense. The Christian does not merely possess life; he has it in the greatest possible abundance because it is the life of God within him. In the New Testament this is called "eternal life." He who can say, "For me to live is Christ" can be truly said to possess life.

## A Right Attitude toward Death

Most people would concede that "life" is a blessing; at least very few are eager to give it up. And "life" is one of the possessions that the apostle Paul tells us is given to us in Christ (1 Cor. 3:22). But in this list of particular blessings of the believer in Christ, he also refers to "death." Who wants to claim death as a prized possession? Did Paul make a mistake? Should he have stopped at "life" as our heritage in Christ?

No, Paul made no mistake here, even as he made no mistake in Philippians 1:21 when he said, "For to me to live is Christ, and to die is gain." Of course, life and death are the common possessions of all men. Yet the unbeliever can never enter into the full enjoyment of life because he neither recognizes nor appropriates the Giver of life. And he dreads death. The idea of it, the certainty and inevitability of it, scare him. The Christian, on the other hand, sees death as the gateway to life everlasting in the presence of the Lord, so that he can say with Paul, "O death, where is thy sting? O grave, where is thy victory?" (1 Cor. 15:55). Paul says that, as all people, and things, and life have something to teach us, so does death.

Obviously Paul does not mean that we as Christians are exempt from physical death. We are subject to sickness and physical deterioration and therefore to the death of the body. However, we who are in Christ are liberated from the fear of death. While it may be said of all other men that they are death's, of the believer alone can it be said that death is his. Sin, unrepented and unforgiven, can be said in a sense to make man the rightful property of death, so that when the hour of dissolution arrives it is as though the lawful proprietor were merely coming to claim his own.

In human society, when a man commits a crime, he forfeits his right to liberty. His person, by right, if not in fact, is the property of the law. Wherever he can be found, the representative of the law may arrest him and claim him as his own to take into custody. Even though the crime may be concealed, or the criminal may elude the arm of the law for awhile, he still has no intrinsic right to liberty or a free life. He is at the mercy of the law he has offended, wherever he can be detected. He knows that resistance will do him no good.

This is similar to the condition of the unbeliever. His unrepented sin gives death a claim upon him. However long death may delay to press this claim, he will come to put in force the right he has established over the person of the sinner, and to claim him as his own. Resistance or escape is impossible. Who can enter into the feeling of amazed, awestruck impotence and abandonment with which the unrepentant soul realizes the thought, "This is death at last, and I am his!"

"Sin entered into the world, and death by sin" (Rom. 5:12). And the consciousness of sin, the voice of conscience, makes death an enemy, the last enemy, feared by all. Because human beings are children of disobedience, they are all their lifetime in bondage to the fear of death, unless they have been delivered from that fear through repentance and reconciliation with God through Christ. They are debtors for whom there is a warrant out for their arrest. When they think of death, they are always trembling that its cold grip is about to come upon them.

On the other hand, if we are Christ's, then death is ours. Death's power over us is gone, for it has no right or ability to detain us in its possession. "The sting of death is sin" (1 Cor. 15:56), but Christ has pulled the sting from death for those who put their faith in Him. Death may be, and often is, objectionable to us as believers for various natural reasons. Life is such a splendid gift that we cannot look at its earthly termination without a feeling of regret. But the sting of death is sin, and in that thought lies the deathliness of death. Without sin we might view death with the uneasiness with which we might suppose a caterpillar to view a chrysalis.

What comfort, then, we derive from Hebrews 2:14, 15:

> Forasmuch then as the children are partakers of flesh and blood, he [Christ] also himself likewise took part of the same; that through death he might destroy him that had the power of death, that is, the devil; and deliver them who through fear of death were all their lifetime subject to bondage.

Behind death stands the devil and his works, that is, the elements of disobedience, guilt, condemnation, punishment, which constitute the power and terror of death. If it were not for sin, men would fear death only as a young bird fears to try its wings. Reconciled to God in Christ, we can sing as did Frances Ridley Havergal when she lay dying,

> Jesus, I will trust Thee,
> Trust Thee with my soul:
> Guilty, lost, and helpless,
> Thou hast made me whole.

There is none in heaven
Or on earth like Thee;
Thou hast died for sinners,
Thou hast died for me.

## What Will Death Mean to You?

What is your reaction when someone brings up the subject of death? Do you shudder and try to change the subject, or can you consider it calmly? What a vast difference it makes in your estimate of death whether you face it with a sense of guilt or of sins forgiven.

Look at the death of a murderer. How terribly repulsive are all the circumstances surrounding it. The condemned man is suffering the penalty of the law he has broken. Then consider the death of a martyr, or of any Christian for that matter. He undergoes very much the same physical suffering and snuffing out of his earthly life. But the martyr reminds you of truth, justice, honor, innocence, loyalty, patriotism, faith, purity. All sense of horror is gone; it is not an execution; it is a triumph, a coronation. The prison gates for him are palace gates.

Christ makes death ours instead of making us the prey of death. He changes death for us from the death of a malefactor to the death of a martyr, a word which really (and originally) means a witness, that is, for Christ. He takes away the guilt and power of sin. He gives to all those who trust in Him the sense of forgiveness and peace. Why, then, fear death when you belong to Him who said, "I am he that liveth, and was dead; and, behold, I am alive forevermore, Amen; and have the keys of hell and death" (Rev. 1:18)?

As we think of death, let us not have the gruesome and un-Christian idea that we remain in our graves waiting for some far-off day of resurrection to restore us to consciousness. Remember Christ's words to the dying thief, "Verily, I say unto thee, Today shalt thou be with me in paradise" (Luke 23:43). And in the account of the rich man and the beggar Lazarus, in Luke 16, the Lord speaks of them both being alive in the world beyond this one after death, while the brothers of the rich man were still alive on earth. The only difference between the rich man and Lazarus was that the first was being tormented, reaping the natural consequences of his sinful life, while Lazarus was resting in paradise. The unbeliever was possessed by death, and the believer possessed paradise in death. Even as the first generation of Christians believed that there was no interval between this life and the entry into the glorious life of the world to come, we too must believe and rejoice in it.

One moment we possess a natural body, and the next we possess a spiritual one. The Lord Jesus was the same person after His resurrection in the new body as in the old. He still had the same way of saying "Mary" and the usual way of breaking bread. He is the firstfruits of all who believe.

Look at death through the eyes of our Lord for a moment. He is the most trustworthy source of information about death because death could not maintain its hold over Him. He rose from the dead; and, if He tells us that we too shall rise, we must believe Him; He cannot lie. His resurrection, His victory over death, makes Him absolutely believable.

The picture Christ gives us of death as experienced by the rich man and Lazarus is most instructive. Here is a beggar, ragged and covered with sores, lying at the door of a rich man and begging for the crumbs that fall from his table. Nobody cares for him. He has no nurses but the dogs that lick his sores. He is a poor, dirty, loathsome object of pity, lying in the gutter.

And then one day death comes to him, and no one pays any attention. The life of the great house goes on. Perhaps the rich man never even glances from his window. No servant comes with a drink or a cushion for his weary head. The busy crowds pass unheeding. It is only a beggar, a dirty beggar lying at the gate. He may be dying. Who cares? What use is he anyway?

But, says the Lord Jesus, if your eyes were open to all that is happening at that gate, you would be filled with a great wonder. For around that dirty beggar are gathered a host of shining forms, the angels of God, waiting to carry his released spirit home. Those whose eyes are not open see only a moment of agony, the twitching of the limbs, the glazing of the eyes, the sudden fall of the head. But the beggar, delivered from his rags and ulcers and his poverty forever, finds himself in the center of a radiant, shining, friendly company who are hurrying to introduce him to Abraham. Was not death for him a wonderful gain, a unique possession?

This earth for the believer, no matter what his physical state, can never be equal to what heaven will be. Yet that unknown quality of the future is what steals the luster from it in this present life. The reason is that there is no language to describe its beauty that we could presently understand. But how different it was for the rich man. For him death must have been a horror. What will it be for you? (see Mackay 1942, 101–3).

### No "Pie in the Sky" Religion

The world's view of the Christian is typically that he is sacrificing the enjoyment of the present life for "pie in the sky." With a smile of doubt, the unbeliever concedes that things above and beyond this present life may belong to the Christian. But he considers him a person who fails to use the present to the greatest possible advantage.

The Scriptures, however, warn us that the future is the fruit of what we have sown here and now. Yet the enjoyment of that fruit need not necessarily be postponed to the future. It begins here on earth and continues hereafter. That is why Paul adds to his list of possessions of the believer, "things present." Things to come are ours only if we make wise use of things present. It is the height of folly to waste today and imagine we can recover its treasure in a far-off unknown tomorrow. The Christianity (so-called) that neglects the present for the sake of the future is corrupt and fruitless. One may doubt if it is genuine Christianity at all.

What the apostle Paul claims is that in Christ we have the richest enjoyment of things present. Our times are largely characterized by materialism. But "things" are not really ours just because we own them legally. Material wealth does not necessarily satisfy us. It is sadly true that we may have riches, honor, power, amusement, yet not have the power to enjoy them.

Our Lord made it clear that it is very difficult for the rich to enter the kingdom of heaven (Matt. 19:23). Those who possess riches may not have God. But those who have Christ, says Paul, own the present, and they are the truly rich. Although those in poverty often sense the need of God, the poor who have God really have everything the world can offer. Men are never more deeply, bitterly, mysteriously miserable than when they have everything the world offers and yet find only emptiness in their soul. Successful men often find themselves wearied of life. Satiated and sickened amid all their so-called wealth, they remind us of bees drowning in their own honey.

The fact is, the human heart can only realize the joy of things present in the light of the infinite, in the light of God's presence, in the power of His blessing. All beautiful things in human life lose their beauty and become dark and disappointing the moment they come between us and God. It is only in the light of God that life shines, only in His blessing that it is rich. In the purity and peace and spirituality that Christ gives we are enabled to enjoy what Providence gives us, to find sweetness and satisfaction in all of life.

In Christ, then, we have the fullest profit of things present. A life of material interests, of material success, considered in itself, is no advantage in any sense. Christ makes things present ours by making them instruments of our higher education.

In Ephesians 1:14 the apostle Paul presents the here and now of the Christian as an earnest or token of the future. "Which [the word of truth which is ours now] is the earnest of our inheritance until the redemption of the purchased possession," that is, what is coming in the future.

Paul realizes that our present state, although imperfect, can be a joyous one because we are in Christ. In our present actions we sometimes demonstrate how little we really have of God, and how little He has of us. We say that we are His, yet we live to please ourselves or someone else. We give God only fragments of our time and efforts.

Such incompleteness of possession is inevitable because we are in a sense only partly redeemed. That is, we are redeemed in our souls, but the redemption of our bodies is yet to come (Rom. 8:23). Now we are imperfect, but the future holds the promise of a better state. This present, in its very imperfection, is a prophecy and a pledge of a perfect future. The facts of Christian experience are such that they inevitably lead up to the conclusion that there is a life beyond.

One of the perfections of the future is the abolition of the present fragmentation of our Christianity and our attachment to personalities instead of to Christ. Probably you have heard of the group who were supposed to have arrived in heaven and been met by St. Peter. In a beautiful meadow they saw some people assembled and asked Peter who they were. Peter replied, "They are Presbyterians." They walked on a ways to a beautiful brook, and one asked, "Who are the people gathered over there?" And Peter answered, "They are Lutherans." Then they came to a tremendously high wall and one asked, "Whose are the voices we hear behind that wall?" "Shh!" said Peter. "Please be quiet!" Then he whispered the name of that denomination and said, "They think they are the only ones up in this place, and we do not want to disillusion them. If they find out that others have made it up here, too, how will they feel?" We do not know whether they were Corinthians, but they certainly possessed the Corinthian spirit.

### Hope for the Future

Did you ever stop to think that the poorest believer in Christ is intrinsically richer than the wealthiest person without Christ? That is the conclusion we draw from 1 Corinthians 3:21–23, where Paul says, "All things are yours; whether Paul, or Apollos, or Cephas [i.e., all Christian preachers and teachers], or the world, or life, or death, or things present. . . ." and that is where we stopped in our last study.

Now we take up the next phrase of verse 22, "or things to come." Not only is the present a possession of the Christian, but also the future. What does Paul mean by "things to come" here? I think we must take it in the very widest and most general sense the future of this world and of all unknown worlds into which this life may open. Christ makes us heirs of the future. As we are found in Him we shall inherit all the wealth and blessedness of the ages beyond.

The Old Testament teaches that, in the Messiah, the world, the ages, will become the possession of the faithful; and the New Testament more clearly and emphatically insists on the same truth. In the epistle to the Hebrews we are taught that Christ is heir of all things, and that He brings many sons with Him to share His glory. The God of our Lord Jesus Christ, says Paul in his epistle to the Ephesians, has set Christ "at his own right hand in the heavenly places, far above all principality, and power, and might, and dominion, and every name that is named, not only in this world, but also in that which is to come: and hath put all things under his feet, and gave him to be the head over all things to the church, which is his body, the fullness of him that filleth all in all" (Eph. 1:21–23). And in Romans 8:16, 17 we read, "The Spirit itself beareth witness with our spirit, that we are the children of God: and if children, then heirs; heirs of God, and joint-heirs with Christ." Christ is the heir, the Lord of the future, and since He is ours, the future is ours also.

No matter what my birth may be,
  No matter where my lot is cast,
I am the heir in equity
  Of all the precious past.

The art, the science, and the lore
  Of all the ages long since dust,
The wisdom of the world in store,
  Are mine, all mine in trust.

The beauty of the living earth,
  The power of the golden sun,
The Present, whatsoe'er my birth,
  I share with every one.

As much as any man am I
  The owner of the working day;
Mine are the minutes as they fly,
  To save or throw away.

And mine the Future to bequeath
  Unto the generations new;
I help to shape it with my breath,
  Mine as I think or do.

Present and Past my heritage,
  The Future laid in my control;
No matter what my name or age,
  I am a Christian soul.

Of course, it takes faith to believe you possess the Future. When the cares and oppressions and seeming contradictions of this life weigh on your spirit, it is hard to envision a time when they will pass into forgetfulness, in that day when "God shall wipe away all tears" (Rev. 7:17). We have not fully entered into our inheritance yet. But we have the earnest of it here and now. Remember this. Belonging to Christ is not all bearing burdens, is not all carrying a cross, is not all feeling restrained in our desires and impulses and inclinations, but is being filled with God Himself.

A legend says that when birds were first created they had no wings. So God made wings and put them down in front of the birds and said, "Now come and take your burdens up and bear them." They took up their wings with their beaks and laid them on their shoulders. At first they seemed to be a heavy load and difficult to bear. But, as they cheerfully and patiently bore them, the wings grew fast, and that which they once bore now bore them. The burdens became pinions, and the weights became wings.

We are the wingless birds, and our duties as Christians are the pinions. When we first take them on they seem heavy loads. But, if we cheerfully bear them in following Christ, the burdens change to pinions. And we, who once thought we were nothing but servants bearing loads, find that we are sons and heirs of God, free to mount up with wings as eagles, running without being weary, and walking without being faint.

This is the blessed inheritance that God invites you to experience the earnest of here and now, and to realize in all its fulfillment of liberation from sin and sorrow in the future, when you see Him face to face.

LESSONS:

1. Paul taught that the world belongs to the redeemed man. True proprietorship is the fit between the created world and the renewed mind which enjoys it.
2. Men have lost their mastery over the world because they have rebelled against God. To the natural man, God is nature—the material universe of motion, laws, and forces. The Christian believes God is behind every event.
3. Circumstances serve God's purpose for each individual life. The natural man is inflated by worldly success and crushed by worldly failure. In the knowledge and strength of Christ, we are freed from the bondage of the world.
4. The unbeliever cannot enjoy life because he neither recognizes nor appropriates the Giver of life; for this reason, also, he fears death. The Christian sees death as the gateway to everlasting life in the presence of the Lord.
5. The Christian does not fear death because he belongs to Christ. Death took both the rich man and the beggar Lazarus out of the world. But Lazarus went to paradise and the rich man to torment, reaping the divine consequences of his sinful life.
6. Christianity that neglects the present for the sake of the future is corrupt and fruitless. Those who possess riches may not have God. The poor who have Christ have everything and are truly rich. Not only does the Christian possess the present; he possesses the future, even death itself. The poorest believer in Christ is intrinsically richer than the wealthiest person without Christ.

## 1 Cor. 3:21b, 23

# *The Supreme Benefit of Belonging to Christ*

*All things are yours . . . and ye are Christ's; and Christ is God's.*

In the days when most European countries were absolute monarchies, the king had power of life and death over his subjects. But though it might be said that he owned their bodies, he could not always command their allegiance. There were always those who wished to overthrow the throne.

In a somewhat similar sense we might say that, though Christ has a right over all men, not all men actually belong to Him. When He mourned that His own countrymen would not come to Him that they might have life, He consoled Himself with the reflection that "All that the Father giveth me shall come to me" (John 6:37). Furthermore He declared, "My Father which gave them me, is greater than all; and no man is able to pluck them out of my Father's hand" (John 10:29). Again He said, referring to Himself as the Son of the Father, "Thou hast given him power over all flesh, that he should give eternal life to as many as thou hast given him" (John 17:2).

In the eternal purpose of God the Father, every one of us who really believes in Christ now was given to Him. As Paul expresses it, "chosen . . . in him before the foundation of the world" (Eph. 1:4). We have been arrested in our course. We have been made to feel that we are sinners. We have been given some measure of sorrow for sin. We have been guided to the cross of Christ where the only remedy is to be found. We have opened our hearts there. There we have laid our burdens. There we have learned that the demands of God's law upon us have been all answered. There we have recognized the love of God toward us. There we have discovered how God can be just, while He justifies even us. There we have discovered that all the duties we have failed in, Christ has performed for us. There the Holy Spirit has taken of the things of Christ and shown them to us. He has united us to Christ. He has grafted us into Him as branches into a tree. We are baptized into Him by the Holy Spirit. We are given the enjoyment of a friendship and fellowship such as no other friendship can equal. What intimacy there is in our friendship with Christ!

So many times we speak of the benefits we receive from God as a result of our receiving Jesus Christ. We conceive of Him as purchasing certain things for us by His death on the cross. We know that the fruits of His sacrifice are pardon, cleansing, and reconciliation. But the supreme benefit that He has obtained for us by shedding His precious blood is this—that He bought us, and that He has redeemed us from the hand of the enemy, in order that we may belong to the enemy no more, but henceforth forever to our rightful Lord. He has bought us that He might give us to God. That is the sublimest view of salvation.

The declaration that we, as believers, are Christ's, viewed negatively, teaches us:

1) *That we are not our own.* We do not belong to ourselves. Therefore we cannot seek our own advantage. Whenever we consider whether or not to engage in some enterprise, to establish some relationship, to purchase something, our criterion should not be, "What is in this for us?" but "How will this affect Christ and His glory?"

2) *That we do not belong to the world.* We are in the world but not of it. In fact, as believers, we do not primarily belong to our natural parents, to our husband, wife, children, friends, country, or even to mankind. The Lord stated this truth when He said, "He that loveth father or mother more than me is not worthy of me: and he that loveth son or daughter more than me is not worthy of me" (Matt. 10:37).

3) *That we do not primarily belong to any church or denomination*, though by virtue of our belonging to Christ we do belong to His church universal. However, far too many believers put the church above Christ. But Paul did not say that our spiritual enrichment came to us by virtue of belonging to the church—any church—but to Christ Himself. As Christians, if the teachings or regulations of our church are in conflict with the Word of God, we should be governed by Christ.

Belonging to Christ should create in us a sense of responsibility. His glory should be our concern. We are His image in the world. An American chaplain in the Civil War asked a wounded soldier, "Would you like me to read you something from the Bible?" The soldier said, "I'm so thirsty, I'd rather have a drink of water." After he had drunk it he said, "Could you put something under my head?" The chaplain took off his overcoat, rolled it up, and placed it under the man's head as a pillow. "Now," said the soldier, "if I had something over me. I'm so cold." The chaplain took off his jacket and covered the man. Then the wounded man said, "For God's sake, man, if there is anything in that Book that makes a man do for another what you have done for me, let me hear it!" Is that not what the world needs today—Christians who exemplify Christ?

Belonging to Christ should also inspire in us a sense of security and safety. The fear of man often makes us cowards. The fear of God makes the righteous as bold as a lion. Christ was the meekest of all beings, yet His courage never flinched. And His courage is available to us, for, as Paul says, "All things are yours . . . and ye are Christ's."

## Sharing the Mind of God

We who belong to Christ are called by two particular names: the bride of Christ and the body of Christ. When I speak of a woman as my bride, I mean she belongs to me and no one else. As Christ's bride we are His exclusive possession. His love is concentrated on us in a particular and unique way. He will protect and provide for us. He will love us in abundance or want, in sickness or health.

But the symbolism of being Christ's body is even more intimate than that of being His bride. What is closer to us than our own body? There can be no closer relationship. When we hurt, Christ hurts. When He hurts, we must hurt. This involves a common consciousness of being. How can we give ourselves to sin, knowing that we are Christ's body?

Now consider the awesome implications of what belongs to you as a born-again believer in Christ: "All things are yours." How can that be? Since all things were created by Christ, they are sustained by Him and serve Him. Therefore the natural consequence of your belonging to Him is that you become heir of all that is His. Yet over and above His gifts you possess the Giver Himself.

If you had to choose between possessing the money of a great and famous man, or being related to him, which would you prefer? Is not having the mind of a great author preferable and more precious than possessing his books? Would you not rather have the genius of a great artist than his most beautiful paintings? In other words, would you not rather have the mind that produces, instead of some of the products of such a mind?

But of course no man can transfer his genius, skill, or abilities to another. How many of us as parents wish we could impart a particular talent or trait of character to a child. The superior nature can never will a share of its inner intellectual or moral power as a legacy to the inferior. And yet this is exactly what we are told Christ does for us. This sharing and communion of minds, inconceivable between us finite and created beings, is not inconceivable between our created minds and God. There is a sense in which we may become sharers of that Mind from which all that is true and good and fair in the universe proceeds. It is given to us not only to see, admire, and share in the works of the Great Author of all, but also to become endowed with the very mind, to be imbued in our inmost being, with the very Spirit and Being of God.

Thus God communicates Himself to the believer in Christ. He diffuses His own Holy Spirit in the spirit of the believer. The happiness of this mysterious nature of ours is never found merely in the possession of God's gifts, the works of His hand, or the bounties of His providence. The soul can find its true satisfaction only in rising beyond the gifts, and claiming the Giver as its own.

When we are eager for the friendship of another individual, it is not because we desire only outward gifts—his money, property, books, or whatever. What do our living, loving hearts care for these? Unless that person gives us something more than these, gives us himself and becomes ours by the bond of deepest sympathy and affection, our hearts are not satisfied.

So it is in the soul's relations with God. We should not seek God for His gifts and bounties but for Himself. The wealth of worlds, to a heart longing for God, would be a miserable substitute for the assurance that God loves him. "As the hart panteth after the water brooks, so panteth my soul after thee, O God. My soul thirsteth for God, for the living God" (Ps. 42:1, 2). And Christ promises to satisfy that thirst. "If a man love me, he will keep my words: and my Father will love him, and we will come unto him, and make our abode with him" (John 14:23). "I in them, and thou in me, that they may be made perfect in one" (John 17:23).

In Christ, God Himself is the immediate possession or portion of the soul. He is the focus that includes all the scattered rays of light. The fountain contains the streams. All finite and created good is contained in Him who is the Supreme Good. All earthly excellence is but a partial manifestation, a more or less bright reflection, of the Great Original. To have a portion in God, therefore, is to possess Him who includes in Himself all created good. The man who possesses some great masterpiece in painting or sculpture need not envy others who have only copies of it. The original is always more valuable than even the finest copy. And in the spiritual realm, he who possesses the Original, God, owns that which includes and is capable of producing all the copies.

Yet we do thank God for the copies—for those men and women who reflect Christ's image so faithfully that they inspire us with a desire to draw closer to God, and to emulate their love and zeal for Christ. Paul himself urged the Corinthians to emulate his example of not seeking his own profit, but the good of others, when he said, "Be ye followers of me, even as I also am of Christ" (1 Cor. 11:1). As Christ's followers, then, "Let us consider one another to provoke unto love and to good works" (Heb. 10:24).

LESSONS:

1. In the eternal purpose of God, the Father gave us to His Son for a possession. The supreme benefit that He obtained for us by shedding His precious blood is this—He brought us back to God. Belonging to Christ creates in us the desire to exemplify Him.
2. God communicates Himself to the believer through and in Christ. He sends His own Spirit into the heart of the believer.
3. We should not seek God for His gifts but for Himself. Christ promises to satisfy the believer who thirsts for God.

1 Cor. 3:21–23

# *No Room for Spiritual Jealousy*

> *Therefore let no man glory in men. For all things are yours, whether Paul, or Apollos, or Cephas, or the world, or life, or death, or things present, or things to come; all are yours; and ye are Christ's; and Christ is God's.*

Christianity proclaims the message of peace. Yet all too often there is strife and contention, envying and jealousy among those who profess to possess the peace of God that passes understanding. What a sorry testimony in the eyes of the world—that Christians who are supposed to love all people sometimes act as if they hate each other!

When you read Paul's Corinthian epistles, you discover how the Christians at Corinth quarreled with each other over the merits of their respective teachers: "I am of Paul, I am of Apollos, I am of Cephas." "Just a minute," says Paul in effect; "let no man boast in any men." These teachers were all men—fallible human beings. Paul wanted the Corinthians to understand that it is a sin, an absurdity to fight over them as if the possession of truth by one deprived the others of their proper regard.

A minister who had to move to an obscure country parish in England because of ill health never gained acceptance among the villagers whom he sought to serve. Being unable to do much work, he procured a preacher from Wales who attracted large congregations. His family was a little jealous of this unexpected preference, but he rebuked them. "Take me to hear him," he said. "God honors him, and I will honor him. Have you ever studied that text, 'He must increase, but I must decrease' [John 3:30]? 'A man can receive nothing except it be given him from heaven [John 3:27].' " How many preachers would be able to accept a more popular man in their pulpit in that spirit?

God's revelation, the gospel, is not diminished when it is shared by many. It is not like a sum of money that, the more who share in it, the less each one gets. The divine treasure of the gospel is not diminished, but rather increased, by reason of the multitude who participate in it. The first prize does not go to one single winner in the Christian race as usually happens in an earthly race. The first prize can go to many without any sense of superiority of the one over the others.

We must recognize the fundamental difference between the distribution of a limited good and an unlimited one. A limited supply of whatever men desire creates envy and jealousy. Your money cannot be yours and mine at the same time. What you gain, I may lose. It is possible for you to be enriched at my expense. But this is not true of spiritual riches. They are an unlimited good. Your spiritual riches, your possession of God's truth, do not mean my spiritual loss.

Power, rank, and social greatness imply their opposites by their very nature. For a man to exercise power, he must have others under him. For a man to be great, there have to be many who are small by comparison. For a man to be noble, there have to be many commoners. One man who attains to a place of power implies that others miss or lose it. The successful man often rises on the ruins of his rivals.

But with respect to spiritual good—the gains and advantages of the spiritual life—it is altogether different. These belong to that class of blessings which possess the qualities of universality and inexhaustibility. The light of the sun is not less bright to me because it beams at the same time on millions of my fellow-men. The beauty I behold in earth, and sea, and sky is not diminished to me because of the multitude of spectators who may share in my delight. Of a thousand men who may look at the same landscape, each may be said to possess all its beauty.

In like manner, those blessings that constitute the Christian's portion—truth, love, beauty, goodness—may become the common possession of millions, each one of whom may be said to possess the whole. The same truths that fill my mind may become the spiritual nourishment of all my fellow believers, undiminished to me though other minds apprehend them.

Jealousy and envy, therefore, should have no place in our hearts when it comes to the possession of these truths. Let no man glory in his own or envy another's spiritual possessions; for to every individual member of Christ's church it may be said, "Whatever others have obtained, the whole illimitable sum of truth and love and joy is still left for you." "All things are yours; whether Paul, or Apollos, or Cephas, or the world, or life, or death, or things present, or things to come; all are yours; and ye are Christ's; and Christ is God's" (1 Cor. 3:21–23).

> All things are mine, for I am His;
> Oh, infinite gifts divine!
> He gave His Son, His only one;
> And all that He has is mine.
> —Annie Johnson Flint

## Is Christ Subordinate to the Father?

The apostle Paul made an astounding statement in 1 Corinthians 3:21, when he declared that the believer in Christ possesses everything. "All things are yours," he asserts. What does he mean by this? Verse 23 helps to make it clear. It is because "ye are Christ's; and Christ is God's."

As a believer you possess all things and you in turn are possessed by Christ. He is the eternal Word who became flesh. When you received Him you became a child of God (see John 1:1, 12, 14). Do you realize your position to the full? You are in Christ, and what that means is set forth in 1 Corinthians 1:1–9.

Christ is the Creator of all things, according to Colossians 1:16. "For by him were all things created, that are in heaven, and that are in earth, visible and invisible, whether they be thrones, or dominions, or principalities, or powers: all things were created by him, and for him." Not only is He the all-inclusive Creator, however, but Paul goes on to say that He is the Sustainer of all things. "And he is before all things, and by him all things consist [i.e., hold together]" (Col. 1:17).

As one commentator says, "The sovereignty over the world was indeed conferred on man in his original estate. But this being lost through sin was restored again by redemption. ('Ye are Christ's; and Christ is God's.')" Perhaps you have never stopped to think of the sweeping sovereignty God gave man when He created him. Read Genesis 1:26, and try to imagine what it must have been like. "And God said, Let us make man in our image, after our likeness: and let them have dominion over the fish of the sea, and over the fowl of the air, and over the cattle, and over all the earth, and over every creeping thing that creepeth upon the earth." That was man's total immediate environment. But through sin man lost much of this dominion over his environment. From man the ruler he was demoted to man the competitor.

But Christ came to remedy this situation. He died so that man might be reconciled to God and become a child of God. Through Christ man can regain his position with God. Observe that Paul does not say, "Ye are Jesus'; and Jesus is God's." He uses the term "Christ" instead of Jesus. "Christ" means the anointed one (*kechrisménos*, from *chríō*, "to anoint in a sacred way"). He was the one whom God the Father foreordained and anointed to become the Lamb that bears our sins. The title "Christ" implies the redemption God's Son accomplished on the cross. It is the reclamation of that which was lost.

Let us begin with that last statement, "And Christ is God's." Actually it is "And Christ God's," for it contains no definite articles or verb. If it were not for the relationship of Christ to God, the possessions described as belonging to the believer would be absolutely impossible and unattainable. Christ could never redeem us and reclaim us to God if He were not uniquely related to God.

Is Paul implying here that Christ the Son is subordinate to the Father? No, the term "Christ" here denotes the work of redemption, the role that He came to earth to play in man's salvation. It is interesting to note that the absence of the definite article before the word *Theoú*, "God's," makes it refer, not to the Father as a distinct personality from the Son, but to the Godhead, the Triune God.

The author, in his book, *Was Christ God?*, explains the distinction between two phrases in John's gospel. In John 1:1, "And the Word was toward *the* God," the word "God," *theoú*, is preceded by the definite article, implying the Father. The purpose is to distinguish "the Word" from "the Father," and to point up their eternal relationship. But in John 1:18a there is no definite article before "God." "God no one has seen at any time." Here reference is made to God in His essence as Spirit, Eternity, and Infinity, and not to any particular personality of the Triune God (see Jelf 1861, 124).

Therefore, when Paul says "Christ is God's," he is declaring that Christ belongs to the Triune God, as the Only Begotten—which means the only one of the same family. In order for Christ to accomplish what He did for all believers, He had to belong to the Trinity, had to be God. What is involved here is not rank but possession. Christ stands between man and God. He had to be specially related to God in order to bring Him to man, and in bringing God to man He also brought all that belongs to God and made it man's actual and potential possession.

If Christ were not a member of the Godhead, He could not possibly have done what He did. He was "in the beginning" (John 1:1). He was "with [or better, 'toward'] the God or the Father." The two were eternally related. He was God. Paul's statement can be better understood if we translate it, "Christ belongs to God or to the Godhead."

## The Work of Christ as God and Man

If Christ were not God, He could not possibly have brought God to man. And in Him, Paul tells those who believe in Him, "All things are yours." Actually, there is no verb at all in the latter part of 1 Corinthians 3:21 and through verses 22 and 23. "All things therefore are yours [or 'is yours,' to be more correct, for when the subject is a neut. pl. in Greek, sometimes the sing. verb is used]." *Pánta*, "all things," therefore, may be taken to refer to the totality of things. "The whole" (it) **is** (sing.) yours. You ought to look at everything that belongs to you in Christ as a whole.

But also this collective pronoun (*pás*, the masc. sing.), when referring to several persons in a number as is the case here where reference is made to Paul, Apollos, and Cephas, has the meaning of "every" (*hékastos;* see Liddell 1889, 1160). Whether you view persons and things as a whole or as individuals, they are yours. And this is ultimately because Christ, the one who was anointed to become your Redeemer, belongs to the Godhead. He is the *Lógos*, God who became flesh, to bear your sins upon His body. If He were not God, He could never have brought God to you, or you to God.

There are some who would rob Christ of His deity because of the constant references He made while here on earth to doing the will of the Father. But these references must be viewed in the light of what Paul meant in 1 Corinthians 3:23 when he said that Christ belonged to God. Christ wanted publicly to declare that what He did and willed was in full accord with the Father. He was "the brightness of his Father's glory, and the express image of his person" (Heb. 1:3). He "thought it not robbery to be equal with God" (Phil. 2:6).

A friend read to Carlyle in his loneliness the opening verse of the 14th chapter of John's gospel: "Let not your heart be troubled: ye believe in God, believe also in me." Carlyle broke in, "Yes, if He was God He had a right to say that. But if He was a man, He knew no more about it than anybody else." Scripture gives us the assurance that Christ did indeed have the right to say that He was God.

But for God to reach man and bestow Himself and all that belongs to God upon man, it was necessary for God to become flesh in the person of the Lord Jesus Christ. He had to be both God and man; He had to bring the two together. As God He could not touch man, and as man alone He could not have reached God. As man, Christ is God's messenger, God's witness to reveal the mind and heart of God toward fallen men. Man by looking at creation can know God's power but not God's thoughts and dispositions toward man.

It is in His incarnation as the Lord Jesus Christ that God was proclaimed to be a Savior. The reason no other religion has a Savior is that Jesus Christ is the unique God-Man. No man can be a Savior without being God also, and no so-called god can be a Savior without also being man. Man in his natural state could never conclude that God could love him. Christ is God "manifest in the flesh" (1 Tim. 3:16).

As man, Christ is God's servant. He was not, however, the first man. That was Adam, in whom the whole human race was united. Had it been Christ, there never would have been a human transgressor. Adam was "of the earth, earthy" (1 Cor. 15:47). He fell into transgression. Therefore the second Adam, Christ, in order that He might save, had to do more than present an obedient life; He had to endure the penalty already incurred by the transgression. That is death, "the wages of sin" (Rom. 6:23). He was God's servant to suffer as well as to be and to do. He cried out, under the pressure of God's wrath against man's sin, "O my Father, if it be possible, let this cup pass from me: nevertheless not as I will, but as thou wilt" (Matt. 26:39).

It was and is the will of God that men should keep His law; therefore the penalty incurred by the breach of the law must be inflicted; and therefore that cup could not pass from Him who had undertaken to endure it. He persevered until He could say, "It is finished" (John 19:30). Thus He was God's servant, obedient in life, obedient unto death.

> Go to dark Gethsemane,
> Ye that feel the tempter's power. . . .
>
> See Christ at the judgment hall,
> Beaten, bound, reviled, arraigned;
> See Him meekly bearing all;
> Love to man His soul sustained;
> Shun not suffering, shame or loss;
> Learn of Christ to bear the cross.
>
> Calvary's mournful mountain climb;
> There adoring at His feet
> Mark that miracle of time,
> God's own sacrifice complete:
> "It is finished!" hear Him cry;
> Learn of Jesus Christ to die.
>
> —James Montgomery

### Who Owns You?

Have you ever heard someone say, "A man's religion is his own affair; it's something between himself and God"? Maybe you have said it yourself. The assumption is that no one has a right to interfere with it. But that is not what the Bible says. The establishment of a meaningful and beneficial relationship with God is something no man can carry on by himself. You need an agent, a priest, a mediator. You cannot negotiate directly with God, the Father Himself. He is too high, too powerful, too holy for you to stand in His presence.

But the priest who stands between you and God has to be more than a mere human. He must be one who has sympathy with you and to whom you can tell what you have done and what you cannot do. You must have a priest to make confession to and from whom you can obtain absolution. You dare not go directly to God.

Jesus Christ is that Priest, in fact the only Priest who is authorized to act as the Mediator between you and God. Before He came, there were priests who served under the "shadow of heavenly things" (Heb. 8:5), and they continued until the "heavenly things" came. These "heavenly things" are in Christ's priesthood. If He were on earth, He could not be a priest (Heb. 8:4) because the only earthly priesthood that God appointed was a type of the heavenly (Heb. 8:5). As long as that earthly priesthood stood, the heavenly was not active. It was a type, and it stood till the heavenly came. It was not to be superseded by another earthly priesthood; it was only to be superseded by the antitype (Heb. 9:23–26), which is a heavenly priesthood, the priesthood of the Lord Jesus Christ. As God's Priest He stands to receive "all who come unto God by him, seeing he ever liveth to make intercession for them" (Heb. 7:25).

As man, the Lord Jesus Christ is also God's King, of whom He says, "I have set my king upon my holy hill of Zion"(Ps. 2:6). He is God's King, reigning and to reign: reigning now invisibly in truth, and to reign in due time visibly in righteousness, putting down all His enemies and ruling over the whole earth.

"And the Lord shall be king over all the earth: in that day shall there be one Lord, and his name one" (Zech. 14:9). Thus "Christ is God's" (1 Cor. 3:23). God is entirely pleased with Christ and with all that are Christ's. Christ is God's "well-beloved" (Mark 12:6), "in whom [He is] well-pleased" (Matt. 3:17), and He is well-pleased with all that are Christ's. This is seen in our Lord's intercessory prayer in John 17, where He asks the Father "that the love wherewith thou hast loved me may be in them, and I in them" (v. 26).

Of whom does Paul speak when he says, "Ye are Christ's"? Not of all men. He is writing to the Corinthian Christians as a whole: "Unto the church of God which is at Corinth," and to all the believers as individuals, "to them that are sanctified in Christ Jesus, called to be saints." That means the local believers. But he also includes believers in Christ everywhere: "with all that in every place call upon the name of Jesus Christ our Lord, both theirs and ours" (1 Cor. 1:2).

Actually Paul is endeavoring here to contrast the advantages of being a Christian over not being one. The person who is "in Christ" owns everything that is Christ's. His spiritual riches come to him by virtue of his belonging to Christ. And the unbeliever's spiritual poverty and misery come to him by virtue of his not belonging to Christ.

This is a declaration of Christ's proprietorship of us. He took the initiative in the first place to create us. The fact that He owns us is the chief part of the privilege He bestows upon us. To belong to God is itself our highest dignity. Creation, however, is something we share with all, and not only with Christians. "All things were made by him; and without him was not anything made that was made" (John 1:3). It is not ownership by creation that Paul is referring to when he says, "Ye are Christ's," but ownership by purchase, by redemption.

However, as by virtue of creation Christ can be said to own everybody and everything, so by His redemption on the cross of Calvary He died for all men. Hebrews 2:9 tells us that Christ "by the grace of God should taste death for every man." Having an elect church, a hidden treasure in the field of this world, He gave all that He had and went and purchased—what? Not the treasure but the field. The whole world is His purchased possession, and He will manifest it in due time.

But even this is not what Paul means when he says, "Ye are Christ's." What then? He refers to those who are Christ's indeed, to those who have accepted His invitation to receive Him as Savior and Lord. "As many as received him, to them gave he power to become the sons of God, even to them that believe on his name" (John 1:12).

### Who Owns the World?

When the apostle Paul urged the Corinthian Christians to follow his example of following Christ, he was not asking for any partisan attachment to himself. Observe his argument in regard to the useless partisan attachments that had developed in connection with the spiritual teachers of Corinth. Why say, "I belong to Paul, to Apollos, or to Cephas"? Strangely enough, he does not include Christ here as he did earlier in 1 Corinthians 1:12. In chapter 3, verses 4 and 5, he mentions only himself and Apollos, and in verse 22 he mentions himself, Apollos, and Cephas. Had he included Christ, it would have nullified his whole argument, which is, if you belong to Christ, you do not have to belong to Paul or to Apollos, or to Cephas. On the contrary, they belong to you, since they belong to Christ, and you are Christ's—and in Christ "all things are yours."

Christian teachers, with all their diversity of gifts bestowed upon them by God for the edification of the body of Christ, are only a fraction of the common property enjoyed by all believers.

Then why fight over Paul, Apollos, or Cephas? Such partialities prove that you do not know the boundless range of your privilege. These teachers are yours. They are part of the great inheritance God gives you freely to enjoy. Belonging to Christ, you may lay claim to them and to all that they can do for you. All their gifts and all their services are bestowed upon them for your benefit.

Paul is yours as a wise masterbuilder, to lay the foundation of your faith. Apollos is yours to build on that foundation, to enrich you with his learning and inspire you with his eloquence. Cephas is yours, with his impetuous devotion and stirring reminiscences, his zeal and experience. All that these men have, all that they are, and all that is in them, can minister to your growth in grace.

Every variety of truly Christian sentiment and character is yours if you are Christians. You, as joint heirs with Christ, have a vested right in them that can never be taken away. Though to the eyes of the world you may seem to have nothing, you truly possess all things.

Though there is one Spirit, one Truth, there are many manifestations. Just as in art, music, literature, and science, the creations of genius need to be as diverse as the wants of the human mind, so of prophets, poets, preachers, and teachers—all are yours, to warn, console, inspire, enlighten, and encourage—to bid you go ever up and on.

It takes all the colors of the rainbow to form pure white light. Truth is a gem of innumerable facets, and though I catch one tiny flash of light and you another; a million eyes could not perceive its full-orbed beauty.

Because all things belong to God and His Christ, Paul includes a second claim for the Christian, and this a specific one. "The world" he says belongs to the Christian. This does not mean the literal physical world, for this earth is not the exclusive property of the believer. In fact, many believers are poor in this world's goods. Of the Lord Jesus Himself it is written, "The Son of man hath not where to lay his head" (Matt. 8:20). When He died, He was buried in a borrowed grave. It was not the Lord, but Satan, who displayed "all the kingdoms of the world, and the glory of them," saying, "All these things will I give thee, if thou wilt fall down and worship me" (Matt. 4:8, 9). But there is a sense in which, according to Paul, we may gain the whole world and not lose our own souls. In fact, we gain the world as a consequence of the gaining of salvation of our souls.

In what way does the Christian own the world? The unbeliever does not see a guiding, planning mind behind the forces in the world. He considers himself the victim of blind conflicting forces. But Christ teaches that these forces are all under the control of a living personal will directed by the love of a Father who is making all things work together for the good of His children. Thus the world becomes truly ours when we learn to look at its outward machinery, not as a play of blind power, mocking our puny might, and working on inflexibly, regardless of our fate, but as a carefully adjusted mechanism that love, no less than wisdom, has devised.

World ownership, as Frederick F. Shannon observes, is a matter of spiritual capacity. The true owner of the world is the soul capable of appreciating it. Individual response to the eternal love and wisdom is owning it. As an illustration, consider a magnificent organ. Who owns it—the person who made it or paid for it? The organist himself? In reality the person who holds an indisputable title-deed to that organ is the man most capable of enjoying the music. As Shannon says:

> God leases the universe to all who can pay for it in the invisible coin of appreciation. Deity hangs a sign in the window of every star, on the breast of every sea, on the summit of every hill, on the leaf of every tree, on the face of every flower, on the peaks of history, on the souls of

immortal men and women—and that sign reads: "To Let! The only rental fee is the capacity to enjoy."

## Are You Really Living?

When Jesus Christ was on earth, He had not a particle of sympathy with the great religious nature-systems of His day. The worship of sun, moon, stars, and other manifestations of nature were perversions of man's instinct to worship. As the apostle Paul expressed it in Romans 1:21–23, men "became vain in their imaginations, and their foolish heart was darkened. Professing themselves to be wise, they became fools, and changed the glory of the uncorruptible God into an image made like to corruptible man, and to birds, and four-footed beasts, and creeping things."

Jesus Christ taught that God sits above, and that nature is simply an organ working out God's will and glory for the fullest, highest welfare and joy of mankind. "You are the world's," says a skeptical science, reducing us to a sad idolatry, a demeaning slavery. You must in effect bend down and worship this material universe, a blind, irrational thing. The conscious must worship the unconscious, the living the dead, the moral the mechanical.

Ernest Renan expressed the arrogance of this philosophy back in 1891 when he wrote: "Science is a religion, science alone will henceforth make the creeds, science alone can solve for men the eternal problems." But this is a dreadful slavery, the worst slavery of all. Out of this false attitude of man to science and nature spring profound humiliations and miseries. The world, like fire, is a grand servant but a bad master. Let it be your servant, and it will wait upon you. It will enrich you. It will exalt you. It will stimulate and develop your whole nature in the most wonderful manner. But make nature your God, and it enslaves your intellect; it starves your affections; it dwarfs and destroys you as all idolatry does.

"You are God's [possession] through Me," says Jesus Christ. He fixes our eyes on the God of heaven. He tells us that God made the world for us, that He rules it for us. And just as we hold to that doctrine, and worship and serve God, so shall the world be ours, ministering to our utmost satisfaction of soul and sense. In the power of the faith of the one true and living God, the world becomes ours.

The natural man often tends to place divinity in nature, but the spiritual man, the Christian, receives God in himself. What Jesus Christ can do for man by indwelling him is demonstrated vividly by the fact of the Incarnation. As A. M. Fairbairn comments: "Christ conceived as the Incarnate Son is a Person so possessed of the communicable life of God as to be the inexhaustible medium of its communication to man."

Man was not made for the world; the world was made for man. But in order for man to realize it, claim it, and comprehend it, he must possess the one who made the world and sustains it.

So far in our studies we have seen that when Paul says, "All things are yours," he has applied this claim to all Christian teachers as being the common possession of Christians; and the world itself as belonging in the most realistic sense to the believer in Christ. Now, in 1 Corinthians 3:22, he adds that "life" is also the Christian's particular possession. What does he mean by "life"? The first and simplest meaning is mere physical existence or duration of being. But this cannot be the full meaning here, for physical existence is the possession of believer and unbeliever alike. It is one of the many common blessings of God and not the peculiar property of the Christian.

Although avoidance of excesses and harmful habits sometimes prolongs the life of the Christian, it is not always true that the holiest men live longest. Often the righteous die young, as do the unregenerate. It is not length of life, therefore, that Paul is speaking of here. It is not the quantity of life but the quality of life that is meant. If the righteous do not live longer, they live more fully in the same space of time than other people. Life should not be measured merely by its duration. It is possible for the longest life to be shorter in true accomplishment than one that attains to fewer years. The child or youth may die older, with more of life crowded into a brief existence, than the man whose dull and stagnant being drags on to an inglorious old age.

Jesus Christ spent only thirty-three years on this earth, and only three of those in active ministry, yet His was the fullest and richest life ever to grace the human scene. He accomplished more in His brief lifetime than could possibly be recorded. As the beloved disciple John wrote, "And there are also many other things which Jesus did, the which, if they should be written every one, I suppose that even the world itself could not contain the books that should be written" (John 21:25).

> We live in deeds, not years; in
> thoughts, not breaths;
> In feelings, not in figures on a dial.
> We should count time by heart-
> throbs. He most lives
> Who thinks most, feels the no-
> blest, acts the best.

### Your Inheritance in Christ

As we conclude our studies on the third chapter of 1 Corinthians, we see that the apostle Paul has presented the life of the believer as a structure built on the one foundation, which is Jesus Christ. But he wants us to realize we are looking at unfinished work. Surely the great Masterbuilder who has laid such a foundation-stone will not abandon the building unfinished.

Every Christian life, at its best and noblest, shows, as it were, the ground plan of a great structure partly carried out. But the very fact that it is incomplete is a prophecy of the day when the capstone shall be set in place and the flag hoisted on the roof tree. On that day we will see the good and bad, so strangely blended in the life and experience of the Christian, lead into a glorious and perfect future (Rom. 8:28).

Paul mentions the future last in his series of what belongs to the believer because it will be the crowning experience of the present. In Ephesians 1:14 he calls it "the redemption of the purchased possession." We now have the possession. We are entitled to it. It is like those trading stamps we receive along with our purchases at some supermarkets. The items they represent—a folding table, a blanket, or whatever—are our possession because they can be purchased with the stamps we have accumulated. But we must take them to the redemption center. So it is with our present salvation. It holds a future inheritance more glorious than the token we now possess. Therefore the sacrifice of Christ has not only a past but also a future.

This future redemption will be at a definite time. The day of redemption of the whole man, which will include the body, is coming on the Resurrection Day. We shall then be delivered from every limitation and sin, and be lifted up into the full light and knowledge of God. "Then shall I know even as also I am known" (1 Cor. 13:12). That is knowledge in full. What a glorious future awaits the believer in Christ.

But remember another lesson also stressed in this great chapter. Whatever you sow you shall reap. If you use cheap material in building your life, the superstructure will burn down. Oh, yes, you yourself will be saved, but so as by fire. But if you use costly material, as symbolized by gold, silver, and precious stones, it will stand. The present, in other words, is the parent of the future.

A man planted a weeping willow beside his door. He had bent down its branches and put them around the hoop of an old wine barrel to teach them to droop. He thought to himself: After a bit, when they have become set, I will take away the hoop. And when he did this, the branches could no longer spring upward. They were fixed.

You, too, are fixing your future now. In that way you truly possess the future. It is not going to be a total surprise to you. Heaven will perfect the partial knowledge and incomplete service of earth, and will be the consummation and not the contradiction of your life here.

The chief characteristic of the Christian life is that we are to share the inheritance of Jesus. It is impossible that we can go our own way in this world and share the inheritance with Him in the next. If we are to have part in a heavenly reward, we must not seek to escape His yoke of service or sorrow in this world. The servant is not greater than his Lord, and we ought not to desire to be more popular or successful in business, or society, or church circles, than Jesus Christ would be were He here. We are joint-heirs with Christ. We must not evade our fellowship with Him in sharing temporary discomforts or burdens, but, like Him, must have our eyes on the goal at the end of the race.

In sharing Christ's inheritance there may be times that are full of trial, like the forty days that Christ spent in the wilderness. But if we share the wilderness with Jesus, we shall also share with Him the Mount of Transfiguration. It is better to go through the darkness with Christ than to walk in the blazing noon without Him.

What is an inheritance? Not the pay you receive for your work. That is something you earn by your own efforts. But even a baby can come into an inheritance. In the terms of a court of law, believers in Christ hold heaven, not by purchase or because they earn it, but by inheritance. It has been won for them by another arm than theirs. It presents the strongest contrast to the spectacle seen in England's palace on a day when the king demanded to know of his assembled nobles by what right and title they held their lands. Stung by the question, they drew their swords, and advancing on the alarmed monarch exclaimed, "By these we won, and by these we will keep them!"

How different the scene which heaven presents. All eyes are fixed on Jesus, and every voice exclaims, "Not unto us, O Lord, not unto us, but unto Thy name give glory" (Ps. 115:1).

LESSONS:

1. Christianity proclaims the message of peace. It is a poor testimony to the world when Christians, who are supposed to love all people, act like enemies. The gospel is not diminished but increased when multitudes spread it. Jealousy and envy over the spread of the faith, therefore, should have no place in our hearts.
2. The apostle Paul spoke of "Christ," the anointed one. He was the one whom God the Father foreordained and anointed to become the Lamb that bore our sins. Through sin, man lost dominion over his environment. The anointed Man, Christ Jesus, belongs to the Triune God. He had to be specially related to God in order to reconcile man to His Father.
3. God became flesh to bear our sins in His body. During Christ's ministry on earth, He publicly declared that what He did and willed was in full accord with the Father.
4. The person who is "in Christ" owns everything that is Christ's. The unbeliever owns nothing but is enslaved by the world, the devil, and his own flesh.
5. The unbeliever does not see a guiding, planning mind behind the forces in the world. He considers himself a victim of conflicting forces. But Christ teaches that forces are all under the control of a living personal will, directed by the love of the Father, making all things work together for the good of His children. The true owner of the world is the soul capable of appreciating it and responding to eternal love and wisdom.

6. Man was not made for the world; the world was made for man. For man to claim it he must be possessed by the One who made it. Then, he shares inheritance of Jesus Christ who owns all things. He becomes a joint-heir with Christ.

# Bibliography

Ainsworth, Percy C. *The Silences of Jesus and St. Paul's Hymn to Love.* London: Charles H. Kelly, 1912.

Anderson, George Wood. *Unfinished Rainbows.* New York: The Abingdon Press, 1922.

Barker, Harold P. *Review and Reward.* London: Pickering & Inglis, n.d.

Blair, Hugh. *Sermons by Hugh Blair.* Vol. 5. Edinburgh: William Blair, 1818.

Brininger, Frederick P. and Charles H. Welch, eds. "Faction, Fellowship, Faithfulness." *The Berean Expositor.* Vol. 8, no. 6. London: Frederick P. Brininger, 1918.

Burns, James. "Co-partnership with God." In *Christian World Pulpit* 133 (1938): 25, 26.

Caird, John. *Sermons.* New York: Robert Carter & Brothers, 1858.

Calvin, John. *Institutes of the Christian Religion.* Vol. 2. Translated by Henry Beveridge. London: James Clarke & Company, 1957.

Caws, Luther W. "The Christian's Wealth." In *Christian World Pulpit* 85 (1914): 92, 93.

Cooper, James S. "God's Fellow Workers." In *Christian World Pulpit* 72 (1907): 343.

Cumming, James Elder. *Through the Eternal Spirit.* Stirling, England: Drummond's Tract Depot, n.d.

Dawson, W.J. *The Comrade-Christ.* London: Isbister and Company, 1894.

DeHaan, M.R. *Seven Laws of Salvation.* Grand Rapids, MI: Calvary Church, n.d.

Duckworth, Rev. Canon. "The Christian's Heritage." In *Christian World Pulpit* 13 (1878): 65–67.

Dudden, F. Homes. *Christ and Christ's Religion.* Edinburgh: T. & T. Clark, 1910.

Edwards, Thomas Charles. *A Commentary on the First Epistle to the Corinthians.* London: Hamilton, Adams & Company, 1885.

Flint, Professor. "Foundations First." In *Christian World Pulpit* 36 (1889): 329–32.

Ford, W. Herschel. *Simple Sermons for Special Days and Occasions.* Grand Rapids, MI: Zondervan Publishing House, 1961.

Friedrich, Gerhard, *Theological Dictionary of the New Testament,* vol. 8, Geoffrey W. Bromiley, translator. Grand Rapids, Michigan: Wm. B. Eerdmans Publishing Company, 1972, 152.

Godet, F. *Commentary on the First Epistle of St. Paul to the Corinthians.* Vol. 1. Grand Rapids, MI: Zondervan Publishing House, 1957.

Gosse, Philip Henry. *The Mysteries of God.* London: Hodder and Stoughton, 1884.

Greenhough, J. G. *The Cross in Modern Life.* London: Hodder and Stoughton, 1896.

_______. *The Mind of Christ in St. Paul.* London: Hodder and Stoughton, n.d.

Hobbs, David. "All Things Ours But Ourselves." In *Christian World Pulpit* 40 (1891): 58–60.

Janes, Bishop. "Man a Worker with God" In *The Biblical Illustrator, 1 Corinthians.* Vol. 1. Edited by Joseph S. Exell. Grand Rapids, MI: Baker Book House, 1964.

Jelf, William Edward. A *Grammar of the Greek Language.* Vol. 2. Oxford: John Henry and James Parker, 1861.

Jordan, G. Ray. *Religion That Is Eternal.* New York: The MacMillan Company, 1960.

Kittel, Gerhard and G. Friedrich, eds. *Theological Dictionary of the New Testament.* Vol. 2. Translated by Geoffrey W. Bromiley. Grand Rapids, MI: Wm. B. Eerdmans Publishing Company, 1964.

_______. *Ibid.,* vol. 3. 1965.

_______. *Ibid.,* vol. 4. 1967.

Lenski, R. C. H. *The Interpretation of 1 and 2 Corinthians.* Minneapolis, MN: Augsburg Publishing House, 1961.

Liddell, H. G. and Scott, R. *The Greek-English Lexicon.* New York: Harper, 1889.

Liddon, H. P. *Sermons Preached Before the University of Oxford, 1859—1868.* London: Longmans, Green, and Company, 1891.

Luther, Martin. *The Bondage of the Will.* Translated by J. I. Packer and O. R. Johnston. London: James Clarke & Co., Ltd., 1957.

Mackay, James. "Death—Is It a Door?" In *Christian World Pulpit* 141 (1942) 101–3.

Maclaren, Alexander. *Christ in the Heart, and Other Sermons.* London: "Christian Commonwealth" Publishing Company, Ltd. & Hodder & Stoughton, 1886.

_______. *A Year's Ministry.* no. 1. London: Hodder and Stoughton, 1884.

Mc'Neile, Hugh. "The Christian's Possessions." In *The Pulpit, for 1853.* 2 (1853) 49–55.

Marston, Annie W. *Messages for Workers.* London: Marshall Brothers, 1913.

Meyer, H. A. W. *Critical and Exegetical Handbook to the Epistles to the Corinthians.* Vol. 1. Edinburgh: T. & T. Clark, 1877.

Miller, J. R. *The Building of Character.* London: The Sunday School Union, n.d.

_______. *Living Without Worry.* London: Hodder and Stoughton, 1914.

Murray, Andrew. *The Master's Indwelling.* New York: Fleming H. Revell Company, 1896.

_______. *The Spirit of Christ.* New York: N.p., 1888.

*Our Hope* (magazine). Vol. 64, no. 5, "Gold, Silver, and Precious Stones." Waretown, NJ: Arno C. Gaebelein, Inc., 1957.

Phillips, Harold C. *Seeing the Invisible.* New York: Harper & Brothers, 1932.

Robertson, A. T. *A Grammar of the Greek New Testament in the Light of Historical Research.* New York: George H. Doran Co., 1923.

Shannon, Frederick F. *The Enchanted Universe and Other Sermons.* Old Tappan, NJ: Fleming H. Revell Company, 1916.

Telfer, Alexander. "A Party-Spirit Unbecoming in Christians, and Ministerial Success Wholly of God." In *The Scottish Pulpit* 5 (1839) 241–52.

Trench, R. C. *Synonyms of the New Testament.* Grand Rapids, MI: Wm. B. Eerdmans Publishing Company, 1953.

Watkinson, W. L. *Noon Day Addresses.* London: C. H. Kelly, 1890.

## Lexicons, Encyclopedias, and References for Greek Readers, from Classical and Koine Greek to Modern Greek

Byzantiou, S. D. *Lexikṓn tḗs Hellēnikḗs Glṓssēs* (*Lexicon of the Hellenic Language*). Athens: Koromēlá, A., 1852.

Dēmētrákou, D. *Lexikón tês Hellēnikês Glôssēs* (*Lexicon of the Hellenic Language*). Athens: Dēmētrákou, 1954.

*Enkuklopaidikón Glōssologikón Lexikón* (*Encyclopedic Glossological Lexicon*). Athens: Morfōtikē Hetaireia, n.d.

*Enkuklopaidikón Lexikón Eleutheroudáki* (*Encyclopedic Lexicon*). Athens: Eleutheroudákis, 1927.

Kalaráki, Michaēl and Nikólas Galanós. Iōánnou toú Chrusostómou Tá Hápanta (Complete Works of John Chrysostom). n.p. 1899.

Liddell, Henry George, and Robert Scott. *Greek–English Lexicon,* as Translated and Enriched by Xenophōn P. Móschos and Michaēl Kōnstantinídes. Athens: John Sideris, n.d.

*Megálē Helēnikē Enkuklopaideía* (*Great Hellenic Encyclopedia*). Pursos (Pyrsos), Athens: Hēlios, n.d.

*Neōteron Enkuklopaidikón Lexikón Hēlíou* (*New Encyclopedic Lexicon "Hēlios"*). Athens: Hēlios, n.d.

Papaoikonómou, George L. *Lexikon Anōmálōn Rhēmátōn* (Lexicon of Irregular Verbs). Athens: Kagiáphas, n.d.

Stamatákou, J. D. *Lexikón Archaías Hellēnikês Glôssēs* (*Lexicon of the Ancient Hellenic Language*). Athens: Pétrou Dēmētrákou, 1949.

## Works by Spiros Zodhiates

*Conquering the Fear of Death.* Grand Rapids, MI: Wm. B. Eerdmans Publishing Co., 1970.

*A Richer Life for You in Christ.* Ridgefield, NJ: AMG Publishers, 1972.

*Was Christ God?* Grand Rapids, MI: Wm. B. Eerdmans Publishing Company, 1970.

# List of Abbreviations

acc. (accusative)

act. (active)

aor. (aorist [2 aor. for second aorist])

cf. (compare)

ch. (chapter)

comp. (composition)

dat. (dative)

e.g. (for example)

etc. (and so forth)

ff. (following)

fut. (future)

gen. (genitive)

i.e. (that is)

imperf. (imperfect)

indic. (indicative)

inf. (infinitive)

KJV (King James Version)

MT (Majority Text)

mid. (middle)

neut. (neuter)

n.d. (no date available)

N.p. (no publisher available)

NASB (New American Standard Bible)

NIV (New International Version)

NKJV (New King James Version)

nom. (nominative)

p. (page), pp. (pages)

part. (participle, participial)

pass. (passive)

perf. (perfect)

pl. (plural)

pres. (present)

pron. (pronoun)

Sept. (Septuagint)

sing. (singular)

TR (Textus Receptus)

UBS (United Bible Society)

usu. (usually)

v. (verse), vv. (verses)

vol. (volume)

# Guide to the Transliteration and Modern Pronunciation of the Greek Alphabet

| Capital Letter | Small Letter | Greek Name | Trans-literation | Phonetic Sound | Example |
|---|---|---|---|---|---|
| Α | α | alpha | *a* | a | as in father |
| Β | β | bēta | b | v | as in victory |
| Γ | γ | gamma | *g* | y | as in yell (soft gutteral) |
| Δ | δ | delta | *d* | th | as in there |
| Ε | ε | epsilon | *e* | e | as in met |
| Ζ | ζ | zēta | *z* | z | as in zebra |
| Η | η | ēta | *ē* | ee | as in see |
| Θ | θ | thēta | *th* | th | as in thin |
| Ι | ι | iōta | *i* | i | as in machine |
| Κ | κ | kappa | *k* | k | as in kill (soft accent) |
| Λ | λ | lambda | *l* | l | as in land |
| Μ | μ | mē | *m* | m | as in mother |
| Ν | ν | nē | *n* | n | as in now |
| Ξ | ξ | xi | *x* | x | as in wax |
| Ο | ο | omicron | *o* | o | as in obey |
| Π | π | pi | *p* | p | as in pet (soft accent) |
| Ρ | ρ | ro | *r* | r | as in courage |
| Σ | σ,ς* | sigma | *s* | s | as in sit |
| Τ | τ | tau | *t* | t | as in tell (soft accent) |
| Υ | υ | ēpsilon | *u* | ee | as in see |
| Φ | φ | phi | *ph* | ph | as in graphic |
| Χ | χ | chi | *ch* | h | as in heel |
| Ψ | ψ | psi | *ps* | ps | as in ships |
| Ω | ω | omega | *ō* | o | as in obey |

*At the end of words

# SPECIAL RULES FOR THE TRANSLITERATION AND MODERN PRONUNCIATION OF THE GREEK LANGUAGE

## COMBINATIONS OF CONSONANTS

| Small Letter | Greek Names | Trans-literation | Phonetic Sound | Example |
|---|---|---|---|---|
| γγ | gamma + gamma | *gg* | g | as in go |
| γκ | gamma + kappa | *gk* | g | as in go |
| γχ | gamma + chi | *gch* | gh | as in ghost |

## DIPHTHONGS (DOUBLE VOWELS)

| Small Letter | Greek Names | Trans-literation | Phonetic Sound | Example |
|---|---|---|---|---|
| αι | alpha + iōta | *ai* | ai | as in hair |
| αυ | alpha + ēpsilon | *au* | af, av | as in waft or lava |
| ει | epsilon + iōta | *ei* | ee | as in see |
| ευ | epsilon + ēpsilon | *eu* | ef, ev | as in effort or every |
| ηυ | ēta + ēpsilon | *ēu* | eef, eev | as in reef or sleeve |
| οι | omicron + iōta | *oi* | ee | as in see |
| ου | omicron + ēpsilon | *ou* | ou | as in group |
| υι | ēpsilon + iōta | *ui* | ee | as in see |

## BREATHINGS (Occur only with initial vowels)

(᾿) Smooth, not transliterated or pronounced.
When words begin with vowels, it may occur at the beginning of words with every vowel or double vowel (diphthong). ἔργον—*érgon*, work; εὐχή—*euchḗ*, vow.

(῾) Rough = h.
When words begin with vowels, it may occur at the beginning of words with every vowel or double vowel (diphthong). No distinction in pronunciation from the smooth breathing. To indicate the rough breathing we use "h" in the transliteration.

(ῥ) Rho = r.

(ὑ) Epsilon = u.
When these begin a word, they always have the rough breathing. There they are transliterated rh, hu, respectively. ῥέω—*rhéō*, flow; ὑπομονή—*hupomonḗ*, patience.

# Scripture Index

## John



## Acts